GEOGRAPHY *and* EXPLORATION

BIOGRAPHICAL PORTRAITS

Editor

Barry M. Gough, historian and teacher, has been interested in exploration since childhood. A noted traveler, he is also a sailor and a student of the history of navigation and cartography. Born and raised in Victoria, British Columbia, he holds a Ph.D. in history from the University of London and is a Fellow of the Royal Geographical Society of London. Author or editor of a dozen books, he is biographer of Sir Alexander Mackenzie. His next book—about international rivalry for the North American west—tells of the interaction among Mackenzie, Thomas Jefferson, and Lewis and Clark. He is Professor of History at Wilfrid Laurier University, Waterloo, Ontario, Canada.

THE SCRIBNER SCIENCE REFERENCE SERIES

VOLUME 4

GEOGRAPHY *and* EXPLORATION

BIOGRAPHICAL PORTRAITS

Barry M. Gough, *Editor*

Charles Scribner's Sons

New York • Detroit • San Francisco • London • Boston • Woodbridge, CT

Developed for Charles Scribner's Sons by Visual Education Corporation, Princeton, N.J.

FOR SCRIBNERS
PUBLISHER: Frank Menchaca
ASSOCIATE PUBLISHER: Timothy J. DeWerff
COVER DESIGN: Pamela Galbreath

FOR VISUAL EDUCATION CORPORATION
EDITORIAL DIRECTOR: Darryl Kestler
PROJECT DIRECTOR: Meera Vaidyanathan
WRITERS: Stephen Currie, John Haley, Rebecca Stefoff
COPYEDITING MANAGER: Helen Castro
INDEXER: Stephen R. Ingle
PHOTO RESEARCH: Susan Buschhorn
INTERIOR DESIGN: Maxson Crandall, Rob Ehlers, Lisa Evans-Skopas
ELECTRONIC PREPARATION: Fiona Torphy

Library of Congress Cataloging-in-Publication Data

Geography and exploration : biographical portraits / Barry M. Gough, editor.
    p.cm. - (The Scribner science reference series ; v. 4)
    Includes bibliographical references.
    ISBN 0-684-80662-2
    1. Explorers-Biography-Juvenile literature. 2. Geographers-Biography-Juvenile literature. 3. Discoveries in geography-Juvenile literature. [1. Explorers-Encyclopedias. 2. Geographers-Encyclopedias. 3. Discoveries in geography-Encyclopedias.] I. Series.
    G200 .G43 2001
    910'.92'2-dc21
    [B]   2001032046

TABLE OF CONTENTS

Table of Contents

INTRODUCTION

BY BARRY M. GOUGH

Since the beginning of time, explorers and geographers have been pathfinders and true discoverers. They have exploded myths, formulated new concepts, and expanded the boundaries of our knowledge of the physical world. The work of these men and women has been largely empirical—building up detail, gathering evidence, and providing new bases on which knowledge can be confirmed.

Methodology and Purpose. Although explorers and geographers share the same general goals, their methods are different. Explorers seek to add to existing knowledge of the world and to confirm or verify theories. Being the first to reach the North Pole or the first to travel into outer space is both exploratory and demonstrative. It extends the frontiers of understanding and proves that man can reach the ends of the earth or soar above it.

Geographers, by contrast, often work from existing statistical or spatial evidence. From this point they may formulate a thesis or proposition about the nature of human and natural developments. A geographer might argue that certain activities of humans can be explained by environmental circumstances or technological innovations. For instance, the Russian geographer Vasily Dokuchaev suggested that agricultural activity differs throughout the world because the earth is divided into five geographical zones, each presenting different soil and climate conditions and unique challenges to the cultivators. Some geographers concentrate on area studies, such as the study of specific regions of the world, and others study how regions, cities, and communities interact. Whatever their specialization, all geographers and explorers have the same purpose: to increase humankind's knowledge of the world.

Sometimes explorers and geographers end up with a thesis they cannot prove. In 1497 the Englishman John Cabot set sail from England intending to reach Cipangu (Japan), but he landed in or near Newfoundland. As a result of this voyage Cabot proved that one cannot sail to Japan along the westward route that he took. Christopher Columbus had a similar experience a few years earlier when he set out to prove that he could sail west from Spain and end up in Asia. Arriving in North America, he believed that he had reached India and called the indigenous people Indians. After each of these explorers reached their destination or discovered something, they modified their theories according to their findings.

Another difference between explorers and geographers is that explorers tend to be physically involved in the achievement of their plan. Geographers, on the other hand, generally work in government offices, universities, or institutes, gathering evidence and writing up their results. An explorer need not be a writer, but a geographer must certainly be.

The Importance of Record-keeping. What sets apart the nearly 100 explorers and geographers featured in this book is that they were extremely well situated to take advantage of opportunities that came their way. They also made great efforts to find explanations of the world around them. Curious and inquisitive, these seekers went beyond the ordinary—investigated the known world, studied the findings of those who had preceded them, and did the research, planning, testing, and exploration necessary. Many wrote reports of activities and discoveries; others had their findings confirmed by associates or by people who had observed their work.

Introduction

A discovery without confirmation does not count. To say you have been on the moon without a photograph to prove it or without an accomplice to verify it will not lead to fame. Such evidence is vital in both exploration and geography. Although Captain James Cook of the Royal Navy kept detailed journals and records of his expeditions, it was the records maintained by those with whom he had sailed that confirmed his achievements. Sir Alexander Mackenzie, the first to make an overland crossing of the North American continent north of Mexico, had to master the methods of scientific navigation in order to record the precise longitude and latitude of his exploratory route and of his ultimate destination. His journals and the writings of his companions were proof of his remarkable achievement.

Sometimes recognition and acceptance take a while. The scientific community of Britain in the mid-1800s considered Charles Darwin, the noted theorist of the evolution of species, a radical and, scientifically, quite unreliable. Gradually, however, other scholars came to accept his point of view. Still, Darwin has been assailed by those arguing for a divine creation of the world and its creatures, and the controversy continues. Clearly, the importance of the achievements of the explorers or the theories and conclusions of geographers are not readily or always accepted, but they often contribute information to existing knowledge.

History. The history of exploration and geography has its own fascination. The contributions of many early figures are told in these pages. They come from Asia, the Middle East, the Mediterranean, and northern Europe. Ranging from Ptolemy, Herodotus of Halicarnassus, and Ibn Battūta to Alexander the Great and Nicholas Copernicus, they made substantial additions to human knowledge. When science and statistical measurement helped provide scientific proof and when sailing ships and marine navigational tools enabled explorers to reach remote locations of the world, an explosion of information occurred.

Starting with the Europeans in the late 1700s, gigantic strides were made in exploring the earth. The marine expeditions of Cook and of Charles Wilkes of the United States Navy are just two examples. The heroic age of polar exploration in the early 1900s, featuring Roald Amundsen, Robert Falcon Scott, Robert Edwin Peary, and Matthew Henson, brought journalism into the pursuit of "firsts." After reporter Henry Morton Stanley found David Livingstone in "darkest Africa" in 1871, Stanley went on to become a noted explorer and later wrote a best-selling book on his travels.

The reporting of exploration may be less sensationalistic than in the days of these "firsts," but the astronauts and cosmonauts who have expanded our knowledge and understanding of space still gain fame. Indeed, we celebrate their achievements and stand in awe of their success. Their success is, in fact, our success. Everyone shares the achievements and benefits of these discoverers—explorers and geographers alike.

Technology. The great mariners of the past who opened new areas for trade and colonization and increased the exchange of commodities owed much to technology. The sextant, the compass, the astrolabe, and the chronometer—these were the main tools of the early explorers. The calculator, the camera (still and moving), the aerial photograph, and above all the computer have been the key tools of the geographers of our time. Geographical research has extended our knowledge of where to plant crops and where to drill for oil. Aerial surveillance and remote sensing equipment also aid in the collection of useful data.

In the future, new technologies will help increase our understanding of the earth, the seas, and of space. The gathering of knowledge about space is accelerating, and in the future we will be learning more about that realm than about our planet. For these reasons, we need to follow the news stories about explorers and geographers. By their works and achievements the future knowledge of the world and of space will be extended.

TIME LINE

EXPLORATION

North America

ca. 1001	Leif ERIKSON arrives in Newfoundland; he explores the area.
1497	The CABOTS lead English expedition to coast of North America.
1535–1563	Jacques CARTIER discovers St. Lawrence River.
1536	Álvar Núñez CABEZA DE VACA becomes the first European to travel across North America.
1540–1541	Francisco CORONADO explores the North American Southwest; discovers Grand Canyon.
1589	Richard HAKLUYT chronicles English overseas exploration.
1603	Samuel de CHAMPLAIN travels along the St. Lawrence River and creates a map of the Hudson Bay and the Great Lakes.
1608–1609	Champlain founds Quebec, a trading post; reaches Lake Champlain.
1673	Jacques MARQUETTE explores upper Mississippi Valley.
1741	Vitus BERING lands on Alaskan mainland.
1767–1784	Junípero SERRA founds missions in present-day California.
1778–1779	James COOK sails around the coast of Alaska seeking an entry into the Northwest Passage.
1789	Alexander MACKENZIE follows Mackenzie River to Arctic Ocean.
1793	Mackenzie becomes first European to cross North America north of Mexico.
1797	David THOMPSON travels through northwestern Canada.
1800–1811	Thompson explores the Rocky Mountains.
1803	Meriwether LEWIS and William CLARK begin their expedition westward across the United States.
1805	Lewis and Clark reach Pacific Ocean.

Central and South America

1492	Christopher COLUMBUS arrives at islands in Caribbean Sea.
1499–1502	Amerigo Vespucci sails along east coast of South America.
1502	Columbus reaches Central America.

Time Line

1513	Vasco Núñez de BALBOA becomes first European to sight the Pacific Ocean.
1519–1521	Hernán CORTÉS conquers Aztec Empire for the Spanish.
1520	Ferdinand MAGELLAN sails through Strait of Magellan.
1526–1529	Sebastian Cabot explores the Río de la Plata region.
1768–1769	James Cook sails to Brazil and around Cape Horn.
1789–1794	Alejandro MALASPINA visits Spanish possessions along South American coastline.
1799–1802	Alexander von HUMBOLDT explores natural life in South America.
1831–1836	Charles DARWIN sails aboard *HMS Beagle* to South America and to islands in the Pacific and Atlantic, studying animal and plant life.

Africa and the Middle East

ca. 400s B.C.	HERODOTUS travels to Egypt and writes *History,* a lengthy account of the wars between Greece and Persia.
334–324 B.C.	ALEXANDER THE GREAT conquers Asia Minor and the Middle East.
ca. 915	AL-MAS'UDI begins his travels in Asia and Africa.
1325–1353	IBN BATTŪTA travels through North Africa and Arabia.
1488	Bartolomeu Dias sails around Cape of Good Hope.
1526	LEO THE AFRICAN writes a treatise on the geography of North Africa.
1770	James BRUCE finds source of Blue Nile River.
1840	David LIVINGSTONE begins 30 years of exploration in Africa.
1849–1855	Heinrich BARTH journeys through North and Central Africa.
1849–1856	Livingstone is the first European to travel across Africa; discovers Victoria Falls.
1857	Richard BURTON leads expedition to find the source of Nile River.
1858	Burton and John Hanning Speke discover Lake Tanganyika.
1862	Speke finds source of White Nile.
1871	Henry STANLEY finds Livingstone in central Africa.
1874–1877	Stanley follows course of Congo River from source to mouth.
1893	Mary KINGSLEY travels through West Africa to Angola and Nigeria.

Asia

ca. 629–645	XUAN ZANG travels through Asia to learn about Buddhism.
ca. 1271–1295	Marco POLO tours China and Southeast Asia.
1497–1499	Vasco da GAMA commands first European fleet to India and back.
1524	Gama is named viceroy of India.
1770	James Cook sails past the Great Barrier Reef to Indonesia.
1865	Nain SINGH begins exploring the Himalaya Mountains, Tibet, and Central Asia for the British.
1866	Nain Singh reaches the Forbidden City of Lhasa, Tibet.

Pacific Ocean, Australia, and Voyages Around the Globe

Polar Regions

Time Line

1895   Robert PEARY explores northern Greenland.

1896   Aboard the *Fram*, Fridtjof NANSEN determines the depth of the Arctic Ocean and the locations of land and water masses near the North Pole, and sets a record for reaching 85°55'N.

1902   Robert Falcon SCOTT reaches Antarctica.

1905   Roald AMUNDSEN sails through the Northwest Passage.

Vilhjalmur STEFANSSON begins exploring Canadian Arctic.

1907   Ernest SHACKLETON sets record for coming within 97 miles of the south magnetic pole.

1909   Matthew HENSON and Peary claim to reach North Pole.

1910   Peary publishes *The North Pole*.

1911   Amundsen reaches South Pole.

1912   Amundsen publishes *The South Pole*.

Scott reaches South Pole.

1926–1929   Louise BOYD becomes first woman to fly over the North Pole.

Space

1961   Yuri GAGARIN becomes first person to travel in space.

Alan Shepard is first American astronaut.

1962   John GLENN becomes first American to orbit earth.

1963   Valentina TERESHKOVA travels as the first woman in space.

1969   Neil ARMSTRONG is first person to land on the moon.

1983   Sally RIDE becomes the first American woman in space, aboard the space shuttle *Challenger*.

1996   Shannon LUCID works for 188 days on the Russian space station *Mir*, the record for hours in orbit by any non-Russian.

1998   Glenn returns to space on the space shuttle *Discovery*.

GEOGRAPHY AND CARTOGRAPHY

ca. 240 B.C.   ERATOSTHENES calculates the earth's circumference and draws the first world map.

ca. 31 B.C.   STRABO works on Geographica, the first known attempt to assemble all geographical knowledge into a single source.

ca. A.D. 140   PTOLEMY writes his *Guide to Geography*, mapping the world and establishing the principles of mapmaking

ca. 1140   Al-IDRISI produces a world map and an accompanying text.

1569   Gerardus MERCATOR publishes first Mercator projection world map.

1828   Carl RITTER founds the Berlin Geographical Society.

1864   George MARSH, America's first environmentalist, publishes *Man and Nature*, suggesting than humans are active agents of change.

1865   Petr KROPOTKIN finds evidence of glacial activity.

1887   Halford MACKINDER becomes the first geography lecturer at a British university.

1891   Paul VIDAL DE LA BLACHE founds *Annales de Géographie,* a French journal of geography.

1899   Alfred HETTNER founds the Heidelberg Geographical Institute.

1901   Albert BRIGHAM begins publishing works outlining the field of human and historical geography.

1903   Ellen SEMPLE publishes *American History and Its Geographic Conditions,* and becomes the first well-known female geographer.

1923   John GOODE publishes a school atlas known as *Goode's World Atlas.*

1935   Nikolay VAVILOV announces that he has located the origins of about 600 species of plants.

1956–1977   Marie THARP publishes maps of ocean floors.

1961   Jean GOTTMANN publishes *Megalopolis* about cities along the Atlantic coast of the United States.

1969   David HARVEY publishes *Explanation of Geography.*

1986   Donald Meinig publishes *The Shaping of America: A Geographical Perspective on 500 Years of History.*

MAPS

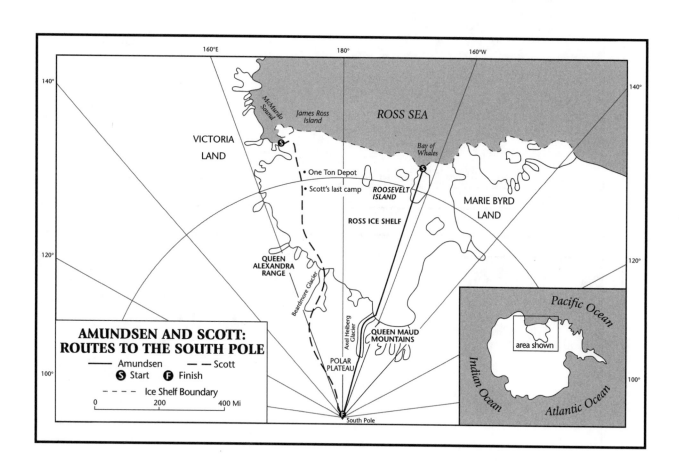

AMUNDSEN AND SCOTT:
ROUTES TO THE SOUTH POLE
—— Amundsen   - - - Scott
S Start   F Finish
- - - Ice Shelf Boundary
0   200   400 Mi

160°E   180°   160°W

140°   140°

McMurdo Sound

James Ross
Island

ROSS SEA

VICTORIA

LAND

Bay of
Whales

• One Ton Depot

• Scott's last camp

ROOSEVELT
ISLAND

MARIE BYRD
LAND

ROSS ICE SHELF

120°   120°

QUEEN
ALEXANDRA
RANGE

Beardmore Glacier

Axel Heiberg Glacier

QUEEN MAUD
MOUNTAINS

Pacific Ocean

area shown

POLAR
PLATEAU

100°   100°

Indian Ocean

Atlantic Ocean

F
South Pole

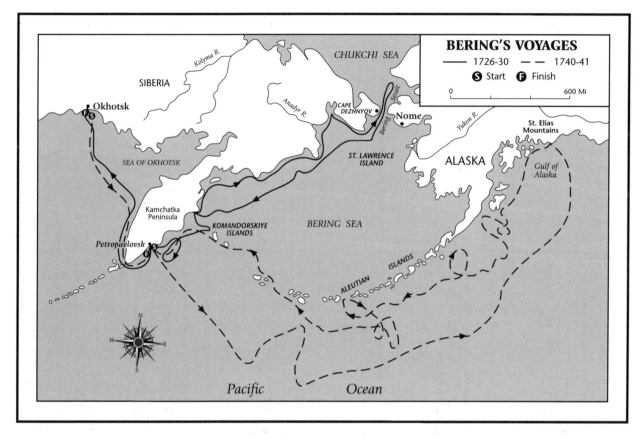

BERING'S VOYAGES
—— 1726-30   - - - 1740-41
S Start   **F** Finish
0   600 Mi

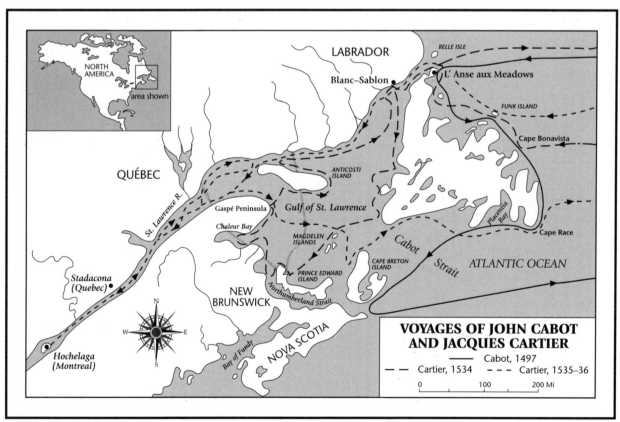

**VOYAGES OF JOHN CABOT
AND JACQUES CARTIER**
———— Cabot, 1497
- - - - Cartier, 1534   - - - Cartier, 1535–36
0   100   200 Mi

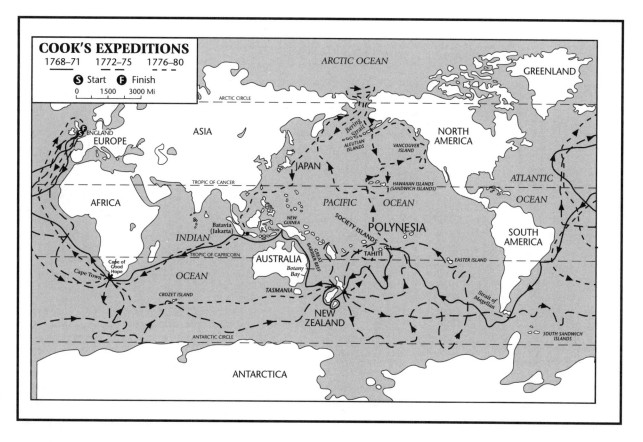

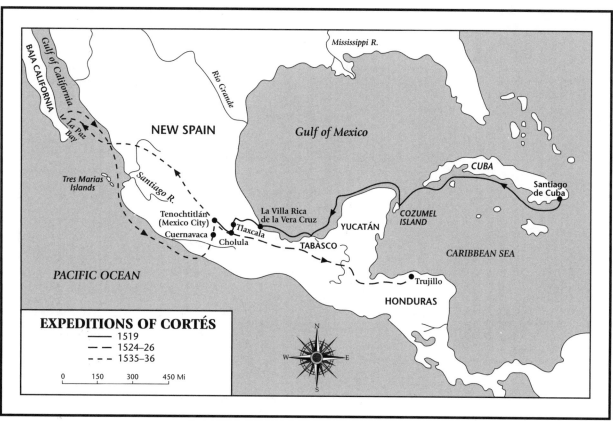

Maps

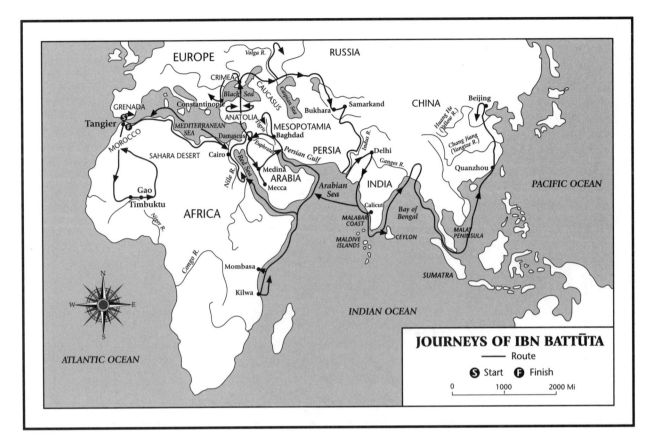

JOURNEYS OF IBN BATTŪTA
——— Route
S Start   **F** Finish
0   1000   2000 Mi

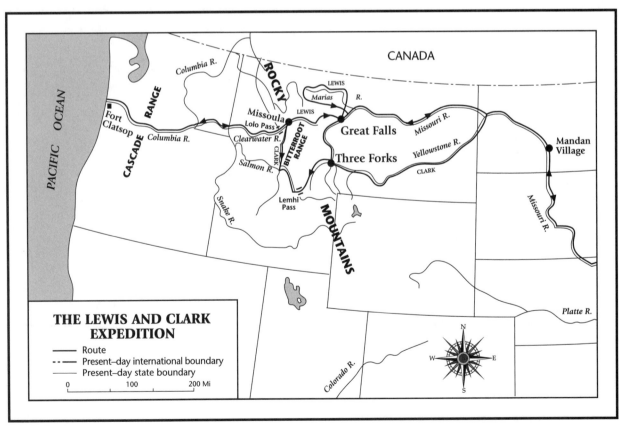

THE LEWIS AND CLARK EXPEDITION
——— Route
– – – Present–day international boundary
——— Present–day state boundary
0   100   200 Mi

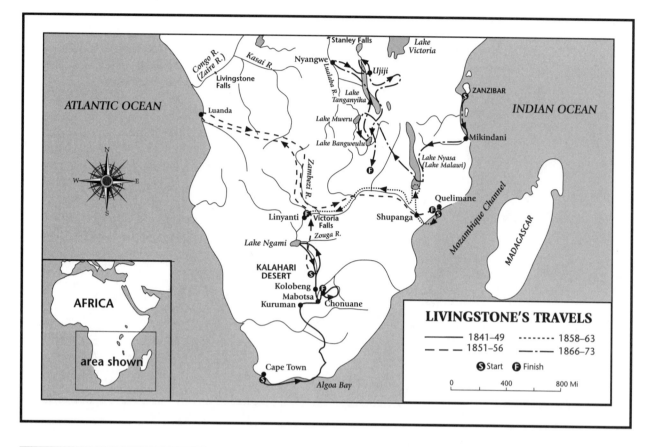

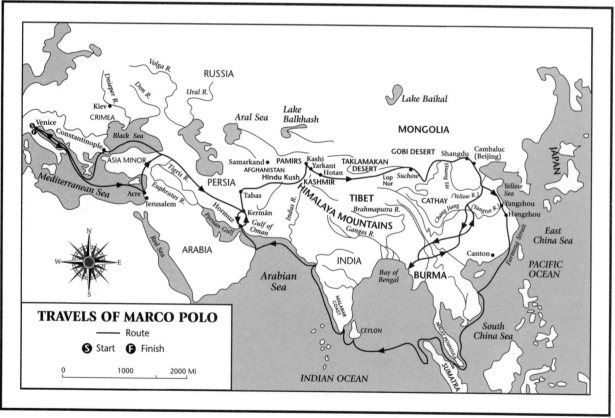

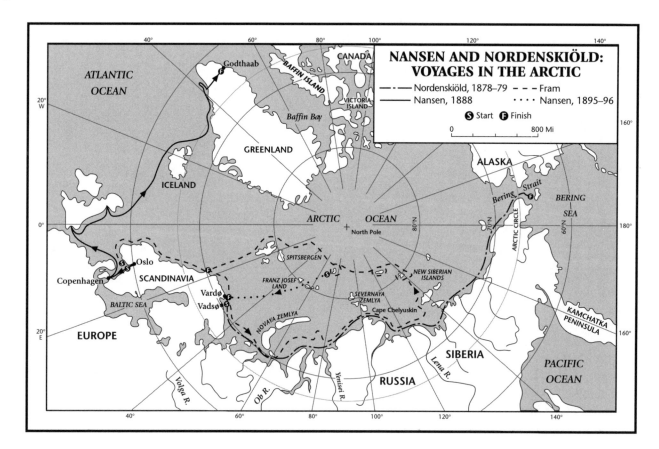

**NANSEN AND NORDENSKIÖLD:
VOYAGES IN THE ARCTIC**

— · — · Nordenskiöld, 1878–79   – – – Fram
———— Nansen, 1888   · · · · Nansen, 1895–96

S Start   **F** Finish

0   800 Mi

ALEXANDER THE GREAT

Alexander III of Macedonia, known as Alexander the Great, was a ruler, a conqueror, a general, and an empire builder, but not an explorer. Yet his desire to rule the world included a driving curiosity about the sciences, including geography. Alexander's military conquests, the voyages of exploration he ordered, and the colonies he established in Africa and Asia greatly enhanced the ancient Greeks' view of the world.

Becoming King. Alexander was born in Pella, Macedonia, a land on the northern border of Greece. At the time, Macedonia was the main power in the Greek world. Alexander's father was King Philip II of Macedonia, and Alexander grew up in a royal household where he was taught for a time by Aristotle, a leading Greek philosopher and scientist. From him Alexander gained respect for science and the search for knowledge.

While still a teenager, Alexander proved his skills as a fighter and commander in the wars in which his father conquered Greek city-states to the south. When Philip was assassinated in 336 B.C., the Macedonian army supported Alexander's claim to the throne. At the age of 20, along with the kingdom, Alexander inherited his father's ambitious plan to invade Asia Minor, today known as Turkey. The Greek colonies there had fallen under the control of the Persian empire, based in present-day Iran. Philip had planned to win back control of Asia Minor from Persia, and Alexander was determined to fulfill that plan.

First, Alexander had to attack some tribes that were waging war on the northern and western borders of Macedonia and Greece. During this campaign, however, a rumor of his death reached the city of Thebes, leading the Thebans to revolt against Macedonian rule. Alexander punished the Thebans by tearing down their city and selling them into slavery. Other Greek city-states promptly pledged their loyalty to Alexander, leaving the king free to begin his assault on the Persians.

The Campaign Against Persia. Alexander's army marched into Asia Minor in 334 B.C. Scientists, historians, engineers, and architects also traveled with the soldiers, suggesting that Alexander did not simply plan a war of conquest; he intended to study the lands he entered and to build cities there for long-term occupation. An admirer of Greek achievements in culture and science, he wanted to spread the Greek language and civilization everywhere. His goal was nothing less than a world empire, united under Greek rule, with himself as emperor.

In a series of battles against the Persians, Alexander's army gained control of western Asia Minor. At the city of Issus, his forces confronted those of Darius, the Persian emperor. Darius retreated, and Alexander marched triumphantly south through present-day Syria, Lebanon, and Israel, overthrowing cities that were loyal to Darius.

When Alexander arrived in Egypt, the Persian officials there surrendered to him, and the Egyptian people greeted him as their liberator. Alexander spent several months establishing his control of Egypt. At the mouth of the Nile River, he founded the city of Alexandria, destined to become a great center of learning in the ancient world. Some sources say that he also sent an exploring expedition southward up the Nile.

After Alexander gained control of the Mediterranean coast of western Asia, he turned inland toward Persia. He captured the city of Babylon in present-day Iraq and marched on to take Persepolis, the Persian capital, forcing Darius to flee eastward. In 330 B.C. Alexander set off in pursuit, but soon he learned that a local ruler named Bessus had killed Darius. Alexander then took the title "lord of Asia" and reorganized his army and his imperial* government.

imperial of or relating to an empire or emperor

Into Central Asia and India. Alexander continued to advance east and north into Central Asia, now in pursuit of Bessus, who was trying to set himself up as king there. After he captured and executed Bessus, his military campaign became an expedition to explore the limits of his empire and to extend its borders still farther east.

On his way to the ancient city of Samarkand in present-day Uzbekistan, Alexander founded numerous cities, most of which he named Alexandria. One was at the present-day site of Herat, Iran, and another in Tajikistan, now a republic in Central Asia. These and other new cities, populated by soldiers from Alexander's armies, would become outposts of Greek culture. Alexander went on to conquer the Scythians, nomads who lived beyond the eastern frontiers of the Persian empire, and the people of Bactria, a kingdom in northern Afghanistan.

In 327 B.C. he turned his attention southward and marched his army across the Hindu Kush mountains, passing from Afghanistan into present-day Pakistan and northwestern India. These realms had never before experienced the Greek influence. Alexander crossed the Indus River, defeated several local rulers, founded new cities, and prepared to continue eastward. If he had done so, he might have reached central India or the Himalaya Mountains. But when his army reached the Hyphasis River in northern India, today called the Beas River, the weary troops, battered by tropical rainstorms, refused to go any farther. Even the will of the mighty emperor, whom some believed to be a god, could not persuade them to continue, and Alexander was forced to return to Persia.

For the return trip, Alexander led part of his force by land along the Indian Ocean coast and across the deserts of Gedrosia, a land that spanned the border between present-day Pakistan and southeastern Iran. The rest of the men traveled by sea in a fleet of ships built by the soldiers and commanded by a mariner named Nearchus. Theirs was the first Greek voyage of exploration along the coasts of the Indian Ocean and the Persian Gulf. Alexander later founded an Alexandria at the mouth of the Tigris River on the Persian Gulf.

Back in Persia, he embarked on a plan to blend Macedonians and Persians into a single race, a policy that displeased many of his Macedonian and Greek followers. Alexander also devoted some energy to planning new expeditions of exploration. At the time of his death from a natural illness or poison—a topic of much debate among both ancient and modern historians—Alexander the Great was issuing orders for an expedition to survey the coast of the Arabian peninsula.

R oald Amundsen of Norway became a hero of polar exploration in the early 1900s, a time when individuals and nations were striving to set new records of achievement in the Arctic and the Antarctic. Amundsen is most often remembered as the leader of the first expedition to reach the South Pole, the victor of one of the greatest geographic races of his day. He was more deeply interested in the Arctic Ocean, however, and there he won fame as the first to sail the Northwest Passage* and one of the first to fly over the North Pole.

The Northwest Passage

Amundsen owed his success as a polar explorer to his thorough knowledge of polar conditions, his careful attention to detail, and his physical fitness and strength. He displayed these characteristics on his voyage through the Northwest Passage, but he had been preparing for that achievement since he was a teenager.

Drawn to the Poles. Amundsen was born in Borge, not far from Oslo, the capital of Norway. Since the days of the Icelandic explorer Leif ERIKSON and the Vikings*, Norway had produced many committed seafarers who ventured boldly into the frigid waters of the far north. Determined to carry on that tradition and to put Norway on the map, the young, patriotic Amundsen undertook physical training to increase his strength and endurance, and he read as much as possible about polar exploration.

He was especially interested in the 1845 expedition of Britain's Sir John FRANKLIN, one of many who had tried to find the Northwest Passage and had died in the attempt. For centuries geographers and explorers had wondered about the passage, a sea route that was believed to exist in the Canadian Arctic, connecting the Atlantic and Pacific Oceans. Because of Franklin's attempt, geographers knew by Amundsen's time that the only Northwest Passage is a tortuous route through the ice-choked maze of islands and waterways in the Arctic. This passage was not the smooth-sailing shipping route that explorers had sought for centuries, and no one had yet traveled completely through it.

Pressured by his mother to study medicine, Amundsen enrolled in the University of Christiania (now the University of Oslo). In the mid-1890s, after the deaths of his parents, he abandoned his medical studies and decided to become a polar explorer. Knowing that seamanship would be a skill critical to that mission, Amundsen trained to become a sailor. By 1897 he had gained enough experience to serve as first mate, the officer second to the captain, on a Belgian-financed expedition to explore the coast of Antarctica. The ship froze in the southern ice,

Roald Engelbregt Gravning
AMUNDSEN

1872–1928

POLAR EXPLORATION

*Northwest Passage water route connecting the Atlantic and Pacific Oceans through the Arctic islands of northern Canada

*Vikings Scandinavian seamen who robbed the coasts of Europe in the eighth and tenth centuries

See Amundsen's route to the South Pole in the "Maps" section.

*scurvy disease caused by a lack of vita-
min C and characterized by bleeding
gums, bleeding under the skin, and
extreme weakness

making Amundsen a member of the first expedition ever to spend a
winter in Antarctica. When the captain fell ill and nearly everyone
aboard contracted scurvy*, Amundsen took charge. He directed the
crew's survival activities, such as hunting, and he commanded the ship
when it finally escaped from the Antarctic ice in 1899.

Voyage Through the Northwest Passage. Qualified as a captain following the voyage, Amundsen laid the groundwork for an expedition
of his own. He planned to sail through the Northwest Passage with the
scientific goal of locating the north magnetic pole, the place in the
Northern Hemisphere to which magnetic compasses point. It is not in
the same location as the North Pole. Amundsen also took his plan to
the Norwegian polar explorer and scientist Fridtjof NANSEN, who
approved it and offered encouragement. Because of his goal, Amundsen easily obtained finances for the expedition. He equipped a 70-foot
vessel named *Gjøa,* and in June 1903 set sail from Christiania (now
Oslo) with a crew of six men.

The *Gjøa* crossed the North Atlantic and cruised along the western
coast of Greenland and the northern coast of Baffin Island. Braving
floating ice, fog, rocky reefs and shallows, and storms, Amundsen then
entered the maze of channels that make up the Northwest Passage. On
King William Island, he found a good harbor and established a camp
where he and his crew spent the next two years taking measurements
that would pinpoint the location of the magnetic pole. Amundsen also
studied the Inuit*, who are indigenous* to the region. He observed their
habits and the tools that enabled them to survive in an inhospitable climate, especially their use of dogsleds for light, fast travel over ice and
snow. The knowledge Amundsen gained from these polar specialists
would later give him an advantage over other explorers who did not
think they could learn anything from a people they considered primitive.

*Inuit people of the Canadian Arctic and
Greenland, sometimes called Eskimo

*indigenous referring to the original
inhabitants of a region

Leaving King William Island in August 1905, the *Gjøa* continued
through the Arctic Ocean, passing along the hazardous northern coast
of Canada. When winter set in, ice held the ship motionless at Herschel
Island off the Yukon coast, but by then Amundsen knew that he had
traversed the Northwest Passage. Using dog teams, he traveled over the
ice to the closest telegraph station, almost 500 miles away in Eagle
City, Alaska, to send word of his success to the outside world.

A Sudden Change of Plan

The voyage of the *Gjøa* made Amundsen famous. Shortly thereafter he
began to plan an even bolder venture—a journey to the North Pole,
which no one had yet reached. Amundsen would use the *Fram,* a ship
that had carried Fridtjof Nansen. His plan was to sail into the polar
waters, where the *Fram* would freeze into the ice and be carried across
the pole by the slow drift of the ice pack. In 1909, however, the American explorer Robert PEARY announced that he had reached the North
Pole using the same method. Although Peary's claim was later challenged, at the time he was hailed as the conqueror of the North Pole.

Determined to make his expedition a success, Roald Amundsen did his best to keep his men comfortable and content during the long, cold polar winters. For example, he packed luxury items such as chocolate and biscuits in the rations and constructed a sauna to help his men relax.

South to Antarctica. Notwithstanding the news of Peary's expedition, Amundsen continued preparing the *Fram* and its crew of eight men for a polar voyage. He told his financial backers that the *Fram* would make a scientific survey of the northern polar region. His was to be a serious voyage of Arctic research, Amundsen said, not an attempt to achieve a goal or set a record. The *Fram* set sail from Norway in June 1910, but instead of heading north toward the Arctic it went south to the Atlantic island of Madeira, where Amundsen had said he would perform some oceanographic* studies before returning north to enter the Arctic.

At Madeira, Amundsen assembled his crew and made a startling announcement. Instead of going to the Arctic, as they had thought, they were going to the opposite end of the world: to Antarctica. Unable to be the first to reach the North Pole, Amundsen wanted to try for the

*oceanographic of or relating to oceanography, the study of oceans

Life at Framheim

As leader of the South Pole expedition, Roald Amundsen believed that an orderly routine was needed to keep tension at bay while the men were confined to the hut during the winter. Quarters were small—each man had just two hooks and a sack to hold his personal possessions—and Amundsen feared that idleness might cause tempers to fray. He scheduled work hours during which the men sewed tents, packed supplies, made skis, and built dogsleds in preparation for the coming dash to the pole. Each man took a turn cleaning the hut. Every evening they gathered for a supper of seal steak, bread and butter, cheese, and coffee, followed by games, conversation, and sometimes music.

*meteorological referring to meteorology, the science that deals with the atmosphere, especially the weather and weather predictions

*sledge heavy sled that is mounted on runners for traveling over snow and ice

South Pole instead. The crew agreed to his plan. Amundsen later said that he had made this decision as quickly as news of Peary's feat had sped along the telegraph cables.

Amundsen knew quite well that the British explorer Robert Falcon SCOTT was ready to launch his own well-publicized Antarctic expedition with the goal of reaching the South Pole. Some have criticized Amundsen for his secret change of plans and for rushing to beat the British team, turning Scott's expedition into a race for the South Pole. Amundsen admitted that he kept secret about switching his goal from the North to the South Pole so that neither his backers nor public opinion could prevent him from making the attempt. He had instructed his brother to tell Scott and the world that he was headed for Antarctica—but only after the *Fram* had left Madeira and could not be called back.

On January 14, 1911, the *Fram* dropped anchor in the Bay of Whales on Antarctica's Ross Ice Shelf. Amundsen's crew built a base camp they called Framheim, "home of *Fram*"; Scott's base camp was just 60 miles away. Amundsen chose this site because it was closest to the pole, rich in animal life, and a vantage point to monitor the meteorological* conditions in all directions. Framheim consisted of a wooden hut in which Amundsen and his team lived, 15 large tents in which they stored their supplies, and shelter for the 97 sled dogs they had brought. After establishing the camp, the group spent three weeks unloading tons of supplies from the ship to the base camp and another three weeks making stockpiles of supplies at several points along their proposed southward route to the pole. Winter then set in, and the expedition members spent the long, dark season indoors, living by the strict schedule of meals and chores that Amundsen set up to maintain discipline and order.

Race to the Pole. In August, Amundsen began to prepare for the expedition's true goal, the attempt to enter the heart of the Antarctic continent and reach the South Pole. A group of eight men set out with two dogsleds in September, but after a few days Amundsen decided that it was still too cold for them to press onward to the Pole, so they returned to Framheim.

In October 1911, Amundsen started again, accompanied by 4 men and 52 dogs pulling sledges*. He sent a second party of four to explore the region known as King Edward VII Land, claiming that if the expedition to the pole were not successful, at least the other party could gain a "first" for Norway. Amundsen's group made excellent time to the southernmost of their supply stockpiles, which was at 82°S (the pole is at 90°S). From there they hauled supplies still farther south until they came to a range of mountains. Amundsen named them Queen Maud Mountains in honor of the Queen of Norway. When he and his men camped at the base of the mountains, they were still 340 miles from the South Pole.

It took them four days to climb to the 10,000-foot summit of the mountains with the ton of supplies they would need for their final dash. Because their dwindling store of food could be pulled by fewer dogs, they slaughtered half the pack to provide food for the remaining ones. Amundsen had planned this use of the dogs very carefully. His understanding that some dogs would have to be sacrificed helped his expedition succeed, but outsiders unfamiliar with the harsh realities of polar travel later criticized his actions as cruel and unfeeling.

During the final weeks of the journey southward, Amundsen and his comrades crossed a foggy, blizzard-torn plateau. At 95 miles from their destination, they passed the southernmost point reached on January 9, 1909, by Ernest SHACKLETON, the explorer who had come closest to the pole before them. They did not know, though, whether Scott and his men might also have passed that point and beaten them to the South Pole.

On December 14, 1911, Amundsen's party reached the South Pole and planted the Norwegian flag there. To their great relief, they saw no trace of the Scott expedition during the several days they spent camping and exploring the vicinity. Amundsen's change of plan had paid off—he had achieved a landmark feat in the history of exploration. He led his men and the remaining dogs safely back to Framheim, and soon the *Fram* was on its way to Tasmania so that Amundsen could announce the news by telegraph. Later Amundsen learned that Scott's party reached the South Pole a month after he and his team had left. Tragically, the British explorers had perished on the way back to their base camp.

Return to the Arctic

Amundsen's achievement made him a hero of exploration. He shared the experience in his book *The South Pole,* published in 1912. The Arctic still beckoned, however, and Amundsen devoted the rest of his life to adventures in the polar north.

Troubles on Ice. Returning to his former plan of drifting across the North Pole in an icebound ship, he built the *Maud* to withstand the crushing pressure of the ice and equipped it for scientific research as well as exploration. Harald Urik Sverdrup, a member of the crew, was an oceanographer and meteorologist who could make observations about the magnetism, weather, and geography of the polar region.

The voyage of the *Maud,* which occurred between 1918 and 1925, was a disappointment to Amundsen, however. Several times the ship froze in coastal ice where it remained unmoving for years at a time, and it required extensive repairs. Unable to accomplish his goal of drifting across the North Pole in the moving ice pack, Amundsen left the *Maud* in 1921. Sverdrup's geophysical* researches, however, did contribute to scientists' knowledge of the far north.

*geophysical of or relating to the structure and physical characteristics of the earth

Aerial Exploration. Having failed to set a North Pole record by sea, Amundsen took to the air. He believed that the new field of aviation offered great potential for polar exploration, and he hoped to become the first person to fly over the North Pole. In 1925 the American adventurer Lincoln Ellsworth had financed a flight north from Norway, but the expedition had to turn back because of mechanical trouble.

*dirigible blimplike airship carried aloft by a large envelope of lighter-than-air gas; unlike a balloon, a dirigible has a motor and a steering device for directed flight

Neil Alden
ARMSTRONG

born 1930

SPACE EXPLORATION

*aeronautical of or relating to aeronautics, the scientific study of flight

A year later Amundsen and Ellsworth tried again, this time flying not in an airplane but in the *Norge,* a dirigible* designed and flown by Umberto Nobile of Italy. During a 72-hour flight, they traveled from Norway to Alaska, crossing over the North Pole. This triumph of exploration, which Ellsworth and Amundsen described in 1927 in *First Crossing of the Polar Sea,* was marred by quarrels between Nobile and Amundsen over who deserved the primary credit for the achievement.

When Nobile crashed in the Arctic two years later, however, Amundsen joined the rescue effort. He boarded a flight that set out from Norway to look for Nobile. Another group of searchers found and rescued the stranded Italian and his men, but Amundsen's plane and all aboard disappeared during the search and were never found.

On July 20, 1969, Neil Armstrong achieved a feat about which most humans can only dream. Uttering the words, "That's one small step for a man, one giant leap for mankind," he became the first person to set foot on the moon, and his name became synonymous with space exploration.

Armstrong was born on his grandparents' farm in Wapakoneta, Ohio, and grew up with an interest in air travel. He earned a private pilot's license on his sixteenth birthday and a year later became a cadet in the U.S. Navy. He enrolled at Purdue University to study aeronautical* engineering, but his studies were interrupted in 1950, when he was called to serve in the Korean War. Armstrong flew combat missions from an aircraft carrier and won three medals for his service in the war.

The war ended in 1953 and Armstrong returned to Purdue to complete his studies. He worked in the Lewis Flight Propulsion Laboratory in Cleveland until 1955, when he moved to California to become a test pilot at Edwards Air Force Base. He flew more than 200 types of aircraft, including the X-15 rocket plane. In 1962 he joined the National Aeronautics and Space Administration (NASA) as the first civilian astronaut (until that time all astronauts were active military officers). That same year, President John F. Kennedy set a goal of "landing man on the moon and returning him safely to the earth."

After four years of training, Armstrong was named commander of the *Gemini 8* spacecraft, which was to dock with an unmanned spacecraft in earth's orbit. The docking was successful, but shortly thereafter the craft began to spin out of control. Acting quickly and calmly, Armstrong used the spacecraft's rockets to stop the spin and made a safe emergency landing in the Pacific Ocean. NASA awarded him its Exceptional Service Medal for displaying courage during the emergency.

Three years later, Armstrong was chosen as commander of *Apollo 11.* The mission's goal was to land the first person on the moon. The spacecraft, carrying Armstrong, Edwin "Buzz" Aldrin, Jr., and Michael Collins, lifted off on July 16, 1969, from Cape Kennedy (later renamed Cape Canaveral), Florida. Four days later, at 4:18 P.M. U.S. Eastern Daylight Time, the "Eagle" lunar landing module of the craft touched down on the moon. At 10:56 P.M., Armstrong stepped out of the module on a plain near the Sea of Tranquility and spoke his famous words. For the next two and a half hours, he and Aldrin set up scientific instruments, collected samples, and took photographs of the moon. The following day, after 21 hours and 36 minutes on the moon, the module left the lunar surface to rejoin the Apollo command module orbiting the moon.

Armstrong and his colleagues returned to earth on July 24, 1969, and they were held in isolation for 18 days to guard against possible contamination by lunar microorganisms*. Armstrong was hailed as a hero and was awarded the NASA Distinguished Service Medal, the Congressional Space Medal of Honor, and the Medal of Freedom, the highest award an American civilian can receive. He retired from NASA in 1971 and settled on a farm in Lebanon, Ohio, with his wife and sons. He later taught aerospace engineering at the University of Cincinnati and served on the boards of several companies. In 1986 he served on the commission that investigated the explosion of the space shuttle *Challenger.*

*microorganism organism invisible without the use of a microscope

---

Vasco Núñez de Balboa belonged to a generation of conquistadors* who, often violently and ruthlessly, brought Mexico and much of Central and South America under Spanish control. His place in the history of exploration is secure because he led the first European expedition that made an overland crossing of the Americas from the Atlantic Ocean to the Pacific Ocean south of the Rio Grande. By proving that a great sea lay beyond Panama, Balboa made an important contribution to Europeans' knowledge of American geography. He also gave new energy to the European effort to find a sea passage around or through the Americas. Within a few years, the Portuguese mariner Ferdinand MAGELLAN would succeed in that effort, sailing into the ocean that Balboa had seen.

Vasco Núñez de
BALBOA
1475–1519
CENTRAL AMERICAN EXPLORATION

*conquistador Spanish military conqueror and explorer

To Darién. Balboa was born in Jerez de los Caballeros in the Castile region of Spain. His father was a low-ranking nobleman who had some status but little wealth. Consequently, the young Balboa went to work in a more prosperous noble household in the port city of Moguer. There, during the mid- to late 1490s, he encountered ships setting sail for and returning from the Americas and sailors who told fascinating stories of the new lands on the far side of the Atlantic. Balboa, like many other young men of his social class, began to dream of winning his fortune in the lands that Spain had begun to explore and colonize in that region.

In 1501 Balboa received his chance to embark for the Americas. He joined a Spanish expedition that set out to explore the coast of Colombia, and afterward he became a settler in Hispaniola, Spain's first American colony. (The island of Hispaniola is today divided between the nations of Haiti and the Dominican Republic.) Balboa was a failure as a farmer, however, and was soon forced to flee Hispaniola to escape his debts. In 1510 he left the island as a stowaway aboard a ship that was carrying supplies to San Sebastián, a new colony recently founded on the Colombian coast by Francisco Pizarro, a conquistador.

When the supply ship arrived in San Sebastián, the crew found that Pizarro had abandoned the colony because of the hostile indigenous* people and the lack of food. Balboa, who held the post of a soldier in the supply expedition, suggested that the colony might be more successful if it were relocated to a village in present-day Panama that he had seen during his first voyage. He knew that the people there were more peaceful and that there were no food shortages. The settlers accepted his advice, moved to that coast, and the following year established the colony of Santa María la Antigua del Darién, which was considered the first stable Spanish settlement in South America.

The South Sea. The settlers chose Balboa as their leader and drove away Francisco Enciso, the commander of the expedition on which Balboa had been a stowaway. Shortly thereafter, King Ferdinand II of Spain sent news that he had named Balboa the temporary governor of Darién. Meanwhile, the overthrown and furious Enciso left for Spain to press charges against Balboa, who realized that only a spectacular achievement or discovery would help him win the king's favor.

To this end Balboa began to recruit slaves from among the Indians and organized a series of gold-hunting expeditions around Darién. He looted jewels and gold from the local peoples, amassing a fortune. Many Indians told Balboa tales of a body of water, a large lake or a sea, that lay south of Darién, and that somewhere on its distant shores was a rich kingdom with much gold—perhaps a reference to the Inca empire of Peru that Pizarro would later conquer. Balboa sent a message to Ferdinand, asking him for men and equipment to undertake an expedition to locate the sea and the gold. Ferdinand, meanwhile, had decided to replace Balboa and send a nobleman named Pedro Arias Dávila, also known as Pedrarias, to govern Darién. Without waiting for authorization and reinforcements from Ferdinand, Balboa set out on September 1, 1513, with 190 men and about 1,000 Indian guides and porters*. When Pedrarias arrived in Darién with orders to send Balboa back to Spain to respond to Enciso's accusations, he found Balboa gone.

Claim to Fame. Balboa and his crew sailed to Acla, a point on the Atlantic shore where the Isthmus* of Panama is narrowest. From there the expedition marched toward the legendary body of water. They traversed swamps, jungles, and mountains and defended themselves against hostile Indians along the way. On September 27, when they had traveled a distance of about 50 miles, Balboa's guides told him that the sea would be visible from a nearby mountain peak. Balboa climbed up alone and gazed southward and saw a limitless expanse of water. He named it the South Sea and claimed it and all the lands on its shores for Spain. Balboa was the first known European to see the eastern shore of the Pacific Ocean, but he did not know that it was the same Pacific that other European explorers had seen from Asia. He only knew that it

Vasco Núñez de Balboa, seen here on his way to the Pacific, is often depicted as befriending the Indians he met and having good relations with Indian chiefs. He was not always compassionate, however, often enslaving the Indians and punishing them severely if they resisted.

*indigenous referring to the original inhabitants of a region

*porter person who carries a load

*isthmus narrow stretch of land connecting two larger landmasses and separating two bodies of water

was an important discovery. After he and his men had wet their feet in the new sea, Balboa returned to Darién in triumph.

A Violent End. Balboa's achievement made him popular with the colonists and restored him to Ferdinand's favor. Unfortunately, it aroused the jealousy of Pedrarias, who became an even worse enemy than Enciso, despite the fact that Pedrarias had given his daughter in marriage to Balboa. Pedrarias did everything he could to stand in Balboa's way, but eventually he gave Balboa permission to explore the South Sea and possibly even seek out the golden kingdom of the south.

Balboa supervised the construction of a fleet of ships, which were then carried in pieces across the Isthmus of Panama, from Acla to the Pacific shore. When he reached the Pacific coast, he received word that Pedrarias wanted to discuss important matters with him, so he returned to Darién. In reality, Pedrarias was devising a plan to secure his own safety, because he had learned that the king was sending an official to Darién to investigate *him*. Fearing that Balboa would give the investigator evidence of Pedrarias's misrule of the colony, Pedrarias declared Balboa a traitor, rushed him through a quick and unjust trial, and had him publicly beheaded.

The German explorer and geographer Heinrich Barth is considered one of the foremost observers of African society and culture. The 3,500-page account of his journey across the Sahara from Tripoli to Lake Chad, *Travels and Discoveries in North and Central Africa, 1849–55*, is one of the earliest and best works of scholarship on the region. However, its value went unrecognized until years after Barth's death.

Early Life and Journeys. Barth was the son of a successful self-made businessman in Hamburg, Germany. He attended the University of Berlin, where he studied archaeology*, history, geography, and law. He was also an accomplished linguist who spoke fluent English, French, Spanish, and Italian. In 1844, when he graduated with a Ph.D. in law, he traveled to London where he spent a year learning and perfecting his Arabic.

From 1845 to 1847 Barth embarked on a tour of the North African coast of present-day Libya and Tunisia. After the tour he returned to Germany and took a post as a lecturer in archaeology at the University of Bonn, but his classes attracted few students. In 1849 he received an invitation to join a British expedition to Central Africa; a colleague had recommended Barth to the Prussian* Ambassador to London, who had passed on his name to the leader of the expedition, James Richardson.

Richardson had led an expedition into the Sahara three years earlier. On that trip, sponsored by the British and Foreign Anti-Slavery Society, he traveled 700 miles into the Sahara. His reports on the trip and on the slave trade in particular made a deep impression in Britain, and the government had asked him to return and learn more about the region. When Richardson met Barth he asked Barth to join him.

Heinrich
BARTH

1821–1865

EXPLORATION OF
AFRICA, GEOGRAPHY

*archaeology scientific study of past human life and activities, usually by excavating ruins

*Prussian of or relating to Prussia, a country that existed from the 1400s until 1947 in the area of present-day eastern and central Europe

Exploring Was in His Blood

Barth's ability to remain calm in a crisis served him well on several occasions. At one point during a side trip, he set out to climb a mountain that local folklore said was the home of evil spirits. Barth reached the top of the mountain, but along the way he had finished all of his water. Worn out and thirsty, he began to lose consciousness and fell to the ground. When he came to, he was consumed by thirst. Thinking quickly, he cut open one of his veins and drank his own blood to quench his thirst. Eventually a local inhabitant found him and helped him return to the expedition.

From the Shores of Tripoli. Richardson, Barth, and a German geologist named Adolf Overweg began their journey from the Tunisian city of Tripoli in March 1850. The group was well equipped with a large number of guides and porters and an abundance of equipment and supplies. They also carried a large wooden boat, built in two separate sections, with which they planned to explore Lake Chad.

From Tripoli the expedition traveled south toward the city of Kano in present-day Nigeria. About 500 miles south, near the desert town of Murzuq, Barth found the ruins of an ancient Roman settlement. Farther south, he found rock paintings made by peoples who had lived there from the Stone Age to about A.D. 100.

Barth and Richardson soon discovered that they disliked each other, and the Germans and British formed two factions. They rode apart, often ate and slept in separate camps, and took different side trips. On one such side trip, Barth became separated from the rest of the Germans and nearly lost his life before he was rescued. In addition to the hostility within the party, the explorers had to deal with attacks by bandits. In the Aïr Mountains, hostile Tuareg people threatened to kill them if they did not give up their Christian faith. Ultimately, the Tuareg were pacified with a third of the party's supplies and allowed the explorers to safely proceed to the city of Ghat.

A Group Divided. Barth and his party then set out toward Agadez, where he was the honored guest of the king. He rejoined the expedition in October 1850 but again parted ways three months later. Richardson chose to go directly to Lake Chad, while Barth and the Germans decided to look for a western route to the lake. Barth would later separate from Overweg to explore in a different direction. The three men agreed to meet near the lake at the town of Kuka (present-day Kukawa, Nigeria) in April 1851, but Richardson died of fever shortly before the meeting.

By May 1851 Barth and Overweg had reunited at Lake Chad, but Overweg was suffering from fever and exhaustion. While Overweg stayed at the lake to recover, Barth continued to explore the areas to the east and south. He traveled south to the town of Yola and became the first European to see and explore the Benue River. Overweg regained his health and he explored the lake by boat. During the 15 months that the group remained at Lake Chad, the British government heard of Richardson's death and named Barth the new leader. The government also sent additional funds for the remaining members of the party.

The expedition prepared to continue to its next destination, the fabled city of Timbuktu in present-day Mali, but Overweg died suddenly of malaria. Barth also suffered from fever and dysentery, but despite his sicknesses and the deaths of his crewmembers, he decided to push farther. In November 1852 he headed west to Timbuktu. He thought it might take him as long as two years to reach the city, but he arrived there in September 1853. Barth reported that the city, a one-time trading center of the Sahara, had lost much of its former splendor.

The Long Road Home. Barth left Timbuktu in May 1854 and headed back to Kuka. En route, he learned that the British government, fearing that Barth and his party were dead, had sent a search party led by the German explorer Eduard Vogel. The two met at Kuka; Vogel decided to remain in the region and explore the lower Niger River and Barth headed back to Tripoli. By September 1855 Barth had returned to London. Vogel, however, was killed in Wadai in central Africa the following year.

In a little more than five years, Barth had traveled 10,000 miles and gathered enough information to make the first reliable large-scale maps of north and central Africa. In *Travels,* published in 1858–1859, he recorded a wealth of information about the history, cultures, and languages of the people who inhabited the areas he visited. Although the work was thorough, it was not a critical success. Frustrated by the lack of recognition for his book, Barth returned to Germany in 1859.

More disappointment awaited Barth in Germany. He was denied full membership in the Royal Academy of Sciences and the German government turned down his requests to be appointed ambassador to Siam or Constantinople. Moreover, when his mentor, the geographer Carl RITTER, died, Barth was not named to succeed him as professor of geography in Berlin, despite his advanced academic degrees and experiences in the field. Barth spent the rest of his life traveling in Europe. Before his death in Berlin at the young age of 44, he published a collection of vocabularies of central African languages.

Faddei F.
BELLINSGAUZEN
1779–1852
NAVIGATION, OCEANOGRAPHY

*oceanographic of or relating to oceanography, the study of oceans

Faddei F. Bellinsgauzen began his naval career at the age of ten and is most famous for his expedition to the Antarctic. Although it is disputed whether he was the first navigator to sight Antarctica, he was definitely the first to describe the Southern Ocean surrounding Antarctica and to conduct oceanographic* experiments there.

Bellinsgauzen was born in Arensburg, on the island of Oesel, Russia (present-day Kingissepp, Estonia). At the age of ten, he left home to become a naval cadet at the Russian military fortress of Kronstadt. After finishing his studies at Kronstadt, he joined the first Russian round-the-world voyage, which was led by Ivan F. Kruzenstern, a young lieutenant commander. Bellinsgauzen was responsible for most of the maps made during the voyage. He later commanded several naval expeditions to the Baltic and Black Seas, correcting many errors on the existing charts of the Black Sea shoreline.

Because of the scientific knowledge and naval experience that Bellinsgauzen had gained from these voyages, he was chosen as commander of the first Russian expedition to the Antarctic in 1819. He was in charge of the *Vostok,* the flagship; a second ship carrying supplies, the *Mirny,* was commanded by Mikhail P. Lazarev. The ships first sailed to England, where Bellinsgauzen met with the botanist Joseph Banks, who had been on Captain James COOK's earlier voyage to the Antarctic region and who provided maps and books to the Russian expedition.

After several months of sailing south, the ships reached a group of islands that Bellinsgauzen named South Sandwich Islands. (Cook had mistakenly believed the group to be one large island.) Relying on icebergs to supply drinking water, the ships continued to sail farther south than Cook's expedition had. In the winter of 1820, Bellinsgauzen sighted a solid ice mass 20 miles away, which turned out to be the Antarctic mainland. Whether he was the first person to sight the mainland is an ongoing scientific dispute. the English claim that Edward Bransfield arrived there first; the Americans say it was Nathaniel Palmer; and the Russians insist it was Bellinsgauzen.

Bellinsgauzen continued to sail along the Antarctic coastline, returning to Australia whenever the weather became too severe. At last, in 1821, having sailed around Antarctica, the expedition turned north and docked at Rio de Janeiro, Brazil, where they rested and overhauled the ships before returning to Kronstadt.

In 751 days, the two ships had sailed more than 55,000 miles through brutal weather, discovering 29 islands and a coral reef, and conducting many experiments. Bellinsgauzen accurately determined the position of the south magnetic pole (not in the same location as the geographic South Pole) and described and classified the Antarctic ice.

When Bellinsgauzen's accounts were published ten years later, many people became convinced of the existence of a continent near the South Pole. The explorer was never again involved in such an important expedition, but he served as an admiral in the Russian navy for 30 years, became governor of Kronstadt, and helped found the Russian Geographic Society. He died in Kronstadt at the age of 72. A sea in the Antarctic, a cape in the southern part of Sakhalin Island (Russia), and an island in the Tuamotus (French Polynesia) were renamed in his honor.

More than a century passed before Russia sent any further expeditions to Antarctica. After the end of World War II, Russian whaling fleets sailed toward Antarctica, and a scientific base was established there during the International Geophysical Year (1957–1958).

Vitus Jonassen
BERING

1681–1741

EXPLORATION OF SIBERIA
AND ALASKA

Vitus Jonassen Bering led two Russian exploring expeditions—one concerned with the exploration of Siberia, Russia's vast eastern territory; and another with one of the most urgent geographic mysteries of his day, the question of whether northeastern Asia and northwestern North America are connected by land or separated by water. The latter voyage not only advanced geographic knowledge but also had economic and political results, paving the way for a fur-trading outpost of the Russian empire in Alaska.

Journey to Kamchatka, 1725–1730

Bering was born in Horsens, Denmark. One of many children, he became a sailor at an early age to earn a living. In his early twenties, Bering joined the Russian navy, a newly formed service that offered opportunities for advancement. Soon he rose to the rank of commander, married, and raised a family. Bering spent the rest of his life in Russia, returning only once to Denmark, to visit Copenhagen in 1715.

In 1724 Peter the Great, Russia's ruler, decided to send an expedition to explore the waters off Asia's northeastern coast to determine whether Asia and America were connected by land or separated by water. Before they could enter those waters, however, the explorers had to cross Siberia, an immense and still largely unexplored frontier of the Russian empire. Bering was placed in command of the mission. He would be carrying on an eastward expansion that had begun several centuries earlier, when English, Dutch, and Russian explorers had begun to probe the Arctic Ocean north of Russia and to venture into the forests of Siberia.

Earlier Explorers of the Northeast Passage and Siberia. By the mid-1500s, Portugal and Spain had claimed the southern sea routes that led from Europe to Asia around the southern coasts of Africa and South America. Dutch and English merchants, seeking other ways for their commercial (or merchant) ships to reach Asia, turned north. Some sought a Northwest Passage* through or around North America. Others searched for a Northeast Passage*, which they hoped to find by sailing east along the northern shores of Europe and Russia.

By the 1550s, English, Dutch, and Russian sailors and traders had begun to make voyages between western Europe and the coastal city of Archangel in northern Russia, sailing around the northern tip of Norway. Geographers knew nothing about what lay farther east of Archangel, but explorers hoped that somehow the Arctic Ocean north of Europe was connected to the Pacific Ocean, which washed the far shores of China and the rest of Asia.

In the 1590s the Dutch explorer Willem Barents pushed farther eastward, sailing north around Novaya Zemlya, a large island off the Russian Arctic coast. Trapped by winter, Barents and his companions survived in a driftwood shelter on the island, but Barents perished on the voyage back to Western Europe. Thereafter Russian voyagers heading east stayed closer to the continental shore, and by the end of the 1500s they had established a route to a fur-trading center at the mouth of the Ob River on the Arctic coast of western Siberia.

The Russians were also pushing eastward by land, driven by the desire for Siberian furs. In the 1580s a Russian force crossed the Ural Mountains, the geographic boundary between Europe and Asia. In 1641 a party of Russian adventurers traversed the continent, arriving at the Sea of Okhotsk, an arm of the North Pacific Ocean. By that time the Russians had also pushed their coastal trade routes as far east as the mouth of the Kolyma River, north of the Sea of Okhotsk.

In 1648 a Russian fur trader named Semyon Dezhnyov led a fleet of ships to the Anadyr region, east of Kolyma, because he had heard that that region was rich in furs. Dezhnyov's own ship went farthest, rounding a cape (now called Cape Dezhnyov) at the northeastern tip of Asia and then turning south. Dezhnyov reached the Anadyr and returned to

During the last Ice Age, sea levels sank, exposing a land bridge between Asia and America. This bridge, which allowed for migration of animals and humans between the two continents, was named Beringia in Vitus Bering's honor. It submerged as ocean levels again rose at the end of the Ice Age.

*Northwest Passage water route connecting the Atlantic and Pacific Oceans through the Arctic islands of northern Canada

*Northeast Passage water route along the northern coast of the Eurasian landmass, lying mainly off northern Russian Siberia

See the routes of Bering's voyages in the "Maps" section.

Bringing Bering to Life

In 1991, Russian scientists and representatives from the Horsens Museum in Bering's Danish birthplace teamed up to search for the explorer's remains on Bering Island. They succeeded in locating his grave and five others belonging to his crew and took the remains to Moscow. There, scientists skilled in re-creating the facial features of skeletons worked on Bering's skull to produce an image of him as he likely looked in life. The following year, all six men were reburied on the island where they had died. The Horsens Museum in Denmark now houses a sculpture of Bering, a cast of his skull, and a reconstruction of his grave.

*caravan large group of people traveling together across a desert or other dangerous region

write a report of his trip. He is the first European known to have sailed through the passage of water between Asia and North America (present-day Bering Strait). His voyage had proved the existence of a waterway between Asia and North America, but his report lay buried in the Russian archives, and no one heard of his discovery for nearly a century. Consequently, in 1724 Peter the Great sent Bering across Siberia to answer the question that Dezhnyov had already answered.

Bering's Expedition. Preparations for Bering's expedition took a year. Another two years passed as Bering and his second in command, Aleksey Ilich Chirikov, led the inland expedition across Siberia to the port city of Okhotsk on the western coast of the Sea of Okhotsk. There the crew built a vessel to carry them to the western coast of the Kamchatka Peninsula, a huge southward-stretching landmass that separates the Sea of Okhotsk from the Pacific. Bering and his men reached Kamchatka and traveled in caravans* across the peninsula. Kamchatka was new territory to Europeans, and Bering was the first to map it.

On the Pacific coast of Kamchatka, the expedition members built another ship, the *St. Gabriel,* in which Bering set out in 1728 to find out what lay between Siberia and North America. He sailed north along the coast and discovered an island that he named after Saint Lawrence. Farther north Bering passed a cape and entered a broad sea. Convinced that there was no more land ahead, he turned back. The cape that he had passed was Cape Dezhnyov and the sea was the Chukchi Sea, a part of the Arctic Ocean. Bering had sailed between Asia and North America through the eastern end of the long-sought-after Northeast Passage, but bad weather had prevented him from sighting North America to the west. Convinced that the two continents were separated by water, but without the evidence to prove his claim, he turned back.

After returning to Kamchatka, Bering set out on another voyage, but he was blown off course. He went south and discovered that it is possible to sail around the southern end of the peninsula into the Sea of Okhotsk. Bering then led his expedition back across Siberia to St. Petersburg, which he reached in 1730.

Bering was convinced that he had discovered the Northeast Passage, but he could not prove it because he had turned south before sighting any known landmark on the Russian Arctic coast. Critics pointed out that Bering could not be certain that he had passed the end of Asia. Perhaps Asia and North America were connected somewhere north of where he had sailed. Bering also received criticism for not having sighted the western coast of North America. That honor went to two Russians, Ivan Fyodorov and Mikhail Gvozdev, who, in 1732, sailed from Cape Dezhnyov to the western shore of Alaska, exploring near present-day Nome, Alaska. They were the first Europeans known to have seen Alaska.

The Great Northern Expedition, 1733–1743

In spite of the criticisms of Bering's expedition, the Danish explorer received the support of the Russian government for a second expedition to more fully explore and map the waters north of Kamchatka. Under the sponsorship of the Russian Admiralty, the government bureau in charge of naval matters, Bering's second trip grew into a large, complex, and ambitious enterprise known as the Great Northern Expedition. The expedition was planned not only to conduct geographic research but also to establish Russian territorial claims and promote Russian commercial interests in the North Pacific.

The Great Northern Expedition had many goals: to map the Arctic coast of Russia and Siberia; to map Siberia's Pacific coast, including the Kamchatka Peninsula and the Kurile Islands between Kamchatka and Japan; to send ships to Japan; and to land in North America. Seven surveying parties, totaling nearly 1,000 men, would fan out to sail along and chart the coasts. Bering, the chief planner and overall head of the expedition, and Chirikov, again his second in command, would attempt to reach North America.

Surveying Siberia. The expeditions encountered many obstacles. Time after time ice blocked the vessels along the northern coast. The captains had to decide whether to turn back to safe harbors and hope to complete their missions the following year or to spend the winter in the Arctic, risking such hazards as bitter cold and malnutrition. Many expedition members, including leaders of two of the seven survey parties, died of scurvy, a vitamin-deficiency disease. Caused by a shortage of fresh fruit and vegetables in the diet, scurvy killed many travelers at sea and in cold climates before explorers learned to combat it with lime juice and other remedies.

Not all of the expedition's work was done by sea. Some groups traveled by dogsled to map the northern coast of the Taymyr Peninsula, a landmass that extends far into the Arctic Ocean. One of these groups, led by Semyon Chelyuskin, reached the northernmost point of the Taymyr, which is also the northernmost point in continental Europe and Asia. It is known as Cape Chelyuskin in his honor.

Despite all the difficulties, the surveying parties produced 62 maps and charts of Kamchatka and the Arctic coast as far east as the Kolyma River. As a result of their work, geographers learned far more about the northern coast of Asia than about the Arctic coast of North America, which remained almost completely unknown in the mid-1700s.

Geographers and navigators benefited greatly from the expedition's work, but the surveys did not open up a commercial shipping passage through the Northeast Passage as the Russian government had hoped that it would. The expedition's reports made it clear that the waters of the Arctic coast were too treacherous for regular travel, chiefly because of ice. In the 60 years after the expedition, only one Russian trader attempted to sail the Northeast Passage east from the Kolyma River. He disappeared, and the Chukchi people later found the skeletal remains of his crew at the camp where they had tried to spend the winter.

The Voyages of Bering and Chirikov. Although Bering left St. Petersburg in 1733 when the expedition began, he spent the next few years overseeing the surveying parties. Not until mid-1740 was he ready to embark on his mission to North America. Bering set sail from Okhotsk to the west coast of Kamchatka Peninsula in the *St. Peter*. Chirikov commanded a companion ship, *St. Paul*. Each ship was accompanied by smaller boats to carry supplies and make landings.

The two ships sailed south through the Sea of Okhotsk and around Kamchatka. They founded the town of Petropavlovsk on the peninsula's east coast and set out again. About three weeks into the voyage, a storm separated Chirikov and Bering. Chirikov continued to sail east and soon sighted Prince of Wales Island off the southern Alaskan coast. He sent two parties ashore in small boats, but neither returned. With his crew reduced in number and suffering from scurvy, Chirikov headed west and returned to Kamchatka, sighting the Aleutian Islands on the way.

After separating from Chirikov, Bering sailed northeast, entering the Gulf of Alaska. He sighted the St. Elias Mountains and sent ashore a party led by Georg Wilhelm Steller, a scientist who made the first reports on the wildlife of Alaska. The short Arctic summer gave Bering little time to explore—he wanted to return to Kamchatka before winter set in and made the Pacific crossing dangerous, if not impossible. Still, he managed to survey part of Alaska's southwest coast, the Alaska Peninsula, and the Aleutian Islands before heading west.

Battered by the storms of early winter and weakened by scurvy, the *St. Peter* and its crew could not complete the crossing. They were wrecked on an island off the coast of Kamchatka. Forced to spend the winter there, the men huddled in shelters made of driftwood piled over pits in the sand. About half the crew, including Bering, died. The following spring, Chirikov sailed from Kamchatka to search for Bering but had to return to port without locating the missing ship or its men. Then a few survivors from the island managed to reach Kamchatka in the small supply boats. They brought word of Bering's discoveries in Alaska and his fate on the island.

The survivors also described the Alaskan coast as teeming with furbearing animals such as seals and sea otters. Within a short time Russian fur traders were crossing the northern sea to load their ships with Alaskan furs. Eventually they founded trading posts and settlements in Alaska, which for a time was part of the Russian empire.

Bering's Legacy. Every map of the North Pacific Ocean reflects Bering's geographic legacy. The island where he died is called Bering Island; it is part of the Komandorskiye Islands (also known as Commander Islands), belonging to Russia. The northern portion of the Pacific Ocean between Siberia and Alaska is known as the Bering Sea, and the arm of it that separates Asia and North America is the Bering Strait. Bering's name has even been attached to a land that no living person has ever seen. When modern scientists realized that low sea levels during past ice ages exposed a land bridge between Siberia and Alaska, they understood that animals and people had migrated from Asia to the Americas across land that is now covered by the Bering Strait. They gave this bridge between continents the name Beringia.

The son of a French notary*, Louis Antoine de Bougainville had no intention of following in his father's footsteps. Instead, he began his career as a mathematician and later distinguished himself as an explorer when he became the first Frenchman to sail around the world.

Born in Paris, Bougainville began his mathematical career when he was barely into his 20s. He expanded and updated the first textbook on calculus* that had been written half a century earlier. Bougainville's writings on the subject were so highly regarded that he was elected to the Royal Society, England's prestigious scientific organization. However, at that point he abandoned mathematics and, at the age of 24, he joined the French army. The army sent Bougainville to Canada, where he fought against the British in the French and Indian War (1754–1763). After the war, he transferred to the French navy and set sail to the southern tip of South America, where he established a French colony in the Falkland Islands. When France handed over the colony to Spain in 1767, he set out on his next adventure: the first French voyage around the world.

Setting out in *La Boudeuse,* Bougainville first stopped at Rio de Janeiro to meet his supply ship. There he encountered the French botanist Philibert Commerson, who was aboard the supply ship. Commerson had collected many plant specimens in Rio de Janeiro, including a climbing shrub with large purple-red bracts that he had named bougainvillea in honor of the explorer.

The two ships set sail in 1767 and traveled through the Strait of Magellan and discovered islands in the Tuamotu Archipelago, a group of French Polynesian islands in the South Pacific Ocean. They sailed to Tahiti, Samoa, and the New Hebrides Islands, and then pushed farther west into regions no other European ship had visited. Bougainville almost reached the Great Barrier Reef but turned north without exploring further or sighting Australia. The expedition then traveled through the Louisiade Archipelago, the Treasury Islands, and the Solomons. Next they arrived in the Moluccas, where Bougainville confirmed the French naturalist Georges-Louis Buffon's suspicion that pouched mammals inhabited the East Indies.

On this expedition, Bougainville became the first explorer to create navigational charts using systematic astronomical observations, which was extremely helpful to future explorers. When the crew members began to develop scurvy* and the ships needed repairs, the expedition stopped for supplies and returned home to France, having successfully completed their goal of sailing around the world. The voyage had been remarkably safe for its time; only seven men died. After his return to France, Bougainville wrote in *Voyage autour du monde* (Voyage Around the World) that "geography is a science of facts; one cannot speculate from an armchair without the risk of making mistakes which are often corrected only at the expense of sailors."

In 1772 Bougainville became secretary to King Louis XV, and seven years later he was appointed captain of the French fleet that supported the colonists during the American Revolution. In 1782 he underwent a court-martial after the navy suffered a defeat near the

Louis Antoine de
BOUGAINVILLE
1729–1811

GEOGRAPHY, MATHEMATICS, EXPLORATION

***notary** public officer who certifies documents to make them authentic

***calculus** advanced branch of mathematics

***scurvy** disease caused by a lack of vitamin C and characterized by bleeding gums, bleeding under the skin, and extreme weakness

island of Martinique. Although he was a supporter of the French monarchy, he managed to escape the massacres during the French Revolution and lived out the rest of his life at his estate in Normandy. Napoleon I made Bougainville a senator and a count of the empire. His other honors included election to the Académie des Sciences and membership in the Legion of Honor. Bougainville died in Paris at the age of 81 and was buried with full honors in the Panthéon, a building dedicated to the memory of great Frenchmen.

Louise Arner
BOYD

1887–1972

ARCTIC EXPLORATION

*fiord deep, narrow, often winding inlet found on mountainous seacoasts (also spelled fjord)

At the age of 68, the American Louise Arner Boyd became the first woman to fly over the North Pole. Her real contributions to geographic exploration, however, came earlier in her career, when she led expeditions that studied and mapped little-known regions of the Arctic.

Boyd was born in San Rafael, California, into a wealthy and socially prominent family. Educated at home and at private schools, she developed an early interest in geography, especially stories of Arctic exploration. She also learned to enjoy riding and shooting. She did not attend college. In 1920, when Boyd inherited her family's fortune, she began traveling. After a few years touring Europe, she took a cruise that gave her a glimpse of the Arctic Ocean and the northern world she called "an immensity of lonely mountains, fiords*, and glaciers." The experience inspired Boyd with a determination to explore that world.

For her first Arctic venture in 1925, she took friends on a hunting trip to Franz Joseph Land, a cluster of islands north of Russia, aboard a rented ship that had been part of an expedition led by the Norwegian polar explorer Roald AMUNDSEN. Three years later, in 1928, she hired the same ship and joined a far-ranging search for Amundsen and his group, who had disappeared while flying toward the North Pole. The remains of neither Amundsen nor his crew were ever found, but the mission was Boyd's entry into the world of polar exploration. She gave her extensive photographic and film records of that voyage to the New York–based American Geographic Society (AGS), beginning a long-lasting, mutually fulfilling relationship with that organization. The AGS was noted for its pioneering work in exploration and mapmaking. Boyd was eager to undertake serious research in the Arctic, and the AGS provided her with scientific guidance and published the results of her work. In return, Boyd received financial help from the society for a series of expeditions to the east coast of Greenland.

On the first expedition, in 1931, Boyd discovered a large glacier and took photographs that the AGS used to make new maps of Greenland's northeastern coast. She visited the area three more times during the 1930s, accompanying scientists recommended by the AGS. The expedition members surveyed the region for mapping and charting purposes. They also photographed and collected samples of the region's geology and its plant and animal life. Boyd's tasks were to gather botanical specimens and take pictures with a special instrument called a photogrammetric camera, which produces images used for making detailed, accurate maps. Boyd had received training in photogrammetric techniques so that she could make a genuine scientific contribution to Arctic exploration. In the later expeditions, Boyd pioneered the use of the newly invented echo sounder to measure the depth of the sea. In addition to using the device to map the ocean floor, Boyd's teams discovered that they could use it to locate schools of fish. She published a detailed account of these expeditions in 1935 in *The Fjord Region of East Greenland*.

The Second World War (1939–1945) interrupted Boyd's explorations. During the war she advised the U.S. government on polar conditions and participated in a U.S. Coast Guard expedition to study the effects of polar magnetism on radio broadcasts. Boyd was nearly 60 when the war ended, and she made no further sea voyages to the Arctic. However, she traveled to many other parts of the world and wrote another book about her explorations in Greenland titled *The Coast of Northeast Greenland*.

Boyd's final visit to the Arctic came in 1955, when she hired a plane in Norway and flew across the North Pole. She proudly announced the feat in a telegram to the Society of Women Geographers. Boyd received honors and recognition from the American Polar Society, the British Royal Geographical Society, and the Explorers Club of New York. She died in San Francisco at age 85.

Albert Perry
BRIGHAM

1855–1932

GEOGRAPHY

The American geographer Albert Brigham is best known for outlining the influence of the field of geography on history and on the development of human society. He is considered one of the founders of the scientific field known today as human geography.

Brigham was born on a farm in the small town of Perry in upstate New York. When he was a child, his mother gave him a copy of *A System of Modern Geography*, by S. Augustus Mitchell, originally published in 1860. Brigham became fascinated by the many drawings and maps in the book, spending countless hours looking at them. Although his mother never traveled as much as 50 miles from home, she instilled in her son an interest in the world that would last his entire life.

When Brigham was 20 he enrolled at Madison University (now Colgate University) to study liberal arts. An excellent student, he was also a gifted speaker and writer. One of the classes that he found most interesting was a natural history* course that portrayed the history of the earth as changing and evolving. Brigham wished to pursue his interest in the subject, but he instead followed his father's wishes and entered the ministry. He later entered the Theological* Seminary in Hamilton, New York, and was ordained to the ministry in 1882. He spent the next three years as pastor in the small town of Stillwater before taking a position in a church in the city of Utica.

Brigham's duties as a minister did not keep him from pursuing natural history as a hobby. He devoted long hours to studying the local geography of the areas where he lived. In 1888 he published a book

natural history systematic study of nature and natural objects in their original settings

theological of or relating to theology, the study of religion

about the rocks and landforms around Utica. The following year he took field classes taught by professors from Harvard University. At that time he became convinced that he could do better as a geographer than as a preacher, and two years later he resigned from the ministry.

Brigham enrolled at Harvard to study geography under the professors who had taught the field courses he had attended. In 1892 he earned his master's degree and took a post at Colgate University as a geology instructor. He would spend the next 30 years at that institution. He also taught summer classes at Cornell, Harvard, and Oxford Universities. In addition, he held classes at scientific institutes including the Royal Geographical Society in London.

Brigham's first geology textbook was published in 1901, followed the next year by his *Introduction to Physical Geography*. In the latter text he presented his ideas about the interactions between people and their physical environment. He further elaborated on the topic in his 1903 work titled *Geographic Influences on American History*. These books established his reputation in the field of human geography.

In the years that followed, Brigham continued to publish on the topic of historical geography. In *From Trail to Railway through the Appalachians,* published in 1907, he summarized the results of several studies on routes across the Appalachian Mountains. During this time he also hosted discussions at the annual meetings of the Association of American Geographers (AAG) concerning the influence of geography on history. These discussions involved not only geographers, but also specialists from the fields of history and anthropology*.

anthropology study of human beings, especially in relation to origins and physical and cultural characteristics

In 1914 Brigham was elected president of the AAG, and in his inaugural address he focused on the difficulties of studying geographic influences on human behavior and history. The following year he visited Cape Cod, which led to the book *Cape Cod and the Old Colony,* published in 1920. The renowned American geographer Preston Everett JAMES considered this Brigham's greatest work.

Brigham retired from Colgate in 1925, but he remained active in promoting his field. The Library of Congress named him a "Consultant in Science" in 1930, and that same year he was chosen as an official delegate of the American Geographical Society to attend a celebration of the 100th anniversary of the Royal Geographical Society in London. The AAG honored Brigham on his 75th birthday by dedicating an issue of its annals to tributes to him from his colleagues. He died in Washington, D.C., two years later.

James BRUCE

1730–1794

AFRICAN EXPLORATION

The son of a wealthy Scottish landowner, James Bruce sought to find the source of the Nile River and to explore the interior of East Africa. His adventures marked the beginning of Africa's modern era of exploration, inspiring many explorers to follow. Despite his critics who doubted the truthfulness of his narratives, he became known as the first European explorer of Ethiopia.

Born in Stirlingshire, Scotland, Bruce played with the idea of becoming a clergyman. He later decided to try his hand at studying law but dropped out to serve as British consul general* in Algiers, Africa, from 1763 to 1765. During that time he studied the continent's environment, and when his two-year post came to an end, he began to ready himself for a mission of scientific exploration in Africa. He studied navigation and medicine as well as the geography, culture, and languages of the region. He spoke both of the Abyssinian (Ethiopia is also known as Abyssinia) languages, Tigrinya and Amharic, and could also speak Arabic fluently. Legend has it that if he covered his bright red hair with the proper headdress, he could pass himself off as an Arab.

*consul general official of the first rank who is appointed by a government to live in a foreign place and who represents the commercial interests of citizens of the appointing country

Exploring Ethiopia. In 1768 Bruce began his travels through Ethiopia, determined to find that the source of the Nile River. Two years after beginning his voyage, Bruce reached Gondar, the Abyssinian capital, only to find that the country was in the midst of civil war. Political instability hampered his plans, but because of his medical skills, he gained the favor of King Takla Hayamot. During his stay, Bruce helped curtail an outbreak of smallpox and served in military campaigns for the king.

After several delays caused by the political unrest, Bruce was allowed to continue his exploration. In late 1770, he arrived at the source of the Blue Nile, the main tributary of the White Nile, but he believed it to be the source of the main river. He was not the first European to arrive at this location, however. Two Portuguese Jesuit priests, Jeronimo Lobo and Pedro Páez, had been there nearly 150 years earlier, but their travels were not well known. Although Bruce may have known there were other explorers to make this discovery before him, he denounced the accuracy of their findings and denied that any European had ever scientifically explored the region. He also claimed that he had explored the region more thoroughly than any of his predecessors.

Bruce kept detailed records of his astronomical and meteorological findings during the mission. He collected seeds from several plants and rendered detailed drawings of buildings, plants, and flowers. Later explorers of the same region have attested to the accuracy of his accounts. The trip home was extremely difficult; his party experienced starvation and dehydration. Bruce himself suffered from a guinea worm–infested leg and was held up in Aswan to recover for months.

Writings. When Bruce returned to London, he expected to be praised for his brilliant discoveries. Yet his reception was less than warm. Several British scholars questioned the accuracy of his accounts, and their skepticism may have been partly because he first shared his discoveries with the French. In 1790 he published a detailed account of his expedition in *Travels to Discover the Source of the Nile in the Years 1768, 1769, 1770, 1771, 1772, and 1773,* a five-volume work. He used a skillful narrative with vivid detail and wrote his account for the lay reader rather than for an academic audience. Its pages are full of obvious embellishments of his personal experience.

James Bruce's difficult and conceited personality was one of several reasons that scholars and readers doubted the sincerity of his works.

Bruce was accused of making up stories about his adventure and was discredited by those who respected the discoveries of the Portuguese Jesuits who had preceded him. The author Samuel Johnson, who had translated Pedro Páez's account of Ethiopia, was Bruce's harshest critic. He went so far as to spread rumors that Bruce had never gone to Ethiopia. Although Bruce was not the first to make these "discoveries," his vivid account has become known as an epic of African adventure literature. Another reason his work was closely scrutinized was the late date of its publication; it was published 12 years after the completion of his mission, causing scholars to doubt its accuracy.

Bruce retired to his family estate and died at Kinnaird House in 1794 at age 63.

Richard Francis BURTON

1821–1890

EXPLORATION OF AFRICA

*diplomat one who conducts official relations and negotiations between nations

British author, explorer, and diplomat* Richard Francis Burton is best known for his role in a major geographic adventure of the mid-1800s, the search for the source of Africa's Nile River. One of the most colorful and controversial explorers of the time, Burton also traveled in and wrote about regions of Asia and South America. He is the author of more than 50 books, whose topics range from accounts of his voyages, to poetry, to translations of literary works from the countries he visited. Although these works are valued for their contributions to the study of Asia and Africa, Burton has come under strong criticism—then and now—for using racist vocabulary and including shocking content.

Early Career. Burton was born in Torquay, England, but grew up in France and Italy. He possessed a gift for learning languages, and by the time he began college at Oxford University, he had become fluent in half a dozen. During the course of his life he mastered about 25. A high-spirited and often strong-willed youth, Burton found university life dull and limiting. In 1842 he was expelled for disobedience.

The 21-year-old adventure-seeking Burton then enlisted in the army of the East India Company, a commercial firm that played a central role in Indian politics during the years that Britain controlled that country. He spent the next seven years in Sind, a region now divided between India and Pakistan, where he learned many languages and explored the customs and cultures of local peoples, often by living among them in disguise. Burton acted as a spy for his commanding officer, gathering intelligence in the region. In 1845, when Burton published a controversial report based on his spying activities, his commanding officer left India and Burton's reputation and career were both damaged. Burton then returned to England, where he wrote four books about India and its peoples.

In 1853 Burton turned his attention to Mecca, an Arabian city that is holy to Muslims and forbidden to non-Muslims. He traveled to Mecca and Medina by way of Egypt, passing himself off as a Muslim pilgrim. He wore Arab clothing and darkened his skin with henna, a natural dye. The following year he became the first European to successfully enter and leave Harar, a holy city in Ethiopia also closed to Europeans.

In company with several other British East India Company officers, Burton next tried to cross East Africa from the Red Sea to the Nile River, but attacks by the people of Somalia forced them to turn back. He immediately wrote about his journeys in Arabia and East Africa, including what is considered his best travel book, *Personal Narrative of a Pilgrimage to El Medinah and Mecca.* Like all his writings, it reveals his love of adventure, keen eye for observation, and deep interest in what would come to be known as the science of ethnology*.

ethnology scientific study of the physical and cultural differences between human races

The Quest for the Nile. Burton spent the next several years training Turkish soldiers to fight for the British against Russia in the Crimean War, which took place around the Black Sea. In 1857 he returned to East Africa with a fellow army officer, John Hanning Speke, one of his companions from the earlier Somalia expedition. London's Royal Geographic Society had sponsored an expedition to solve one of the most pressing geographical puzzles of the time: to locate the sources of the White Nile. Burton was the mission's leader.

The expedition left Zanzibar on Africa's Indian Ocean coast and headed inland toward Kazeh (present-day Tabora, Tanzania), battling various illnesses along the way. Burton fell desperately ill with malaria, and Speke suffered from temporary near-blindness. Still they pushed farther inland, and in early 1858 they reached Lake Tanganyika; Burton and Speke became the first white people to see that great body of water. Burton hoped that the lake would prove to be the Nile source, but a quick exploration of its northern shores showed that it was not.

Seriously ill, the expedition returned to Kazeh to regain their health. Speke recovered quickly and set off northward, following African accounts of another, larger lake, while Burton remained in Kazeh. A few months later Speke found Lake Ukerewe, which he renamed Lake Victoria in honor of England's queen. When locals told him of a large river that flowed from the lake's north side, Speke correctly assumed that the lake must be the source of the Nile. He returned to Kazeh to share the news with Burton, who, consumed with jealousy, argued that Speke had no evidence to support his claim. The two men returned to the coast, and Speke hastened to England to announce that he had located the Nile source. When Burton reached England and disputed Speke's claim, the feud between the two explorers and former friends became public. Notwithstanding the debate, the Royal Geographic Society funded Speke to explore Lake Victoria on his own. Burton later described the journey in *The Lake Regions of Central Africa.*

Burton traveled to the United States and visited the Mormon settlement of Salt Lake City, Utah, which he described in *City of the Saints,* published in 1861. He then returned to England, married an aristocratic woman named Isabel Arundell, and entered a new stage of his career by becoming a diplomat.

The Mysterious Death of Mr. Speke

Even after John Speke returned from his second expedition to Lake Victoria, having verified that his initial claim was correct, Burton was not sure that lake was the source of the Nile. In September 1864 the two were to debate the issue at a meeting of the British Association for the Advancement of Science. After the meeting began, but before the debate occurred, Speke was killed by a gunshot wound to his chest during a hunting expedition. The death was ruled an accident, but many people pointed out that Speke was an experienced hunter, unlikely to mishandle his gun. Sure that Speke had committed suicide, Burton said, "The charitable say that he shot himself, the uncharitable say that I shot him."

Later Career. Burton's first assignment was as consul, or representative of the British government, in Fernando Po, an island off the coast of West Africa. During this time he traveled to the Gabon River region and studied the Fang people, who practiced cannibalism. He also journeyed to Nigeria, Cameroon, and Angola. Burton wrote five books about these regions and their peoples. His descriptions of African customs and rituals, including sexual practices as well as those surrounding birth, marriage, and death, were unusually frank for the Victorian age and brought him some criticism.

Next posted to Brazil, Burton traveled widely in South America and continued to write. Later he served as consul in Damascus, Syria, and in the city of Trieste in the empire of Austria-Hungary (now in Italy). Burton remained in Trieste until his death. In the late 1870s he tried unsuccessfully to look for gold in Arabia and later in West Africa.

Literature was the main occupation of Burton's later years. In addition to writing about his travels, he translated a number of works from Arabic or Asian languages. One of these, *The Thousand Nights and a Night,* is considered the best English-language version of the stories that are sometimes called the *Arabian Nights.* Drawing from his own vast knowledge of western Asian and Muslim cultures, Burton added notes on subjects ranging from philosophy to sexual behavior. Hoping to educate the West to the sexual wisdom of Eastern cultures, Burton translated the *Kama Sutra, Ananga Ranga,* and *The Perfumed Garden.* Because his willingness to discuss sexuality was shocking to some, many of his publications were printed in secret. Isabel Burton, always concerned with presenting a "proper" public image of her bold and inquisitive husband, burned most of his journals and private papers after Burton's death, depriving the world of his private thoughts about his adventures as an explorer. Burton died in Trieste, Italy, at age 69.

Álvar Núñez
CABEZA DE VACA

ca. 1490–ca. 1560

NORTH AMERICAN EXPLORATION

Álvar Núñez Cabeza de Vaca was one of the most remarkable early explorers of North America. Along with a handful of survivors from an expedition to Florida, he wandered across the continent until he reached Mexico. Cabeza de Vaca and his group became the first Europeans to cross North America from the Gulf of Mexico to the Gulf of California.

Early Life. The son of noble Spanish parents, Cabeza de Vaca was born in Extremadura, Castile, in present-day Spain. His family belonged originally to the peasantry, but was elevated to the level of aristocracy for their help in driving the Muslims from Spain. He enlisted in the army as a young man and fought in Italy, earning a promotion for bravery. He later returned to Spain to defend King Charles I against an uprising of nobles. In 1527 Charles named Cabeza de Vaca royal treasurer of Governor Pánfilo de Narváez's expedition to Florida. (At the time, Florida stretched from its present-day location to present-day Veracruz, Mexico.) The mission set out on June 27, 1527, to explore that vast stretch of land and to claim it for Spain.

An Ominous Start. The expedition, which consisted of 5 ships and 600 men, set sail from the Spanish port of San Lucar de Barrameda and made its first stop at Santo Domingo on the Caribbean island of Hispaniola (today the island is divided between the countries of Haiti and the Dominican Republic) to gather additional supplies and horses. During their 45-day stay there, 140 members of the crew deserted, choosing instead to remain on the island. The rest of the crew sailed westward to Santiago, Cuba, where Cabeza de Vaca set out with two ships to another island, Trinidad, for supplies. That mission was hit by a hurricane, wrecking the two ships and drowning 60 of the 90-member crew. Narváez picked up the survivors and the expedition spent the winter at Spanish settlements along the Gulf of Mexico. In spring 1528, five ships (Narváez had purchased two ships to replace the wrecked ones) carrying about 400 men set out for Florida.

On April 12, they arrived at Florida and Governor Narváez claimed the land for Spain. After exploring the region for a short time, he launched an inland expedition with 300 men because the Indians had told him that he would find food and gold at the nearby northern city of Apalachen. He ordered the ships to sail along the coast and meet him and his men farther north. Cabeza de Vaca strongly objected to this plan, but Narváez and the other expedition leaders prevailed. The decision proved disastrous because the inland party never again saw the ships. Cut off from their supplies, the party heading for Apalachen suffered losses from hunger, disease, and hostile attacks.

The Shipwreck. By June it became apparent to the survivors that the only way they could leave Florida was by sea, so they decided to build barges*. They built makeshift furnaces and melted down metal from stirrups and other bits of equipment to make axes. Plant fibers and hair from horses' tails served as rope to lash planks together, and shirts and pants became sails. On September 22, 1528, five barges and the surviving 250 men set out into the Gulf of Mexico, but rough weather drove them apart. In November, two boats carrying Cabeza de Vaca and 90 men washed ashore on an island off the coast of Louisiana (present-day Galveston Island). The crew on the remaining barges either perished at sea or washed ashore and was killed by hostile peoples.

After a failed attempt to relaunch their craft, Cabeza de Vaca and his men decided to stay with the Karankawa people who inhabited the island. During this time the Karankawa convinced a reluctant Cabeza de Vaca, who had a meager amount of medical knowledge, to treat some of their ill. His cures were apparently successful, although he often did little more than make the sign of the cross or say a few prayers. This marked the beginning of his career as a healer. Later in Mexico, his curing powers made him popular among those he encountered. Cabeza de Vaca also spent this time gathering ethnographic* information on the Karankawa.

Crossing Mexico. Later that same winter, Cabeza de Vaca sailed to the mainland, where he fell ill. His companions, fearing he had died, left the

The Head of the Cow

In late medieval Spain, offspring were given either the father's or mother's surname, usually the more prestigious of the two. Cabeza de Vaca took his mother's name, which came from the incident that raised the family into the nobility. In 1212, a family ancestor helped Christian forces by guiding them through an obscure and unguarded pass in the direction of the Muslim army. He then marked the pass with a cow's skull. The Christian army attacked and defeated the Muslims. As a reward, King Sancho of Navarre made the family aristocrats. He gave them the noble name Cabeza de Vaca, Spanish for "cow's head."

barge large flat-bottomed transport boat

ethnographic of or relating to ethnography, the branch of anthropology dealing with the scientific description of different cultures

island and set out along the coast toward Mexico. Cabeza de Vaca recovered but remained a captive of the indigenous* people. He escaped a year later and began to make a living as a trader, carrying goods between the constantly warring tribes of the region. During the four years he spent there, he also took trips to the island, hoping to convince the two crewmen who remained there to accompany him to Mexico.

Finally in 1532, Cabeza de Vaca and his sole companion, Lope de Oviedo, set out for Mexico along the same route that the other survivors had taken four years earlier (the other crew member on the island died). Finally they met up with the other survivors, but all the men were enslaved by Indians and had to wait a year and a half, until September 1534, for an opportunity to escape. They then spent eight months with the Avavares people of southern Texas before continuing west along the Rio Grande.

In late 1535 the party, which by this time consisted only of Cabeza de Vaca and three others, decided to make their way farther inland. With the help of Indian guides, they began their trek from present-day San Antonio and traveled up to present-day New Mexico or Arizona. From there they turned south to Sonora, a Mexican province, and finally arrived at the Gulf of California on the Pacific coast. Traveling southward along the eastern coast of the gulf, they reached the city of Culiacán, and by late June 1536, Cabeza de Vaca and the others had arrived in Mexico City, telling the tale of their adventures.

Later Life. Cabeza de Vaca returned to Spain in 1537, where King Charles I awarded him the governorship of the Río de la Plata, in present-day Paraguay. Three years later, the explorer led a group of 250 men to South America and took them on a 1,000-mile march through unknown territory, losing only two men. However, he was not so lucky as a governor. He angered colonists by forcing them to treat their Indian servants humanely, and by imposing an effective and fair tax collection system. Some of his own officials arrested him and sent him back to Spain. In 1551 he was convicted of charges that included poor administration of the colony and was banished to North Africa. The charges were later overturned and he was allowed to live in Spain with a small income. Cabeza de Vaca died in Seville.

Writings. Cabeza de Vaca wrote two books about his experiences in South America. The more interesting of the two, *Naufragios* (Shipwreck), contains the story of his journey to Florida. In great detail, Cabeza de Vaca relates everything of interest he encountered there. For example, he was the first European to see and describe the American bison. He also told stories he had heard about golden treasures in the famed Seven Cities of Cíbola. These accounts later sent many explorers into the American southwest in search of nonexistent riches.

Naufragios also records his close observation of the Indians and their customs. He saw that they were not the uncivilized barbarians that the Europeans believed them to be. He learned to admire their ability to survive in the wilderness and considered them as worthy of respect as Europeans. Cabeza de Vaca also saw that, in many cases, they acted in a more Christian manner than the Spaniards who were trying to convert them. The book remains not only a fascinating adventure tale but also a remarkably objective and unprejudiced early view of Indian culture. His second book, *Comentarios* (Commentaries), contains the story of the time he spent as governor in Paraguay.

John Cabot and his son Sebastian were two of the most noted early English explorers. The elder Cabot led the first voyages to North America since the Norseman Leif ERIKSON visited what is now Canada around A.D. 1000. Cabot's expeditions established England's claim to North America. His son Sebastian may have accompanied him on these trips, and later led and sponsored naval expeditions of his own that helped England establish trade with Russia in the mid-1500s.

John Cabot

Born Giovanni Caboto in the Italian city of Genoa, John Cabot moved to the city of Venice at age 11. Later he went to work for a trading firm in that city and the job required him to travel to the eastern Mediterranean and Arabia, hubs of the spice trade between Europe and Asia. Over time, Cabot became expert in the skills of navigation and became a master pilot of ships. He also seems to have conceived, independent of Christopher COLUMBUS, the idea of reaching Asia by sailing west from Europe.

From Venice to Bristol. Cabot's whereabouts between the mid-1480s and mid-1490s are a matter of dispute. Some scholars suggest that he had moved to England as early as 1484, but documents from the archives of the city of Valencia, Spain, record that a Venetian named Johan Cabot Montecalunya lived there between 1490 and 1493. It is probable that during this stay in Spain, Cabot met Columbus after Columbus's triumphant return from his voyage. Some scholars suggest that this meeting might have inspired Cabot to sail westward to Asia.

Cabot then tried unsuccessfully to obtain support from both the Spanish and Portuguese crowns for his plan to establish a short westward trade route to Asia. He then considered that England, being the last stop on the trade routes from Arabia, probably paid the most for Asian spices. Consequently, the English had the greatest incentive to support such a voyage to Asia. He also reckoned that he could reach Asia faster by setting sail from England, mistakenly believing that all spices came from northern Asia.

Discovering North America. Around 1495 Cabot moved to the port of Bristol, England, with his three sons Sebastiano (or Sebastian), Ludovico, and Sancto. He hoped to persuade the merchants of the city to back his plan, but he met with little success. However, when the news of Columbus's return from his own trip across the Atlantic

THE CABOTS

John Cabot
ca. 1450–1499
EXPLORATION OF
NORTH AMERICA

Sebastian Cabot
ca. 1474–1557
EXPLORATION OF
SOUTH AMERICA AND CANADA

See the route of John Cabot's 1497 voyage in the "Maps" section.

Signs of Life

Scholars question why John Cabot ended his first voyage to Newfoundland without exploring farther. Although he saw signs that the land was inhabited, he never ventured farther inland than the distance of a crossbow shot. This suggests that, with a small crew, he might have wished to avoid encounters with hostile natives. Interestingly, Cabot left his mark on the land as well. On a voyage to the area five years later, the explorer Gaspar Corte Real found Indians in possession of an Italian sword and silver earrings made in Venice. These must have been left by Cabot, the only Venetian to have yet visited Newfoundland.

reached England, the excitement of that voyage stirred the imagination of England's King Henry VII, who then agreed to meet with Cabot.

Cabot convinced the king that he could duplicate Columbus's success and find a shorter, direct sea route to Asia. On March 5, 1496, Henry granted Cabot royal permits to undertake the journey. The terms of Henry's contract with Cabot were generous. He authorized the explorer to seek out unknown lands and claim them for England. In return, Cabot would have a monopoly over all trade he established with the inhabitants of the lands he discovered.

Cabot's first attempt, made with a single ship, was a failure. Faced with poor weather, a shortage of food, and disagreements with his crew, he was forced to turn back. On May 17, 1497, he set out again with a crew of 18 in a small vessel, the *Matthew*. His son Sebastian may have been on this voyage with him. On June 24 the expedition made landfall somewhere in Canada. Scholars are unsure of the exact location of the landing, but various theories suggest that it may have been in Labrador, Newfoundland, or Cape Breton Island.

Cabot went ashore and saw signs that the land was inhabited, but he found no people. He claimed the area for England before continuing to sail south along the coast. After more than a month of exploration in the region known today as Cabot Strait, he returned to England, arriving in Bristol on August 6, 1497. He reported that the waters surrounding the areas that he had just claimed contained enough fish to end England's dependence on fish from Iceland, and falsely claimed that these lands contained valuable woods and silk. Cabot was convinced that he had reached the northeastern coast of Asia and felt that he could reach Cipangu and Cathay (Japan and China), the reputed sources of Asian wealth, during his next expedition.

Cabot's Second Voyage. Henry was pleased with Cabot's report and rewarded him with a promotion to admiral and with approval for a follow-up expedition. The king also named the lands that were discovered New Isle, but by 1502 he had begun to call it "the newe founde lande," the name by which it is known today.

In July 1498, Cabot set out again, this time with 5 ships and a crew of about 200. The expedition lost one ship shortly after leaving England, but the rest arrived safely in North America. Cabot sailed north up the coast before ice forced him to turn around and sail south. He then made his way past Newfoundland and sailed as far south as Cape Hatteras in present-day North Carolina. However, nothing more is known about the voyage. Even the final fate of Cabot and his companions is a subject of debate. Some scholars believe he returned to England, but others argue that he probably perished at sea. There is no definite evidence to support either position.

Despite the fact that he never achieved his goal of reaching Asia, Cabot merits a place as one of England's great explorers. He was the first European to reach North America in nearly 500 years, and his efforts ultimately led to England's colonization of the continent. Many

This painting depicts John and Sebastian Cabot departing from Bristol on their first voyage of exploration. Their personal narratives from the voyage have since been lost, but their work lives on in *The Principall Navigations, Voiages and Discoveries of the English Nation,* Richard Hakluyt's study of English exploration in North America.

of the places he discovered—including Labrador and Newfoundland—still bear the names Cabot gave them on his voyages.

Sebastian Cabot

Sebastian Cabot, the son of John Cabot, was born in Venice and moved to Bristol, England, with his father and brothers. Some historians believe that he may have been a member of his father's first voyage to North America. In later life he tried to take credit for his father's discovery, but historians soon realized that it was John Cabot, not Sebastian, who had led the English ships across the Atlantic to North America. What is certain, though, is that Sebastian embarked on his own voyage to South America and was largely responsible for establishing trade links between England and Russia.

Early Career. Sebastian Cabot served as royal cartographer (mapmaker) to England's King Henry VIII, whose father had sponsored John Cabot's voyages. In 1512, Sebastian accompanied the English army to Spain to help King Ferdinand II of Aragon in his fight against the French. Ferdinand later planned to sponsor a voyage to North America commanded by Cabot, but the expedition was canceled due to Ferdinand's death.

Cabot remained in Spain, and in 1518 he was promoted to the rank of captain and appointed to Spain's Council of the Indies*. He returned briefly to England to try to enlist royal support for an expedition to North America. Although unsuccessful, he continued to seek backers for his plan. Five years later he approached the Venetians, but they too turned him down.

***Council of the Indies** group that prepared and issued all legislation that governed Spain's colonies, approved all important acts and expenditures by colonial officials, and acted as a court of last resort in civil suits appealed from colonial courts

Journey to South America. In 1525 Cabot finally got approval from Charles I of Spain to lead an expedition to eastern Asia. Cabot was asked to find the fabled lands of spices and riches, establish trade relations, and map the coast of South America. His plan was the same as his father's—sail west until reaching Asia. Cabot set out from the port of Cádiz with 3 ships and about 150 men on April 5, 1526. Rather than bringing him wealth and fame, however, the voyage would bring Cabot grief.

The expedition sailed from the Spanish port of Sanlúcar de Barrameda toward the Río de la Plata region of South America, in what is now Paraguay and Argentina. On September 29, they reached the city of Recife in Brazil. There Cabot heard the Indians tell tales of fabulous riches that lay inland, perhaps referring to the Inca kingdom of Peru. Ignoring his orders to head for eastern Asia, Cabot decided to stop here and look for the treasures. The other members of the expedition disagreed with his plan, so Cabot left them aboard ship and went inland to explore. His companions returned to Spain, where they informed the king of Cabot's disobedient actions.

For three years Cabot explored the Río de la Plata. He traveled up the Paraná River to the point where it meets the Paraguay River and built two forts there. He never found the riches for which he was looking, but he did encounter hostile Indians. Finally, in August 1530, running low on food and supplies, he abandoned the attempt and returned to Spain.

Cabot received a chilly reception in Spain; he was charged with misconduct based on the testimony of his fellow voyagers and was criticized for his failure to successfully complete his mission. The king banished him to Africa for four years, but pardoned him after one year in exile. Cabot returned to Spain, where he retained his titles and the pension that went with his position as captain and council member. He remained in Spain for the next 15 years, after which he settled in England.

The Merchant Adventurers. In England, King Edward VI, who had succeeded Henry VIII, offered Sebastian Cabot the title of great pilot and gave him a royal pension. However, he did not provide royal funds that would have enabled Cabot to undertake voyages. Over the next several years, Cabot remained in contact with other European rulers about the possibility of leading new expeditions.

In 1552, two English adventurers, John Willoughby and Richard Chancellor, approached Cabot for advice on a journey they were planning. The two men conceived the idea of seeking a sea route to China by sailing north of Russia. By this time Cabot had become too old to undertake such a trip himself, but he gave Willoughby and Chancellor information to help plan the expedition. Cabot then founded a company called the Merchant Adventurers (also known as the Muscovy Company) to help raise money for the voyage.

Two years later, he organized the first journey in search of the so-called Northeast Passage*. A second voyage was launched the following year. The conditions on these expeditions were extremely difficult. The ships were forced to navigate through ice in the freezing tempera-

*Northeast Passage water route along the northern coast of the Eurasian landmass, lying mainly off northern Russian Siberia

tures of the Arctic. Several ships were lost and many sailors died along the way. The explorers never found the Northeast Passage, but Chancellor did eventually reach Russia and established a friendship and trade pact between Russia and England.

The trade with Russia was steady but unspectacular, involving exchange of English cloth for wax, flax, rope, and other goods from Russia. However, it proved profitable for Cabot because Edward VI's successor, Queen Mary Tudor, granted his company a monopoly over all trade to the north. Cabot enjoyed his success only briefly, though. He died two years later, in 1557.

The Cabots' Reputations. After John Cabot's disappearance during his second voyage to North America, Sebastian Cabot took credit for much of his father's work during the first voyage. However, scholars today recognize the importance of the senior Cabot's pioneering journeys to North America. They know that he was a skilled navigator and mapmaker. His voyages opened up new fishing waters and eventually resulted in England's colonization of the North American continent.

In time, however, Sebastian Cabot's exploits became renowned while those of his father were forgotten. Although his only expedition was a failure, he made up for his lack in leadership skills with his self-promotion and charm. Even at the young age of 15, he persuaded Henry VII to give him a monetary award for "diligent service and attendance," but there is no mention of what "service" was being rewarded. Although he never found the shorter, cheaper route to Asia, his voyages influenced later European explorers to seek riches in South America.

Like many early European explorers, Jacques Cartier set out to find a western route to Asia across the Atlantic Ocean. Like them, he failed in this attempt, but he succeeded in penetrating deep into Canada. Cartier's voyages ultimately resulted in the discovery of the St. Lawrence River and in the establishment of France's claim to Canada.

Early Voyages

Little is known of Cartier's life before his first expedition to North America. He was born in the busy port of Saint-Malo on France's northwestern coast, and probably learned navigation as a member of one of the many voyages of discovery sponsored by France in the early 1500s. He was already an experienced seaman by the time he received a royal commission to explore North America in 1534.

The First Voyage. Cartier left Saint-Malo on April 20, commanding 2 ships and 61 men. His goal was to explore "the New Lands (North America) to discover certain islands and countries where there are said to be great quantities of gold and other riches." He was also to search for a Northwest Passage* to Asia. Cartier was familiar with the Atlantic crossing, taking just 20 days to reach Newfoundland.

Jacques
CARTIER
1491–1557
EXPLORATION OF CANADA

*Northwest Passage water route connecting the Atlantic and Pacific Oceans through the Arctic islands of northern Canada

In this painting by Johann Matejko, Jacques Cartier is shown standing before a map of the lands that he explored during his three voyages of discovery.

✷ **See the routes of Cartier's voyages in the "Maps" section.**

Cartier sailed north along Newfoundland's coast into the Strait of Belle Isle and entered the Gulf of St. Lawrence. About this time he encountered the first Indians he was to see on this voyage. He described the men as "well enough formed but untamed and savage. They wear their hair bound on top of their heads like a fistful of twisted hay, sticking into it a pin or something and adding some birds' feathers." Modern scholars have identified them as Huron.

Cartier turned south and sailed along the western coast of Newfoundland, crossing the gulf to the Magdalen Islands (also called Les Îles de la Madeleine) and Prince Edward Island. However, he would not realize that these were islands until his second voyage. He believed instead that they were part of the mainland. Continuing west along the northern coast of Prince Edward Island, the expedition arrived at Chaleur Bay on July 6, where it encountered some 50 canoes carrying Micmac. The Micmac greeted Cartier and his group with friendship, and the following day the French and Indians met on the Gaspé Peninsula, north of Chaleur Bay, to trade and celebrate. Around the same time, about 200 Huron were on the peninsula fishing, and Cartier established friendly relations with their chief, Donnacona.

The friendly mood was broken a short time later, however, when Cartier planted a 30-foot cross on the land and claimed the territory for France. Donnacona complained about the cross, but Cartier calmed him by lying that the cross was merely an unimportant landmark. On July 12, Cartier continued his exploration of Chaleur Bay but realized dejectedly that it was not the route to China as he had hoped.

Cartier remained in the Gaspé Peninsula until July 25, when he headed back to France via the Gulf of St. Lawrence. Although he did not return with gold or spices, he did have two treasures with him—Donnacona's sons Domagaya and Taignoagny. The Huron princes told the French tales of the rich Kingdom of the Saguenay that lay to the west of the Huron lands. Intrigued by these tales, France's King Francis I sponsored Cartier's second voyage to Canada the following year.

The Second Voyage. On May 19, 1535, Cartier sailed from France, this time commanding 3 ships and 110 men and guided by Donnacona's sons. His goal was to penetrate the interior of Canada by exploring a large river that he had been told led to the rich lands in the west. Fifty days later the expedition made landfall in Newfoundland. However, the ships had become separated on the voyage and Cartier had to wait two weeks until the vessels reunited.

Cartier once again sailed along the Belle Isle Strait, but this time he turned west to search for the mouth of the great river. He sailed upstream until he reached the Huron village of Stadacona, the location of present-day Quebec City, where he established a base. Cartier was greeted warmly by Chief Donnacona, who also warned him not to continue upriver. Apparently, another Indian chief, who claimed dominion over Donnacona, lived upstream at Hochelaga (east of present-day Montreal Island). Donnacona feared that if Cartier went to Hochelaga, he might lose his alliance with the French to that leader.

None of Donnacona's warnings persuaded Cartier to call off his plans to continue upriver, however. In a last bid to deter the French, Huron shamans* dressed as devils came out to surround the ships and shout warnings. Accounts of the expedition later noted, "they howled and yelled so loud you would have thought that hell had broken loose." Domagaya and Taignoagny came aboard to tell Cartier that the Huron god said that ice and snow upriver would be the death of anyone who ventured there, but all their warnings went unheeded. The chief's sons then volunteered to guide Cartier's party to Hochelaga, but Cartier did not trust them. He sent them ashore and on September 19, 1535, proceeded west.

At the village of Hochelaga, the party was again greeted warmly and treated to an extensive celebration of "fires burning, dancing, and calling out *aguyase,* which is their term for a joyful welcome." A few days later Cartier climbed a mountain that he named Mount Royal (site of present-day Montreal) and from its summit, he could see rapids farther up the St. Lawrence. Concluding that this could not possibly be the route to Asia, he turned back without exploring any farther.

Cartier and his men spent the winter in their base near Stadacona. The weather turned out to be far worse than they had imagined; they had expected a mild winter, because Quebec is at a more southerly latitude than Paris. But the weather was bitterly cold and, to make things worse, almost all of Cartier's men contracted scurvy*.

Moreover, relations with the Huron had also begun to deteriorate. Cartier feared they would attack if they know his men were ill, so he ordered his men to make noise whenever the Huron came near their camp. Surprisingly, Domagaya came to their aid. He told them how to cure scurvy by drinking tea made from the bark and needles of the white cedar tree. However, the mistrust between the two parties prevented him from revealing this secret until 25 of the Frenchmen had died.

During that winter Donnacona added to his sons' tales of the fantastic Kingdom of the Saguenay. He claimed that he had visited the kingdom and seen its vast amounts of gold, rubies, and other riches. He claimed that the people there were white and dressed in woolen cloth. The Huron were great storytellers and greatly embellished their tales to impress and intrigue Cartier and his crew. One Indian even told them of mythical lands inhabited by pygmies who had only one leg, and of a land where the people lived only on liquids. Cartier, who swallowed the stories whole, decided that King Francis needed to hear the stories from the Indians themselves.

Cartier sailed for France as soon as the ice in the St. Lawrence broke the following May. He again returned with Huron, but this time they did not come willingly; Cartier had kidnapped ten Huron, including Donnacona, hoping that their stories would convince Francis to finance another expedition. However, France was in the midst of a war with Spain and could not spare either money or men. It would be another five years before Cartier returned to Canada.

*shaman priest who uses magic and believes in an unseen world of gods, demons, and spirits

*scurvy disease caused by a lack of vitamin C and characterized by bleeding gums, bleeding under the skin, and extreme weakness

Canada or *Kanata*

Cartier named the area around his first settlement Canada (present-day Quebec City), a term he derived from the Huron-Iroquois word *kanata* (meaning "village" or "settlement"). Later, Canada and New France were used synonymously to refer to the French possessions in the region—the St. Lawrence River valley, the Great Lakes, and until 1713, Acadia. In 1763, however, when Britain conquered New France, the British called the region Quebec. The name Canada was restored after 1791, when Britain divided Quebec into Upper and Lower Canada.

Cartier's Final Voyage

Francis was initially interested in Cartier's expeditions solely because they held the possibility of uncovering great wealth. However, after a time he decided to attempt to colonize these lands. In October 1540 he named Cartier captain-general and asked him to establish a French colony in Canada. However, three months later he appointed a nobleman named Jean-François de La Roque, sieur de Roberval to take charge of the expedition. Cartier would be answerable to Roberval.

Return to Canada. Roberval permitted Cartier to begin the voyage while he awaited delivery of artillery and other supplies. Cartier left Saint-Malo on May 23, 1541, leading 5 ships carrying 1,500 people and enough food and supplies to last two years. It took three months for the ships to cross the Atlantic Ocean, arriving at the Stadacona base on August 23.

Cartier and his crew were again welcomed by the Huron and their new chief, Agona. When asked about the members of their tribe that he had forcefully taken to France, Cartier lied. Although all but one had died, he told them that they "had remained in France where they were living as great lords; they had married and had no desire to return to their country." He did admit, however, that their leader, Donnacona, had died. Cartier presented the chief with a red cloak trimmed with yellow and white tin buttons and small bells. He also left two French boys with the chief to learn the local language so they could later act as translators. The boys' fate is unknown, but they probably returned to France with Cartier.

Surviving the Winter. Cartier set up a new base at the entrance to the Rouge River. He called the base Charlesbourg-Royal. From here he took along several Indian guides and set out to find the wealthy Kingdom of the Saguenay. However, as on his previous voyage, he encountered a number of rapids along his route that eventually made passage too difficult to continue. His guides suggested that he continue up the St. Lawrence River instead of tackling the calmer waters of the Ottawa River, which also supposedly led to Saguenay, possibly in an attempt to make Cartier abandon his search. Ultimately, Cartier gave up and returned to Charlesbourg-Royal where he again found that the Huron were no longer friendly toward the French. They no longer sold furs or game to the visitors, and Cartier was convinced that Agona was planning to attack the settlement. Meanwhile Roberval, who was to join Cartier and the crew as soon as he had obtained his supplies, had not yet left France. Cartier and his group were forced to spend the winter at Charlesbourg-Royal, despite the threat of attacks by the Huron.

Cartier's second winter in Canada was almost as miserable as the first. He was unable to maintain discipline among his men, who angered the neighboring Huron. The Huron were further displeased when they realized that the French intended to stay and establish a colony in their lands. They attacked the base several times that winter, killing 35 members of Cartier's group. The party received some consolation for these hardships when they found what they believed to be large quantities of gold and diamonds in the area.

Abandoning the Colony. By spring 1542, Cartier had begun to worry that Roberval had still not arrived. Because of the hostility of the Huron and because he believed he had found a large amount of wealth, Cartier decided to abandon the plan to colonize Canada and to return to France. However, when he arrived at Newfoundland he met Roberval, who then ordered Cartier to return to his base upriver.

Unwilling to follow the orders given to him, Cartier secretly left Newfoundland and steered a course for France. Roberval stayed on and built a fort near Stadacona where he spent the winter. However he, too, failed to penetrate past Hochelaga and ultimately gave up the idea of founding a colony. Cartier arrived in Saint-Malo that September. Shortly thereafter he realized that the gold he had found was worthless pyrite (also known as fool's gold) and that the diamonds were actually quartz. The disappointing results of the expedition dampened France's interest in Canada for many years.

Cartier never received another commission to explore for the French crown. He retired to his estate near Saint-Malo, where he appears to have become a local celebrity. Records from that town indicate that he at one time hosted a party whose guests included the English navigator Sebastian CABOT. Cartier spent the rest of his life looking after business affairs. He died during an epidemic in 1557.

Samuel de Champlain—founder of the Canadian city of Quebec, geographer, and empire builder—was responsible for establishing and securing the first permanent French colonies in the Americas. His efforts led to 150 years of French domination over vast parts of present-day Canada and the United States.

Early Life and Career

Little is known about Champlain's early years. He was born in the town of Brouage on France's Atlantic coast to parents who may have belonged to the lower nobility. According to his later writings, he acquired an early interest in "the art of navigation, along with a love of the high seas." He learned the art of seafaring from his uncle.

Early Voyages. Champlain undertook his first sea voyage sometime before he turned 20, when he traveled with his uncle to Spain. There he boarded a chartered French ship accompanying a Spanish fleet to the West Indies and New Spain*. During the expedition he also visited the Bahamas, Panama, Puerto Rico, Mexico, and Colombia, becoming an accomplished navigator. Around 1602 France's King Henry IV named Champlain royal geographer.

Samuel de
CHAMPLAIN
1567–1635
EXPLORATION OF CANADA

*New Spain Spain's colony in the Americas that included all of Mexico north of the present-day state of Chiapas and parts of the present-day United States

Samuel de Champlain, portrayed as an authoritative commander in this painting by Haskell Coffin, is known as the "Father of New France."

The following year a merchant and fur trader named Francis Gravé invited Champlain to join him on a voyage to Canada's St. Lawrence River (then called the River of Canada). Gravé planned to visit a fur company's trading post at Tadoussac near the mouth of the Saguenay River. Champlain accepted. When the two men reached Tadoussac, Champlain, who had no official position on the voyage, left Gravé to conduct his business and began to explore Canada.

Champlain first traveled up the Saguenay River and later voyaged up the St. Lawrence to the village of Hochelaga (present-day Montreal). He also ventured up the Iroquois River, known today as Richelieu River. On these exploratory missions he spoke to local Indians about the geography of northeastern North America. Based on this information he compiled a map that included the Hudson Bay and the Great Lakes.

Planning a Settlement. Indians also told Champlain about a land to the south that had a pleasant climate and mild winters. They showed him a metal that he believed to be silver, claiming that it came from the same land. Champlain reckoned that if Canada, already a rich source of valuable furs, also contained precious metals, it would be an ideal place to establish a permanent French settlement.

Champlain was also aware that explorers before him had found that the southern part of the continent sloped to the west. Based on this information, Champlain believed that if he followed the coast southward it might take him to a direct water route to the riches of Asia. Given the possible advantages, Champlain decided to found a colony in this land to the south. He returned to France to report his findings and to gather the resources necessary to mount such an expedition.

Acadia. After hearing Champlain's story, Henry IV agreed to establish a colony in northeastern Canada. He gave Pierre Du Gua de Monts, the viceroy of New France*, exclusive trading rights to the area in return for settling colonists there. In 1604 de Monts sent Champlain to scout a site for the colony in the area the French later named Acadia (present-day Nova Scotia).

*New France French colony in North America that included the Great Lakes, the St. Lawrence River valley, and until 1713, Acadia (present-day Nova Scotia)

Champlain explored the northern coast of the Bay of Fundy and found a river (the St. John) flowing into it from the north. The Indians told him that the river led to the St. Lawrence. Champlain continued west along the coast until he reached the point where the St. Croix River enters the bay. He chose a site next to the river for the colony. The first winter that Champlain and his 79 men spent at that camp proved deadly. Nearly half of the men died of scurvy*.

The following spring Champlain moved the settlement to the south side of the Bay of Fundy and named it Port Royal. He remained there for the next two winters, which although not as bad as the first, still claimed a number of lives. During this time, Champlain continued his search for a better site for the colony, sailing down the Atlantic coast as far as south as Cape Cod, Massachusetts. On these voyages he mapped about 900 miles of coastline. But while Champlain was busy exploring new lands, the Port Royal settlement struggled to survive.

*scurvy disease caused by a lack of vitamin C and characterized by bleeding gums, bleeding under the skin, and extreme weakness

Quebec

In 1607 Henry IV revoked de Monts's commission to govern Acadia. De Monts then decided to establish a new trading post on the St. Lawrence River farther upriver from Gravé's trading post at Tadoussac, hoping to take business away from Gravé. On July 3,

1608, Champlain arrived at a point where the St. Lawrence was less than a mile wide, and there he founded de Monts's new trading post, Quebec.

The Early Years. As at Acadia, the first winter at Quebec took a heavy toll on the men. Of 25 settlers, only 9 survived, including Champlain. However, new recruits joined them the following summer. Meanwhile, Champlain had made trade and military alliances with the Algonquin, Huron, and Montagnais Indians. In June 1609 he set out with a party of Indian allies and explored farther up the Iroquois River. On July 8 he discovered the lake that now bears his name. There his group fought and defeated a force of some 200 Iroquois warriors. This victory, and one the following year, greatly strengthened the Indians' respect for Champlain and the French.

In 1611 Champlain went back to Hochelaga, where he built a small square around which the city of Montreal eventually developed. He then continued up the St. Lawrence, becoming one of the first Europeans to penetrate beyond that river's Lachine Rapids. At this time, Champlain became convinced that the river and its tributaries contained the long-sought-after route to Asia. In fact, in 1612, he obtained a commission to "search for a free passage by which to reach the country called China." Meanwhile, however, the fur trade had begun to suffer heavy losses and Quebec's sponsors decided to abandon the colony.

Saving the Colony. Champlain sailed to France to persuade Louis XIII, who had succeeded his father, Henry IV, in 1610, to prevent the collapse of the colony. Louis stepped in and saved the colony, and the following year he named Champlain lieutenant to the viceroy of New France. That same year Champlain entered into a marriage of convenience that brought him a handsome dowry that he later used to keep his colony alive. When Champlain returned to Canada in 1611, he explored the Ottawa River into the present-day province of Ontario, hoping to restore Quebec's failing fur trade. In 1613 he returned to France and persuaded the Récollets, an order of Catholic priests, to send four of their members to Quebec to convert the local people to Christianity.

Champlain and the Récollets arrived in Quebec two years later, and that summer he embarked on what would be his final expedition of discovery. He traveled west to Huron territory, the area between Georgian Bay and Lake Ontario, and explored both of those bodies of water. He found out that even larger lakes lay farther to the west, but the Huron prevented him from traveling any farther. They were at war with the inhabitants of that region and were afraid the French might ally themselves with the Huron's enemies. Using scant information provided by the Huron, Champlain produced a flawed map of the region. However, he collected a treasure of information on their customs and religion, which he later wrote about in his accounts.

Champlain spent the winter of 1615 with the Huron, and during that stay the Huron persuaded him to join them in an attack on an Iroquois village south of Lake Ontario. The attack failed and Champlain was wounded in the battle. During the years that followed, he struggled to keep the colony in operation and fought to keep his command.

Final Challenges. Between 1616 and 1620, Champlain spent most of his time in France trying to raise money and workers to maintain the struggling Quebec colony. His efforts finally paid off in 1627 when France's first minister Cardinal Richelieu created the Company of One Hundred Associates, a group of 100 wealthy men who each agreed to invest a large amount of money in the colony. The funds saved the colony from bankruptcy. Louis XIII also reconfirmed Champlain's authority in Quebec, but forbade him from undertaking any missions of exploration; Champlain was to serve strictly as an administrator.

Shortly afterward, war broke out between France and England, and in 1628 English privateers* laid siege on Quebec and seized the ships bringing supplies to the colony. Outnumbered and out of ammunition, Champlain was forced to surrender Quebec. He was taken prisoner and held in England until 1632. Fortunately, he managed to convince the English that the colony was seized after the war was formally over, and England agreed to return the area to France.

The following year Champlain returned to Canada to try to salvage the devastated colony and reestablish his alliances with the Indians. By this time, though, his health was poor, and he died in Quebec on Christmas Day, 1635. By that time, the colony extended along both shores of the St. Lawrence River and its population had grown to 150. Quebec lived on and is today the oldest city in North America north of St. Augustine, Florida.

*privateer privately owned ship hired by a government to attack enemy ships; also the crew of such a ship

See Lewis and Clark.

CLARK, *William*

Christopher COLUMBUS

1451–1506

EXPLORATION OF THE AMERICAS

No explorer in history is more famous—or more infamous—than Christopher Columbus. He was not the first European voyager to reach the Americas, but his expedition established lasting contact between what Europeans came to think of as the Old World and the New World, with far-reaching results for people on both sides of the Atlantic Ocean. Columbus himself never admitted that he had found an unknown land and opened it to European colonization, however. He arrived in the Americas while searching for a sea route to Asia, and to the end of his life, after four voyages to American shores, he claimed that the islands and coasts he had visited were part of Asia.

"The Enterprise of the Indies"

Europeans of Columbus's day were taking an increasing interest in Asia and Africa. Christian Europe felt threatened by the growth of the

Islamic world. Muslims controlled North Africa and the lands of the eastern Mediterranean, including the birthplace of Christianity. Moors, Muslims from North Africa, had invaded Spain, which was driving them out slowly and with difficulty. An ancient Christian empire based in Byzantium, in present-day Turkey, had fallen to Muslim Turks, who also controlled much of central Asia.

The spread of Islam had cut off Europe from trade routes to Asia. The Turks prevented the Europeans from using the overland route to China that the Venetian traveler Marco POLO and others had followed in earlier centuries. Muslim powers also controlled access to the Red Sea, the gateway to a sea route to the Indian Ocean and southern Asia. Europeans could still obtain Asian spices and silks and African ivory and gold, but they could do so only through costly exchanges with Muslim merchants and middlemen. Consequently, they longed for a direct route to the Indies, the term they used to refer to India and the lands east of it. Columbus offered to provide such a route with a plan that he called "the enterprise of the Indies."

Columbus's Background. Cristoforo Colombo was born in Genoa, a port city on the western coast of Italy. He later became known by the Spanish and English versions of his name, Cristóbal Colón and Christopher Columbus, respectively.

Columbus's father was a weaver of wool and a merchant. No details are known about Columbus's early life or education, but he probably received basic schooling in reading and writing during his childhood. As an adult he was well read; volumes from his personal library have survived, some bearing notes in his handwriting. As the oldest child in the family, Columbus could have joined his father in the family wool business, but instead he chose a seafaring career—not a surprising choice for a young man growing up in one of the busiest ports on the Mediterranean Sea.

At about the age of 14, Columbus began his life as a sailor. He visited various Mediterranean ports, including the Greek island of Khíos, and by 1476 he had begun serving in a Genoese trading fleet bound for England. Columbus's ship was wrecked off the coast of Portugal, but he survived by clinging to wreckage and drifting ashore. Shortly thereafter he settled in Lisbon, Portugal's capital. His brother Bartholomew joined him and they worked together as makers of maps and charts. Columbus also continued to go to sea on merchant ships, visiting England, Ireland, and possibly Iceland.

Portugal in the late 1400s was a good place for a sailor with an interest in geography. For decades the Portuguese royal family had sponsored voyages of exploration southward along the west coast of Africa, hoping to find a sea route around Africa to Asia. These ventures had produced Portuguese colonies on the West African coast and on islands off that coast. Columbus voyaged to many of these outposts, gaining experience sailing in the winds and water currents of the tropical Atlantic Ocean.

Painting titled *Columbus Received by the Catholic Kings After his First Travel,* by Ricardo Balaca y Orejas Canseco (1844–1880). Christopher Columbus is shown announcing his discovery to King Ferdinand and Queen Isabella of Spain.

In about 1479 Columbus married an Italian-Portuguese woman whose father had been governor of Porto Santo, an island in the Madeira group. He is believed to have lived there for a time with his wife and their son, Diego. After only a few years of marriage, Columbus's wife died. By that time he had formed his grand plan for discovering a sea route to the Indies and was trying to find someone to pay for it.

Sailing West to Reach the East. Columbus's idea was simple and based on the knowledge that the earth is a sphere. Instead of trying to reach the eastern lands by sailing east, he decided that he would go west. By traveling westward around the world from Europe, he concluded that he would arrive on the east coast of Asia.

Others before Columbus had suggested that a westward route could lead from Europe to Asia. The ancient Greeks had known that the world is round, and Europeans had been aware of this geographic fact for centuries—the notion that Columbus or his sailors feared that the world was flat and that they might sail off its edge is a myth. Greek geographers had also raised the possibility that the ocean west of Europe was the same body of water that washed Asia's eastern shores. In Columbus's own time, an Italian philosopher and geographer named Paolo Toscanelli had proposed voyaging to the Indies by sailing westward around the globe. Columbus, who had a keen interest in geographic writings, was well aware of all these ideas, which inspired his own.

Columbus may have also possessed another piece of information that suggested that it was possible to reach land by sailing west across the Atlantic—other Europeans had already done so. Centuries earlier the Vikings* had established colonies in Greenland, a large island in the North Atlantic Ocean. Around A.D. 1000, a group of Greenlanders led by Leif ERIKSON landed on several landmasses west of Greenland. Although Erikson's feat had not yet entered the general European body

*Vikings Scandinavian seamen who robbed the coasts of Europe in the eighth and tenth centuries

43

North and South Columbia?

Columbus was lucky to run into the Americas—his ships would probably have never made it from Spain to Japan. But he was unlucky enough to lose many of the honors he felt rightfully belonged to him. One honor escaped him completely. Columbus's stubborn insistence that he had reached Asia kept him from admitting that he had found a world new to Europeans. If he had done so, the continents we call North and South America might now bear his name. Instead they are named for Amerigo Vespucci, an explorer from Florence, Italy, who visited and described the coast of South America in 1500.

of knowledge, people in northern Europe spoke of it sometimes. Columbus may have heard these stories during his northern voyage.

Once Columbus decided to attempt the westward voyage to the Indies, the only remaining questions concerned distance. How far was Asia from the west coast of Europe? How long would Columbus have to sail to get there? Columbus's answers were seriously incorrect because of two errors in his geographic knowledge—he believed that the world was considerably smaller than it is and he misinterpreted the descriptions of Asia found in the writings of various geographers and of Marco Polo. Columbus concluded that Asia was wider than it actually is and that Japan, the easternmost part of Asia, lay farther from the continental mainland than it does. Because of all these miscalculations, he believed that Japan was only one-quarter of its actual distance west of Europe. The Virgin Islands, located in the Caribbean Sea, lie about where he had expected to find Japan.

Scholars debate whether some part of Columbus's error was deliberate. They believe that the explorer might have manipulated his calculations to make the proposed voyage seem shorter and more likely to succeed, and therefore more attractive to sponsors. About one thing there is no doubt, however—Columbus firmly believed that whatever lay across the Atlantic was part of Asia. Neither he nor anyone else suspected the existence of two large continents in between.

Columbus's Four Voyages

Columbus tried to interest the rulers of Portugal, the leader in European exploration, in his scheme. However, the king and his advisers turned down Columbus's request. Tradition says that the Portuguese found Columbus's plan too expensive and his measurements of distances too unrealistic. Moreover, Portugal had spent years developing a route to the Indies by way of Africa and may have been unwilling to invest in an alternative route. In 1488, just a few years after the Portuguese crown rejected Columbus's plan, the Portuguese navigator Bartolomeu Dias became the first to sail around the southern end of Africa, proving that the Indies could be reached by that route.

Columbus gave up on Portugal and moved to Spain with his son Diego. There he formed a relationship with a Spanish woman who bore him a second son, Ferdinand. Meanwhile, Columbus tried desperately to win the support of the Spanish crown for his expedition. Although he eventually received support for his ideas from prominent members of the Spanish church and court, King Ferdinand and Queen Isabella were too busy fighting the last of the Moors to give him much attention.

Finally, in January of 1492, the Spanish defeated the Moors, and the king and queen listened to Columbus's proposal. They rejected it at first because they probably found his demands for rewards too high. However, they changed their minds and agreed to finance the cost of outfitting an expedition, although there is no truth to the legend that Queen Isabella pawned her jewels to pay for Columbus's voyage.

Columbus had finally found a backer, and the greatest adventure of his life was about to begin. He would spend the next 12 years juggling two roles—navigator and administrator of the first European colony in the Americas.

First Voyage. On August 3, 1492, the expedition left Palos, a port in southern Spain. It consisted of about 90 men in 3 sailing vessels, the *Pinta,* the *Niña,* and the *Santa María.* None of the vessels was more than 70 or 80 feet long. The crew consisted of government officials and experienced seamen. After stopping at the Canary Islands, a Spanish colony off Africa's coast, the fleet set sail into the Canary Current, a powerful westward flow that Columbus had encountered on earlier voyages to the islands. The current sped their journey westward.

On October 12, after 36 days at sea, a lookout on the *Pinta* sighted land. Columbus claimed that he had seen it first, pocketing the reward that had been offered to the one who fist sighted land—one of many high-handed acts that created tension between him and his men. The explorers stopped at the island that they named San Salvador. Most historians agree that it was either Watling Island or Samana Cay in the Bahamas Islands. Columbus was pleased to note that the islanders possessed small items of gold jewelry. Believing that he had reached the Indies, he called the local people Indians, a term that came to be used for all the indigenous* peoples of the Americas.

*indigenous referring to the original inhabitants of a region

Columbus soon left the small island to search for the great Asian port cities, splendid palaces, and bustling markets that Polo had described. He landed on Cuba, which he thought was some remote part of Japan or China, and then pushed on to the island of Hispaniola, now divided between the nations of Haiti and the Dominican Republic. The *Santa María* ran aground there and had to be abandoned. Unable to carry all his men in the two remaining ships, Columbus left 39 of them and some supplies in a hastily built fort. He named the settlement La Navidad ("The Christmas") because it was established on December 25, 1492. On January 16, the *Niña* and the *Pinta* set out to return to Spain.

The navigator had planned to return east across the Atlantic at a point farther north than his outward journey. He knew that north of the Canary Islands the winds usually blew from the west and would help carry him back to Spain. Fortunately he found an ocean current that took his fleet far enough north to catch those westerly winds.

Columbus's return journey to Spain was less than peaceful. A storm battered his ships off the European coast and they became separated. When Columbus arrived in Lisbon, the Portuguese captured and held him for a time before sending him on to Spain. He did impress the Spanish court, however, with the Indians and gold ornaments he had brought from his expedition and with his account of his travels along the outskirts of Asia. He received the rewards he had been promised as well as the title "Admiral of the Ocean Sea."

Second Voyage. Ferdinand and Isabella promptly sent Columbus on another mission, this time to colonize Hispaniola—which, according to the terms of Columbus's reward, was to be his to govern. A fleet of 17 ships and a 1,200-strong crew (including the explorer's brothers—Bartholomew and Diego) left the port of Cádiz on September 25, 1493. The expedition discovered several islands, including Puerto Rico, before arriving in Hispaniola, where Columbus found that the men he had left there on his first voyage were dead and the fort destroyed. The Indians had killed most of them, perhaps in response to their looting and violence. Columbus founded a new settlement, Isabela, and began searching the island for gold, enslaving the Indians who resisted.

In late April the following year, Columbus left his brother Diego in charge of the colony and went to explore Cuba, which he still believed was part of Asia. Later when Bartholomew arrived in Isabela, he found the colony in chaos and took a hand in governing it. Meanwhile, Columbus had found little in the way of riches and no real evidence that he was in Asia, but he forced his crew to swear that they believed Cuba was China.

Back on Hispaniola, Columbus's brothers were proving to be poor administrators. Many of the settlers resented them, and an investigator from Spain was troubled by the high death rate among the Indians and other signs of mismanagement. On March 10, 1496, Columbus returned to Spain to defend his administration of Hispaniola before the king and queen. He again left Diego and Bartholomew in charge of Hispaniola.

Third Voyage. In Spain, Columbus managed to persuade the king and queen to remain confident in him, even though his voyages had not yet produced a profit. They granted Columbus's request to make a third expedition, but with a stern warning that they expected him to deliver on his promises of a trade route to the Indies and cargoes of valuable goods. Columbus left Spain on May 30, 1498, with six ships. Three went straight to Hispaniola to strengthen the settlement there.

Columbus steered the remaining three ships southwestward in the hope of striking a different part of the Asian coast—or at least a sea passage to India through the barrier of islands. He arrived at the island of Trinidad and then sailed along a stretch of coastline to the south. A large river emptied into the sea on that coast, and Columbus knew that such a river must drain a big landmass. He admitted, "I believe this is a very large continent which until now has remained unknown." He had encountered the northern coast of South America and Venezuela's Orinoco River. The explorer still claimed, rather desperately, that Hispaniola and the other islands to the north were the outskirts of Asia. By 1500, however, many other European adventurers and explorers had reached the Caribbean Sea and the coasts of North and South America, and everyone but Columbus realized that these were new and unknown lands, not obscure corners of Asia.

After leaving the Orinoco, Columbus continued to Hispaniola, where he found disaster. Bartholomew and Diego had failed to govern effectively or even to maintain order. Settlers were rebelling, Indians were hostile, enslavement was on the rise, and the colony was not producing the wealth that had been expected from it. Despite stern measures such as hangings, Columbus could not restore order. In 1500 an inspector from Spain arrested Columbus and his two brothers, seized their property, and sent them back to Spain in chains.

During the voyage Columbus wrote a long letter to his royal sponsors in which he revealed that he had come to see himself as having a mystical, even holy, destiny. Interpreting the discoveries of the third voyage in terms of the Bible and other ancient texts, Columbus claimed that he had sailed to the borders of Paradise and that the river he had seen flowed out of the Garden of Eden.

Fourth Voyage and Afterward. When Columbus arrived in Spain, Ferdinand and Isabella released him from his chains. They restored his property but not all of his titles or his authority. They also agreed to sponsor one more voyage in search of gold and a passage to India, but they ordered Columbus not to return to Hispaniola, which they had turned over to a new governor.

The fourth fleet consisted of four small ships of poor quality—Columbus had fallen out of favor. The explorer took his brother Bartholomew and his son Ferdinand with him when he set out again from Cádiz on May 11, 1502. Despite his orders, he went first to Hispaniola to warn the new governor of an approaching hurricane. The governor ignored the warning, however, and 25 ships were destroyed in the Spanish harbor. In the months that followed, Columbus sailed along the Central American coast, battling storms, illness, and hostile Indians. He lost two of the ships, and the remaining two, overcrowded and barely seaworthy, ran ashore on the island of Jamaica, which Columbus had visited during his second voyage. The stranded mariners spent more than a year on Jamaica, bargaining with the Indians for food, before a few of them reached Hispaniola in canoes and arranged for a rescue mission. In 1504 Columbus made his final Atlantic voyage, the return to Spain, as a passenger on someone else's ship.

The explorer's last years were bitter. He was rich, but until his death, which occurred at his home in the city of Valladolíd, he never stopped fighting for the return of his titles, honors, and lands. He also never admitted that he had failed to reach the Indies.

Columbus's legacy has both positive and negative elements. He was a brilliant navigator who performed heroic feats of seamanship, and he was a loyal servant of his adopted country and his faith. He also launched 500 years of European colonial domination in the Americas, dooming the great majority of Indians and their cultures to destruction. Many historians have pointed out, however, that despite his gifts as an explorer, Columbus was also a man of his time. If he had not made the fateful voyage, someone else would have done so, very likely with the same results. But it was his destiny to change the world, although he did so in an unexpected way.

James COOK

1728–1779

NAVIGATION

James Cook was perhaps the greatest seafarer in English history. During three historic voyages he undertook the most extensive explorations of the Pacific and Antarctic Oceans ever. In addition to discovering and mapping many new lands, Cook's expeditions answered many of the important questions of world geography during his day.

Early Life and Training

There was little in Cook's background or early youth that suggested that he would become a premier seaman. It was only as a teenager that he was drawn to the sea and into the life that would make him famous.

See the routes of Cook's expeditions in the "Maps" section.

From Land to Sea.   Cook was the son of a Scottish farmhand who had immigrated to the town of Marton-in-Cleveland in Yorkshire, England. When James was young, the elder Cook took a job as foreman in a farm in a nearby village. His employer noticed that young James had a quick mind, and he paid for the child's schooling until age 12. After leaving school, Cook worked on the farm with his father for several years. He then began an apprenticeship at a general store in Straithes, a fishing village just north of the port of Whitby in northeastern England.

In Whitby, Cook was exposed to ships and the sea, and he soon left his apprenticeship on land for one at sea. At the age of 18 he went to work for John Walker, a shipowner whose colliers (coal ships) carried coal between Whitby and London. Cook's apprenticeship on the tricky and dangerous waters in the North Sea was ideal preparation for sailing in any condition. The sturdy Whitby colliers on which he trained became his ships of choice on his later expeditions. During the winter months when sailing was impossible, Cook spent his time studying mathematics.

By the time he was 21, Cook had earned the rating of able seaman, and three years later he was promoted to the rank of mate (the master's assistant). Six years later, in 1755, he was offered command of a bark, a type of sailboat. Although this was a promising start for someone who aspired to a career as a merchant seaman, Cook had grander dreams. He felt that a career in the Royal Navy would offer a more interesting life. That same year he entered the navy as an ordinary sailor.

Early Naval Career.   Working on the HMS *Eagle,* Cook quickly earned promotions to master's mate and later to boatswain (ship's officer who supervises anchors, ropes, and cables). The following year, when England and France began fighting the Seven Year's War (1756–1763), the navy ordered Cook to map the estuary* of Canada's St. Lawrence River in preparation for an attack on the French fort at Quebec. His work paved the way for England's successful amphibious invasion.

*estuary wide part of a river where it nears the sea

Cook's survey of Canada was so masterful that he received a cash bonus for "making himself the 'master of the pilotage.'" After the war he earned command of the HMS *Grenville,* with which he surveyed the coast of Newfoundland. In 1766, while sailing along the Canadian coast, he observed an eclipse of the sun. He sent a report of the details to London's Royal Society, an organization of scientists. This act earned Cook the recognition that led directly to his first great voyage.

The First Voyage

In 1768 the Royal Society was preparing to mount a series of expeditions to study an upcoming astronomical event in which the planet Venus was expected to transit, or pass across, the sun. By measuring the time the transit took, astronomers believed they could calculate the distance from the Earth to Venus. Because England was not an ideal place from which to study the phenomenon, the society decided to send scientific teams to Newfoundland, northern Norway, and Tahiti.

To Tahiti and Beyond. Cook's report on the solar eclipse caught the attention of the Royal Society, which turned to him to command the expedition to Tahiti. Cook was promoted to the rank of lieutenant and placed in charge of a four-year-old Whitby collier renamed the HMS *Endeavour.* His orders were to transport members of the Royal Society and their scientific equipment to Tahiti to observe the transit. The party included not only astronomers, but also botanists, such as the eminent Joseph Banks, who would collect scientific specimens, and artists who would sketch landscapes on the trip.

Observing the transit was only the public objective of the voyage, however. In a second set of sealed orders, Cook was charged with finding the mythical great southern continent called *Terra Australis.* Many philosophers argued that a giant continent must exist in the southern hemisphere to balance out the landmasses in the northern hemisphere. Cook was to see if such a continent truly existed.

Cook in Tahiti. The *Endeavour* left England on September 13, 1768, and sailed across the Atlantic Ocean to Rio de Janeiro, Brazil. There the *Endeavour* was mistaken for a pirate ship, causing some delays in the voyage. Cook then rounded the treacherous Cape Horn on the southern tip of South America without incident and sailed west across the Pacific until he reached Tahiti in the cluster of islands that Cook named the Society Islands. On April 13, 1769, the *Endeavour* landed in Tahiti.

The initial reception by the islanders was cautious, but when a local chief recognized one of the English officers from an earlier expedition, the Tahitians warmly welcomed the crew. During their several months' stay, the English learned a great deal about the life and customs of the people. They became the first Westerners to see tattoos, with which the Tahitians decorated themselves. It is probably from this trip that sailors developed the custom of sporting tattoos.

Cook spent his time on the island mapping its coast; the scientists collected botanical specimens; and the artists sketched the landscape. On June 3, the astronomers witnessed the transit of Venus and recorded their observations. After completing those tasks, the crew began to ready the *Endeavour* for the second part of the mission—to discover the truth about *Terra Australis.* However, they could not leave at once

Respecting Differences

During Cook's first voyage to Tahiti, he and his crew discovered that the Tahitians did not have the same ideas about property as Europeans. They considered all property to belong to the group, so small thefts were common. Cook looked the other way when such incidents occurred, except for one. When the main piece of equipment for observing the transit of Venus was stolen, Cook sent search parties to all parts of the island. Soon the disassembled pieces were all returned. Although he used threats and warnings to retrieve the instrument, he never resorted to violence. His tolerance for different cultures set Cook apart from other explorers of his day.

since many had contracted a sexually transmitted disease and needed to recover. Until that time Cook had taken many precautions to keep the crew free of sickness. In fact, one of his remarkable achievements was that he lost few men, and none to the dreaded disease called scurvy. He accomplished this by forcing his men to eating foods containing vitamin C, such as fresh vegetables and sauerkraut. He also required the crew to keep their quarters clean and aired out. Cook later wrote a paper for the Royal Society on the prevention of scurvy.

***Searching for* Terra Australis.** Finally, in mid-August, when the crew had recovered, Cook was able to resume the journey. The *Endeavour* sailed south for a month, but bad weather forced him to turn back without sighting *Terra Australis*. Cook then headed west to New Zealand, and arrived in Poverty Bay on the eastern coast of North Island. However, he encountered hostile Maori* warriors there and was unable to explore inland. The *Endeavour* continued sailing until it reached the South Island of New Zealand, and from there Cook turned north and sailed along the east coast of Australia (then known as New Holland). Throughout the journey, he mapped the New Zealand coastline.

On April 29, 1770, Cook anchored his ship at Stingray Bay just south of the city of Sydney. He renamed it Botany Bay after the scientists on board discovered many previously unknown types of plants there. Here the party encountered two Aborigines*, whom they frightened away by firing their muskets (shoulder-mounted firearm). On May 7, they left the bay and continued sailing north along the coast. A few days later, the ship ran aground on the Great Barrier Reef and Cook brought the vessel into Cook Harbor. The crew was forced to remain in Cooktown in northeastern Australia for two months to repair the ship.

The ship was still leaky after its repairs, but Cook pressed on. He sailed past the northeastern tip of Australia, which he named Cape York, and turned west and found and named the Endeavour Strait*, which separates Australia and Prince of Wales Island. Cook continued west until he reached Jakarta, Indonesia, where he was again forced to land to make additional repairs to the ship. There his crew came down with a fever that killed many of them on their return voyage to England. The *Endeavour* left Indonesia in December and arrived home on July 13, 1771.

The Second Voyage

Searching for *Terra Australis* was a secret goal of Cook's first voyage, but it was the declared intent of his second. If he found land, he was to claim it for Britain; but if he was unable to locate the mythical continent, he was to sail as far south as he could and circumnavigate the Antarctic Ocean until ice or weather forced him to turn back.

Heading South. Cook received two new vessels for the voyage, the *Resolution* and the *Adventure*. Both were Whitby colliers of the type

*Maori original inhabitants of New Zealand

*Aborigine original inhabitants of Australia

*strait narrow waterway that runs between two landmasses and links two bodies of water

that he sailed to Tahiti, but smaller. Joseph Banks, the botanist from Cook's first voyage, and two astronomers were to join the expedition. However, when Banks and Cook began to argue about how many people Banks could bring along, Banks withdrew from the mission. The astronomers brought with them four chronometers, new scientific instruments that were supposed to measure longitude using the position of stars and the time of day. These instruments would prove to be invaluable. Cook left England on July 13, 1772, heading for Cape Town, South Africa.

About 109 days later, the two colliers reached Cape Town, where Cook heard that a French explorer had discovered land in the Indian Ocean and had named it *La France Australe* (Southern France). This information encouraged Cook to believe that a southern continent might actually exist. Cook left Cape Town on November 23, and by December 11, the crew of the *Adventure* had reached the edge of a vast pack of ice. The *Resolution* followed shortly thereafter and on January 17, 1773, the two ships became the first known vessels to cross the Antarctic Circle. They sailed along the ice for two months but found no entrance that led farther south.

Assuming that *La France Australe* could not be part of a larger southern continent, Cook sailed back to New Zealand. He reached Dusky Sound on the South Island on March 25, 1773, and spent the next several months exploring islands in the South Pacific. During this time, the crew encountered a storm and the two ships became separated. On November 27, Cook, aboard the *Resolution,* again headed south, reaching the ice pack in mid-December. He spent about six weeks navigating his vessel through icebergs, storms, and dangerous seas, but his search was futile and he was again forced to abandon his quest.

Returning Home. Based on his observations during those six weeks, Cook concluded that the ice pack extended all the way to the South Pole. He again steered for New Zealand, where he spent the winter. In November 1774 he sailed across the Pacific to Tierra del Fuego, an island off the southern tip of South America. From there he sailed northeast into the Atlantic, where the crew sighted land. At first they thought it might be the southern continent, but it turned out to be an island covered in ice. Cook named the island South Georgia.

A disappointed Cook decided to again sail south to locate *Terra Australis*. By January 1775, he had found a group of islands that he named South Sandwich Islands. He spent a week exploring there, but gave up and steered a course north to England, arriving there on July 30, 1775. Cook's voyage proved that there was no southern continent unless it lay beyond the ice at the South Pole. On the three-year, 60,000-mile trip, he became the first to circumnavigate the Antarctic Ocean.

Cook's Final Voyage

When Cook returned after three years at sea he was promoted to Fourth Captain, a high rank that was essentially a desk job. He accepted it only under the condition that he be allowed to return to active duty if his country called on him. In early 1776 he got that chance.

Return to the Pacific. Cook's third voyage had two goals—to return a Tahitian who sailed to England in the *Adventure* after that ship became separated from *Resolution,* and to explore the northwest coast of America and the northeast coast of Asia. Explorers had long looked for direct northern sea routes from Europe to Asia. A Northwest Passage supposedly existed among the Arctic islands north of Canada, and a Northeast Passage was rumored to lie north of Russian Siberia. Cook was to find evidence of these routes.

Cook set out on July 12, 1776, in the *Resolution,* reaching Cape Town on October 18. The *Discovery,* an ex-collier, followed a few weeks later, arriving on November 10. The two ships together left Cape Town on November 30 and sailed in a southeasterly direction. Two weeks later they spotted islands that Cook named Crozet Islands after the French explorer who arrived there first. The expedition continued eastward until it reached Tasmania, an island south of Australia, in January 1777. Thereafter, Cook stopped at several points in the South Seas, including New Zealand, Tahiti, the Friendly Islands, and a group today known as Cook Islands. The crew spent the summer and fall of 1777 in Polynesia, learning about the peoples' customs, religions, and culture.

Looking for the Passages. The vessels left Polynesia in December 1777 and sailed north, crossing the equator. On January 18, 1778, Cook spotted some of the smaller Hawaiian Islands, becoming possibly the first European to see them. However, he continued on since he was determined to reach North America when the weather was still warm. When he reached the North American coast, he sailed around Alaska and into the Arctic Ocean. However, after eight weeks of fruitless searching, Cook was forced to turn back due to heavy ice.

The *Resolution* and the *Discovery* then headed back for Hawaii, which Cook renamed the Sandwich Islands in honor of his friend the Earl of Sandwich. It took eight weeks to find a suitable harbor, but he finally put in Kealakekua Bay on the big island of Hawaii. When Cook landed there he was greeted as if he were a god. On February 4, 1779, after a month of enjoying the Hawaiians' hospitality, Cook set out for northern Asia, but storms damaged his ship and he had to return to Hawaii.

Cook arrived in Hawaii on February 13, just in time for a harvest celebration for the god Lonoikamakahiki, for whom he had been mistaken earlier. The high chief of the island of Kaua'i gave Cook his daughter as a gift. She later bore Cook a child. However, the good feelings between Cook and the Hawaiians were not destined to last.

The Death of Cook. Cook's final voyage had a tragic ending. One day his crewmembers discovered that some of the islanders had stolen one of the ship's longboats (rescue boat) for its iron. During the theft, they had killed two watchmen. Cook decided to take the high chief hostage until the boat was returned. The chief agreed to go with Cook, but the chief's wife ran up and begged him not to go. A fight broke out, but no one is really sure how it began or who was responsible. According to one report an islander was killed farther up the shoreline by Cook's crew and the Hawaiians then attacked Cook and his party. Cook suffered a fatal wound during the tussle that followed and died on the beach.

It was a strange end for Cook, who had earned a reputation as one of the few explorers who dealt humanely with the peoples in the lands that he discovered. Shortly thereafter, the ships set sail for the Kamchatka Peninsula, from where the crew sent word of Cook's death, and then to England, arriving there on August 22, 1780.

Legacy of an Explorer. Cook's voyages of exploration helped answer many questions of the day and opened possibilities for trade in the Pacific and in the American northwest. His journals contained a wealth of information on the customs of various peoples that he encountered in the Pacific. He also mapped thousands of miles of coastlines. Finally, he proved that traveling long distances by sea was not only practical but could also be healthy.

Nicholas Copernicus's *De revolutionibus orbium coelestium* (On the Revolutions of the Heavenly Spheres), published the year of his death, overturned existing notions about the structure of the universe, the motions of the planets, and the earth's place in the cosmos. He challenged the theory that the earth was the fixed center of an unchanging universe, and in doing so, he inspired the work of many important figures of the scientific revolution.

Copernicus was born in Torun, Poland. In 1483, when his father died, he went to live with his uncle, who began to prepare him for a career as a church official. In 1491, Copernicus entered the University of Cracow, but he left before earning a degree. At his uncle's urging he went to the University of Bologna in Italy to study church law. Privately, he pursued his interest in astronomy.

In Bologna, Copernicus was greatly influenced by Domenica Maria de Novara, principal astronomer at the university. Because Novara was responsible for making annual astrological predictions (astrology at this time was closely associated with astronomy) for the city of Bologna, Copernicus learned much about astrology from him. Novara also introduced Copernicus to the most important books on astronomy.

In 1497, Copernicus recorded his first astronomical observation—a lunar eclipse in Bologna, and three years later, he observed another in Rome. After a short visit to Poland, he returned to Italy and resumed his studies in medicine and law at the Universities of Padua and Ferrara, receiving a degree in church law from Ferrara in 1503.

Copernicus the moved to Poland to take a position in the church. He spent the rest of his life in the service of the church, but in his spare time he continued to make astronomical observations. From the towers of churches and other buildings, he studied the movements of the sun,

Nicholas
COPERNICUS

1473–1543

ASTRONOMY

moon, stars, and planets. By 1514 he had gained enough respect as an astronomer to be invited to a church council to help reform the calendar. He did not attend that meeting, but his observations served as a basis for the development of the Gregorian calendar some 70 years later.

In 1514 Copernicus issued *Commentariolus,* challenging the Greek astronomer PTOLEMY's geocentric (earth-centered) system, which had dominated Western thought for more than 1,000 years. Copernicus announced that the sun, not the earth, was the center of the universe. He also described how the rotation of the earth appeared to make the heavens rotate in the sky and explained how the earth's revolution around the sun accounts for the motion of the other planets in the night sky. *Commentariolus* resolved many of the difficulties that scholars had been experiencing with the Ptolemaic system, but it raised new questions, some of which Copernicus answered in his later works.

Copernicus spent the next 25 years perfecting his ideas before publishing a full version of his heliocentric, or sun-centered, model of the universe. He published the main elements of his theory under the name of his assistant, George Joachim Rheticus. *Narratio prima* (First Narration) appeared in 1540. The ideas in this work marked a dramatic break with the Ptolemaic system and contained an argument for the new heliocentric theory based on scientific observation and measurement. Although Copernicus knew that he could not rule out other theories, he provided the most logical possibility based on existing knowledge.

In 1542, when Rheticus returned to Germany, he took with him the finished manuscript of the Copernican theory in its final form. Published the following year, *De revolutionibus orbium coelestium* (On the Revolutions of the Heavenly Spheres) presented the Copernican astronomical system. The work contained an anonymous preface, written by the book's publisher, insisting that the idea of a moving earth was only a mathematical hypothesis and that astronomy was incapable of explaining heavenly phenomena. In doing so, however, the publisher had changed the emphasis of the work. Opposition to *De revolutionibus* was not as great as was expected, but many feared that changing the natural order of the universe might result in chaos. By presenting the idea as a hypothesis, the publisher might have minimized the opposition to the new theory. Nevertheless, Copernicus had set in motion a chain of events that led to a revolution in scientific thought, as scholars and scientists began to question traditional beliefs and use observation, experiments, and mathematical calculations to uncover explanations for natural phenomena.

Francisco Vázquez de CORONADO

1510–1554

EXPLORATION OF
NORTH AMERICA

The wealthy, respected governor of a province in New Spain*, Francisco Vázquez de Coronado is best known for his pioneering expedition into the North American Southwest. Motivated by tales of fabulously wealthy cities, he spent two years exploring the region now occupied by the states of Texas, New Mexico, Arizona, and Kansas. Although he never found the treasures he was seeking, Coronado left behind a valuable description of the area before it was conquered by the Europeans.

Early Days in Mexico. Coronado, the son of noble parents, was born in the city of Salamanca, Spain. At age 25 he came to the Americas and was immediately named assistant to Antonio de Mendoza, the viceroy* of New Spain. Coronado wasted little time in making a name for himself. He married the daughter of the colonial treasurer and inherited a large estate. He later suppressed a major slave revolt and within four years of his arrival became governor of the province of New Galicia.

In 1536, the year after Coronado had reached Mexico City, the Spanish explorer Álvar Núñez CABEZA DE VACA and his three companions arrived there after completing their nine-year odyssey. Cabeza de Vaca and his group were the first Europeans to travel across the continent from Florida, on the Atlantic coast, to California, on the Pacific coast. They told tales of incredible riches, including a story of immense riches in the Seven Golden Cities of Cíbola to the north. Fray Marcos de Niza, a priest whom Mendoza had sent north in 1539, confirmed these tales. The viceroy ordered an overland expedition and placed Coronado in charge of exploring and claiming the region for Spain.

The Search Begins. Coronado began to outfit his mission. He assembled a party consisting of about 300 Spanish soldiers, more than 1,000 Tlaxcalan, and several hundred black and Indian slaves. He also took along large herds of horses, cattle, pigs, and sheep for food and transportation. The expedition left the city of Compostela on February 23, 1540, and headed north along the western slopes of the Sierra Madre. A fleet was sent simultaneously up the Gulf of California to look for a waterway that might lead from the coast to the golden cities. In August the fleet discovered the mouth of the Colorado River.

Coronado's group began the long, arduous journey along the mountains until they reached the border of present-day Arizona. They then headed northeast, expecting to find Cíbola. Frustrated with the sluggish pace of the large group, Coronado decided to travel ahead with a smaller group of about 100 lightly equipped men. The rest of the expedition was to follow at a slower pace. On July 4, 1540, the first party arrived at the Hawikuh pueblo* inhabited by Zuni. Coronado, however, was not the first Spaniard to see the pueblo; Estevan, one of the survivors of Cabeza de Vaca's expedition, had led a small group there the year before. However, the Zuni had killed Estevan after he became too familiar with some of the women there.

Confrontation and Disappointment. When Coronado arrived, the Zuni were in the middle of their summer ceremonies. Before the assembled Indians, Coronado read the *requirimento,* a proclamation from the Spanish government that demanded that the Zuni accept the Catholic Church and become subjects of the Pope and the Spanish king and queen. The Zuni resisted and began firing arrows at the Spaniards, but they were quickly overpowered. On July 7, Coronado and his men stormed the pueblo, but they found no gold or riches.

Coronado then divided his force into several smaller groups and sent them out in different directions to search for treasure. These small-

*New Spain Spain's colony in the Americas that included all of Mexico north of the present-day state of Chiapas and parts of the present-day United States

*viceroy governor of a province or colony, ruling as the representative of a king or queen

*pueblo community dwelling, several stories high, built of stone or mud by Indians of the southwestern United States

In this illustration titled *Coronado's March,* the artist Frederic Remington (1861–1909) captures Francisco Vázquez de Coronado's overland trek through the American Southwest in search of the Seven Golden Cities of Cíbola.

er expeditions explored much of the American Southwest between Arizona and California. On one of these journeys, García López de Cárdenas became the first white man to see the Grand Canyon. However, none of the groups found any treasures and the parties reassembled to spend the winter at Tiguex, a village on the Rio Grande near the present-day site of Santa Fe, New Mexico. Many hostile peoples attacked them throughout the winter, but the Spaniards were able to repel them.

During one of the side trips Coronado took that winter, he met a Plains Indian whom he named "the Turk." The Indian told him the fantastic story of an incredibly rich land called Quivira that lay far out on the distant plains. According to the Turk, a river six miles wide flowed through Quivira and contained fish as big as horses. On the river there were canoes that could hold up to 40 men. He claimed that the rulers of Quivira were transported by sail-driven canoes with golden eagles on their prows (the front of the boat) and that the king, Tatarrax, slept under a tree whose branches were strung with golden bells. Tatarrax supposedly worshiped a golden cross and the image of a woman called the goddess of heaven. In Quivira, even the ordinary folk had dishes, jugs, and bowls of gold.

Impressed by the story, Coronado left most of his men in Tiguex and set out on April 23, 1541, with a group of about 30 soldiers and the Turk as his guide toward present-day Kansas, where he hoped to find the mythical kingdom of Quivira. The group traveled from Tiguex to Cicuye (present-day Pecos, New Mexico), crossed the Pecos River, and arrived more than a month later in a small Indian village. Intimidated by the Spanish horsemen, the Indians gave Coronado food, pottery, and some turquoise, but no gold. The Turk then admitted he was attempting to lure the group to the plains, where he hoped they would die. Coronado and his men killed the Turk and headed farther north to find Quivira.

Return to Mexico. Coronado and his men traveled through parts of Oklahoma until they reached the Arkansas River, which they followed downstream where they finally met some Quivira peoples. The Indians took Coronado to their village, which consisted of little more than grass huts and not the rich civilization that the Turk had described.

By this time it had become clear to Coronado that he would not find any riches on this journey, and in April 1542 he returned to Mexico City. The viceroy considered the expedition a total failure, and Coronado resumed his duties as governor of New Galicia. He retired two years later and moved to Mexico City. There the Spanish royal court accused Coronado of atrocities against the Indians who had accompanied him on his expedition, but later found him innocent. Coronado remained in Mexico City until his death in September 1554.

Hernán Cortés ushered in the era of Spanish conquest of Central and South America with his victory over the Aztec Empire in 1521. A restless adventurer since his boyhood, Cortés used a mixture of cunning, cruelty, and personal magnetism to realize his ambition of conquering rich lands for Spain. However, like many other early explorers who gained wealth and power from their achievements, Cortés's success brought him little peace or satisfaction.

Early Life and Career. Cortés was born in the town of Medellín in southwestern Spain. He was the son of noble parents who, according to his secretary, "had little wealth, but much honor." At age 14 Cortés entered the University of Salamanca as a law student. Intelligent and clever, he was also "ruthless, haughty, mischievous, and quarrelsome" and "given to women." Around this time Cortés became captivated by stories of Christopher COLUMBUS's voyages of discovery.

Struck by boredom and wanderlust, Cortés left school for the east coast port of Valencia. He planned to serve in Spain's war in Italy, but instead roamed the region for a year. In 1504 he boarded a ship bound for the Caribbean island of Hispaniola (today divided between the nations of Haiti and Dominican Republic) in search of wealth and power.

Hispaniola and Cuba. On Hispaniola, Cortés settled down to life as a farmer. He joined the town council, becoming a man of some importance. In 1510 he joined the expedition led by Diego Velázquez that conquered Cuba. Velázquez became governor of Cuba and Cortés was named *alcalde* (mayor) of the city of Santiago de Cuba. Cortés also received a grant of land, some Indian slaves to work it, and several gold mines. He became a man of considerable influence, and a possible rival to Velázquez.

During the years that followed, Velázquez sponsored many expeditions, including one that discovered the mainland of Mexico. In October 1518 he ordered Cortés to assemble an expedition to

Hernán
CORTÉS

ca. 1484–1547

EXPLORATION OF MEXICO

See the routes of Cortés's expeditions in the "Maps" section.

The Looting of Tenochtitlán

When Cortés invaded Tenochtitlán, his men entered the palace and "they asked Montezuma about the city's resources . . . They questioned him closely and then demanded gold. Montezuma guided them to it . . . When they arrived at the treasure house . . . They gathered all the gold into a great mound . . . and seized every object they thought was beautiful . . . They searched everywhere and coveted everything; they were slaves to their own greed. All of Montezuma's possessions were brought out: fine bracelets, necklaces with large stones, . . . the royal crowns and all the royal finery . . . They seized these treasures as if they were their own."

explore the mainland and to establish trade with its inhabitants. Within a month Cortés had recruited 300 men and had bought 6 ships. Wary of Cortés's influence, however, Velázquez planned to remove him from command, but Cortés left port before he could do so. Cortés first sailed to other Cuban ports to further outfit his expedition and then left for Mexico.

Contacting the Aztecs. Cortés departed from Santiago de Cuba on February 18, 1519, with 11 ships, a 508-member crew, and 16 horses. He landed at the town of Tabasco on the Yucatán Peninsula where he met local Indians. One of them, a woman named Malinche (later baptized Marina), became his mistress and interpreter. The inhabitants of Tabasco told Cortés stories about the wealthy Aztec Empire to the west. They also revealed to him that the Aztecs had many enemies that the Spanish might be able to recruit as allies.

Cortés next sailed up the coast and founded the town of La Villa Rica de la Vera Cruz (present-day Veracruz). He formed a town council, which then named him captain-general. This appointment made Cortés independent of the authority of Velázquez, whom Cortés feared might try to stop him from continuing farther inland. By now Cortés had little concern for trade or exploration; he had become determined to conquer the Aztec Empire. To ensure that his crew would not desert him in this endeavor, however, Cortés ordered that his ships be burned.

During the next few months, Marina and other Indians guided Cortés and his party west toward the Aztec capital of Tenochtitlán. Along the way they met many Indian groups who were subjects of the Aztecs. Using a combination of force and persuasion, Cortés overcame any resistance and enlisted them as allies. His force grew to more than 200,000. As they neared Tenochtitlán, Cortés began to receive messages from the Aztec king Montezuma II discouraging him from continuing. Cortés ignored the warnings and on November 8, 1519, he entered the city with a small Spanish troop and about 1,000 Indian allies.

The Conquest of Mexico. Unfortunately for the Aztecs, when Montezuma saw Cortés, he believed the Spaniard was the Aztec god Quetzalcoatl. According to Aztec legend, Quetzalcoatl was a bearded, light-skinned god who had left many years before but who would return from the east to reestablish his authority over the Aztecs. Montezuma gave Cortés and his troops unrestricted access to the city. Seizing the opportunity, Cortés took Montezuma prisoner and demanded a huge ransom for his release. The move took the Aztecs completely by surprise, and they began to gather treasures for the ransom.

In April 1520 Cortés learned that Velázquez had dispatched troops led by Pánfilo de Narváez to the mainland to arrest him and bring him back to Cuba. Leaving a small force in Tenochtitlán, Cortés returned to the coast, where he snuck into the enemy camp and captured Narváez. He then recruited help from among the expedition sent to arrest him. Having thwarted Velázquez's attempts to stop him, Cortés went back to Tenochtitlán.

Cortés found the city in revolt against the Spaniards. The captain he had left in charge had massacred unarmed Aztecs during a celebration and the population had turned on the Spanish invaders. Cortés brought Montezuma out to restore calm, but the king was fatally wounded by a stone thrown at him from the crowd. Cortés was forced to withdraw from the city on the dark, rainy night of June 30, 1520, having lost many men. That night later became known as *Noche Triste,* or "Sad Night."

Cortés rejoined his allies, and in December 1520 he led a force that laid siege* to Tenochtitlán. He first blockaded the city with 13 boats and launched an invasion that overwhelmed the defending Aztec forces. On August 13, 1521, Spanish forces captured Cuauhtémoc, Montezuma's successor, and the Aztecs surrendered.

siege long and persistent effort to force a surrender by surrounding a fortress or city with armed troops, cutting it off from supplies and aid

Governor of Mexico. Cortés had gained control of a vast and wealthy empire thousands of miles from Europe. He could have retained the Aztec Empire and declared himself independent of Spain, but instead he claimed the territory for Spain's King Charles I. Meanwhile, his enemies, particularly Velázquez, were working against him. Velázquez tried to turn Charles against Cortés by claiming that Cortés would try to defy the king's authority. Cortés, anticipating such attacks, wrote letters to Charles defending his actions. Ultimately, Charles accepted Cortés's arguments and named him governor of Mexico in 1523.

As governor, Cortés sought to expand his domain by sending troops to conquer Guatemala and Honduras in the south. When one of his commanders rebelled against him, Cortés led a force to Honduras to confront him. He was away from Mexico City (Cortés built the city on the ruins of Tenochtitlán) for nearly two years. During this time his health began to decline, as did his position. His enemies in the city had convinced the Spanish king to send investigators to examine Cortés's administration of the colony. In 1528, when one of the investigators died, Cortés was accused of poisoning him and was forced to relinquish his gubernatorial powers.

A Losing Fight. That same year Cortés returned to Spain to seek an audience with Charles to present his side of the story. Charles received him warmly and gave him several titles, but refused to rename him governor of Mexico. In 1530, when Cortés returned to Mexico, he found the colony in chaos. He also found himself the object of many accusations of misconduct, including the murder of his first wife.

After helping to restore order in Mexico City, Cortés led and financed many treasure-hunting expeditions. Between 1535 and 1536 he tried to start a colony in Baja California. The mission failed, and Cortés gave up his political career and retired to his estate outside the city. In 1540 he returned to Europe and fought briefly for Spain in Algeria. He spent the rest of his life battling lawsuits and accusations and still seeking the status and riches he believed he had been denied. Cortés died in Seville in 1547.

Charles Robert
DARWIN
1809–1882
SCIENTIFIC EXPLORATION

*naturalist one who studies objects in their natural settings

*natural selection theory that within a given species, individuals with characteristics best adapted to the environment survive and successfully produce more offspring than other individuals, resulting in changes in the species over time

*natural history systematic study of nature and natural objects in their original settings

Charles Darwin was a British naturalist* at a time when scientists of Europe and America were sailing to far reaches of the earth on voyages of discovery. They collected specimens of plants and animals unknown to them, which they brought home to study and display, and worked not just to map but also to understand the places they explored.

Darwin made only one voyage of exploration, but that voyage led to a new understanding of the natural world. His famous contribution was his theory of evolution, the process by which new species appear as existing ones evolve over time. He also outlined the chief method by which it occurs, a process called natural selection*. Darwin's work has had enormous influence not only on later scientific work but also on society and culture. He forever changed the human view of the natural world—and of humankind's place in the great web of interconnected life.

Preparation for Discovery. Darwin was born in Shrewsbury, England, into a prominent family. He did not distinguish himself at school—in fact, his teachers considered him slow at learning. He was more interested in collecting insects and other natural history* specimens and performing chemical experiments than in Greek, Latin, and history. At the age of 16, Darwin enrolled in the medical school of the University of Edinburgh, Scotland, but bored by the lectures and disgusted by the surgical demonstrations, he left after two years. He then went to the University of Cambridge to study to become a clergyman, but he did not fare well in those classes either. Meanwhile, his interest in natural history had grown stronger than ever.

The Voyage of the Beagle. Darwin graduated from Cambridge in 1831, and a botanist from the university arranged for him to sail on the *Beagle,* a Royal Navy ship on a surveying mission around the world for the government. Fortunate naturalists of the time traveled this way, and Darwin was eager to go. He equipped himself with the gear of a traveling scientist, including books, materials for collecting and preserving plant and animal specimens, and a geologist's hammer for breaking off rock samples. In December 1831 HMS *Beagle,* commanded by Captain Robert FitzRoy, departed from England on a mission that was scheduled to take two years but would last for five.

The *Beagle* expedition was to complete the charting of certain coasts of South America. On the way across the Atlantic Ocean to South America, the captain stopped at several island groups. At the first stop, in the Cape Verde Islands off the African coast, Darwin observed a layer of rock well above sea level that contained the fossil remains of sea creatures. This and later observations seemed to Darwin to confirm the new theory proposed by the British geologist Charles Lyell, that the present surface of the earth had been formed over a period of millions of years by processes such as the rising and erosion of landmasses.

After the *Beagle* reached South America, it cruised along the continent's eastern and western coasts as the captain carried out his mapmaking duties. This schedule enabled Darwin to spend long periods ashore in various regions—a welcome break from the seasickness that frequently troubled him aboard the *Beagle*. These shore visits were his adventures in exploration.

Walking in Brazil's rain forests, Darwin was amazed by the abundance of insect life and the number of species. As he rode across the plains of Argentina, he found the fossils of long-extinct creatures. When the *Beagle* sailed along South America's Pacific coast, Darwin witnessed an earthquake that raised the land several feet and knocked down the Chilean city of Concepción. He had a firsthand glimpse at nature's ability to reshape landscapes. Later he crossed the Andes Mountains, where he saw marine fossils 12,000 feet above sea level and could only imagine the forces that had raised them to that height.

Next the *Beagle* began its crossing of the Pacific, stopping at the Galápagos Islands off the coast of Ecuador, where Darwin observed and gathered samples of animal life. Identical in climate and physical features and located close to one another, the islands should have been inhabited by identical species. But he noticed that the finches (songbirds) on different islands had varied physical characteristics and diets. Some ate insects, while others ate seeds, and their sizes and bill shapes varied depending on their diets and ways of life. Darwin first thought they were varieties of a single species, but later he learned that they were separate but related species. This observation would hold the key to the theories he later developed.

The *Beagle* then crossed the Pacific Ocean, stopping in several island groups and in Australia. Eventually it rounded the southern tip of Africa and returned to England in 1836.

Fruits of Scientific Exploration. Darwin never traveled again. He moved to the English countryside, raised a family, and spent the rest of his life on a journey of the mind. He spent years classifying, studying, and writing about the samples he had collected and the observations he had made during his voyage on the *Beagle*. In 1839 Darwin published *Journal of Researches into the Geology and Natural History of the Various Countries Visited by H.M.S. Beagle,* a lively and popular summary of his experiences and observations. He also published three geological works on the coral reefs, volcanic islands, and other landforms he had seen during the expedition.

Darwin's main interest, however, was what he called "the species problem"—the question of how various plant and animal species arise. The evidence he had collected at the Galápagos Islands was key because it proved that animals belonging to a single species, when isolated by geographic barriers into separate populations, developed distinctive features and over time formed multiple new species. In July 1837, with the voyage still fresh in his mind, he began to write on the subject. He spent more than 20 years forming his theory of evolution, publishing *On the Origin of Species by Means of Natural Selection* in 1859.

Controversies Brew. One of the most influential in the history of science, the book stirred up a storm of protest. Two aspects of the work

During his five-year voyage aboard the HMS *Beagle,* Charles Darwin had the opportunity to observe hundreds of species of animals in their natural habitats. Here, the *Beagle* is seen observing sharks near St. Paul's Rocks, a group of volcanic islands off the northeastern coast of Brazil.

were especially disturbing. First, the notion that humans and apes had descended from a common ancestor took humans out of their privileged position as beings created in God's image to rule the earth. Second, although Darwin's theory did not deny the existence of God, it claimed that the process of life could be explained by natural instead of divine means. The turmoil caused by Darwin's views lasted for some time—indeed, some religious groups still claim on the authority of the Bible that evolution does not occur.

The fact of evolution, however, has been well established, and scientific debate today centers on its mechanisms rather than on its existence. One of the most important advances in evolutionary biology since Darwin's time has been the growth of genetics*, which has revealed how individual variations occur among organisms and how characteristics pass from parents to offspring—questions Darwin himself never satisfactorily answered.

Before his death at his home in Downe, Kent, Darwin wrote many more books on evolution and botany. He also witnessed controversy and intellectual excitement over his work on evolution, and he lived to see his evidence that species evolve, as well as most of his ideas about how evolution occurs, accepted by the scientific world.

*genetics branch of biology that deals with heredity

Vasily Vasilievich DOKUCHAEV

1846–1903

SOIL SCIENCE, GEOGRAPHY

*topography scientific study of the physical, natural features of a place or object

*geomorphology study of the physical features of the earth's surface

*seminary school for training people for the priesthood, ministry, or rabbinate

*ecclesiastical of or relating to a church

*curator caretaker

*mineralogy study of the properties of minerals

*crystallography science that deals with the forms and structures of crystals

Vasily Dokuchaev is best known for his classification of soils and for his theory that soil is the result of the interplay between geological and biological activity. He showed that climate, topography*, the action of water, and the activities of plant and animal life all play roles in the formation of soil. His work had profound implications for geography and agriculture. Dokuchaev is credited as one of the founders of the field of geomorphology*.

Early Life and Career. Dokuchaev, the son of the village priest, was born in Milyukovo in the Russian province of Smolensk. He was educated at a local church school and later entered the seminary* in the city of Vyazama. In 1867, when he graduated from the seminary, he was accepted at the St. Petersburg Ecclesiastical* Academy and he seemed destined to follow in his father's footsteps. However, shortly after he entered the academy, he decided not to become and priest and instead chose to study natural sciences at St. Petersburg University.

Four years later Dokuchaev earned a master's degree and became a curator* of the university's geological collection. Also appointed assistant professor of geology, he taught courses in mineralogy* and crystallography*. During this time he developed the first course ever on the soil deposits of the Quaternary, the geological period that began nearly 1.6 million years ago and stretches to the present day.

In 1878 Dokuchaev published his first major work, a multiyear study of the geology, mountain formations, and surface waters of European Russia (the far western portion of Russia). He examined and critiqued earlier theories on the formation of river plains in the region, and advanced his ideas about the origin of various landforms and their relations to physical and geographic conditions of the past. This was one of the earliest works in the field of geomorphology.

In 1883 he was appointed head of the Department of Mineralogy and Crystallography, and four years later he began to teach soil science. According to other geographers of the time, "Dokuchaev deserves a major place among the world's geographers because of his innovative studies of soil. . . . He was the first scientist to realize that soil is not just disintegrated rock deposits and decomposed rock." He believed that studying soils was important because it held the key to higher crop yields and economic productivity as well as to crop improvement.

Soil Science and Agriculture. Thereafter Dokuchaev began his work on soils by studying the topsoil of European Russia, particularly the rich black soil known as *chernozem,* a term he helped popularize. He spent several years preparing notes for a soil map of Russia and conducted extensive studies of the chernozem zone in Russia. In 1883 Dokuchaev's work resulted in *Russky chernozyom* (Russian Chernozem), a book that was widely praised and that won many honors. Village councils in the Saratov and Voronezh provinces took note of his work. This attention led to large-scale research on the natural conditions in these regions, performed mostly by students of Dokuchaev's. Their work improved the practice of agriculture and confirmed and furthered Dokuchaev's ideas.

From 1882 to 1896 he conducted scientific expeditions to various sites in Russia. He compiled a description of the natural history of each region, taking into account factors relating to soil, geology, water, and plant and animal life. By analyzing all of these factors, he assessed the agricultural potential of each area. The materials he collected formed the basis of natural history museums throughout Russia. Dokuchaev led the effort to establish these organizations and argued for the creation of a separate soil institute and museum.

Theories of Soil Formation and Classification. During his extensive study of soils, Dokuchaev began to understand that many factors play a role in soil formation. He wrote that soils "are the result of the totality of activity of the bedrock, the living and inanimate organisms (plant as well as animal), climate, the age of the country, and the topography of the surroundings." He concluded that soils were geobiological (geological and biological) formations that change over time and in response to varying environmental conditions.

Dokuchaev then proposed a classification of soils into normal, abnormal, and transitional, and further subdivided them into sections and types depending on the agents that were responsible for their formation and on the interaction between the agents. He suggested that the different soil types were found in different zones of the earth. The zones formed belts that circled the earth at different latitudes. The polar belts were located at the poles, followed by the temperate and subtropical belts and the equatorial belt, which is nearest the equator.

steppe arid land found in regions of extreme temperatures

According to Dokuchaev, these belts form five basic geographical zones—boreal, taiga, chernozem (steppe*), arid desert, and lateritite (tropical). He showed the locations where the zones change and stressed that each zone presented distinct challenges to agriculture. Dokuchaev argued that agricultural activity should take into account the peculiarities of the zone in which it occurs.

Later Life. In 1891, when a severe drought struck Russia, Dokuchaev set aside his scientific work to deal with the problem. The government asked him to design ways to conduct farming, forestry, and water management in the chernozem zone during the drought. Dokuchaev set up experimental plots in which he studied the geology, soil, and climate of the area. This work enabled him to determine the influence that climate had on agriculture. Of particular importance were his findings about the role protective forest belts played in promoting agriculture.

In 1897 poor health forced Dokuchaev to resign his post at St. Petersburg University. His health improved enough the following year to enable him to lead an expedition to study the soil of Bessarabia, the region between the Dniester and Prut Rivers and extending from the Black Sea to Poland. He later led several other expeditions into the Caucasus and the area east of the Caspian Sea. Dokuchaev suffered from severe depression during the last three years of his life and died in St. Petersburg at the age of 57.

ERATOSTHENES
ca. 276 B.C.–ca. 195 B.C.
GEOGRAPHY, MATHEMATICS

Sometimes called the "father of geography," Eratosthenes was a pioneer in mapping and measuring the earth. He was the first to develop maps using a grid system, indicating the location of landmarks in terms of latitude and longitude. Eratosthenes is probably best known, however, for estimating the circumference of the earth with amazing accuracy. His geographical achievements were largely the result of his mastery of mathematics, another field in which he excelled.

Eratosthenes was born in the city of Cyrene in present-day Libya. His family was wealthy, and as a young man he traveled to Athens to study under some of the finest Greek scholars of the time. When Eratosthenes was in his early 30s, the king of Egypt invited him to tutor his son. The king also gave him a position at the famous library in Alexandria, the greatest storehouse of knowledge in the ancient world. A few years later Eratosthenes became the head librarian.

A keen student of both mathematics and geography, Eratosthenes used his knowledge of the former field to solve problems in the latter, such as calculating the earth's circumference. To do so, he positioned a thin rod at two locations in Egypt that he believed lay on the same line of latitude—Alexandria and Aswan. He also knew the distance between the two cities. On one day of the year, the rod at Aswan cast no shadow, but the one at Alexandria did. He measured the angle of the shadow and found it to be 7°12', or 1/50th of a full circle. He then multiplied by 50 the distance between the two cities to obtain his final measurement. Although he made a few errors (for example, Aswan and Alexandria are not on exactly the same latitude, and he assumed the earth was a perfect sphere), his result—29,000 miles—differed from the modern measurement—about 25,000 miles—by a mere 4,000 miles.

Using two intersecting lines to divide the known world into four quadrants, Eratosthenes compiled a world map. He subdivided the quadrants into smaller sections to form a grid similar to the one used on all modern maps. Based on information from travelers' reports and measurements taken by other scholars, he determined distances between many of the points on the map. Although the information on which the measurements were based was not precise and therefore compromised the accuracy of the distances, it was the first truly modern map.

Eratosthenes also used his geographical and mathematical skills to divide the earth into the various climate zones recognized today—arctic, temperate, and tropic—and to measure their width from the poles. Among his other contributions to geography were accurately measuring the tilt of the earth's axis, drawing the route of the Nile River down to the present-day city of Khartoum, and correctly suggesting that lakes farther south were the source of the river. According to Greek sources, Eratosthenes, afflicted by blindness in his old age, committed suicide by voluntarily starving himself to death.

L eif Erikson, also known as Leif the Lucky, is generally considered the first European to set foot in North America, preceding Christopher COLUMBUS by almost 500 years. Some recent scholarship disputes this claim, however, claiming that the Icelandic merchant Bjarni Herjolfsson was the first to reach present-day Canada. Nevertheless, it is undisputed that Erikson was the first to explore this new land; traces of the first European settlement in North America—believed to have been founded by Erikson—have been discovered in Newfoundland.

The Story of Erik the Red. Erikson was born in Iceland to Erik the Red, the man who discovered and colonized Greenland. When Leif was still an infant, his father was exiled from Iceland for committing a murder. Banished for three years, Erik the Red and his family spent the time exploring Greenland, finally settling there around 985 or 986. From this point, the story of Erikson's life becomes confused because of the differences in the two sagas that claim to tell his tale.

One version of Erikson's life is contained in *Eirik the Red's Saga.* According to this account, Erikson made his first major voyage in 999. He was sailing east from Greenland to Norway when his ship was

Leif
ERIKSON

ca. 980–ca. 1020

EXPLORATION OF
NORTH AMERICA

Abandoning America

Despite the promise of natural resources in Vinland, the Norse made only one attempt to colonize the Canadian coast. Several years after Erikson's visit, the Scandinavian explorer Thorfinn Karlsefni led a group of about 130 people to Baffin Island. They then sailed farther south and finally settled somewhere along the Gulf of St. Lawrence. They met no people the first winter there, but encountered friendly inhabitants the following summer. The next year larger numbers of hostile people arrived, however, and fighting broke out between the two groups. The settlers drove off their attackers but abandoned the colony after three years. It would be the last European settlement in North America for over 500 years.

blown off course by a storm and he landed in the Hebrides Islands off the coast of Scotland. Erikson remained in the Hebrides for a month until the weather permitted him to continue. In Norway he met with King Olaf I, who had recently converted to Christianity. The men discussed the Christian faith and Erikson, who was never a great believer in the Norse gods, converted to Christianity. Thereafter Olaf commissioned Erikson to return to Greenland and win over his family and neighbors to the new faith.

On his return from Norway, Erikson was again blown off course and he sailed past Greenland. He encountered "lands of which he previously had no knowledge," where he came across wild wheat and grapevines. He named this region Vinland and then turned back toward Greenland. There he fulfilled his mission of converting the Greenlanders to Christianity. One of his first converts is believed to have been his own mother, who then built the first Christian church in Greenland.

The Other Story. The second version of Erikson's story is derived from the *Saga of the Greenlanders,* which many scholars consider a more reliable source. In fact, *Eirik the Red's Saga* is now believed to be a more recent revision of the older saga. The *Saga of the Greenlanders* was written in Iceland around 1200, while *Eirik the Red's Saga* was composed nearly 100 years later.

The *Saga of the Greenlanders* identifies an Icelandic trader named Bjarni Herjolfsson as the first European to land on North America. According to this version, Herjolfsson discovered unknown lands southwest of Greenland around 985 or 986. When he returned to Greenland, he spoke about his adventures. He said that he set out from Iceland trying to reach Greenland, but mist obscured the North Star, which early mariners used to set their course, and turned his ship off course. After sailing for several days without bearings, he encountered a land covered with trees instead of ice. Because Herjolfsson knew it could not be Greenland, he did not land there. Continuing on, he spotted another landmass, but again it did not resemble Greenland. It was flat and forested. When the weather cleared enough for Herjolfsson to see the stars, he turned around and sailed back to Greenland.

Impressed and intrigued by the story and the possibility of finding timber, Erikson decided to explore the lands about which Herjolfsson had spoken. (Greenland did not have large trees and its people had to depend on driftwood for fuel.) Some time around 1001 or 1002, Erikson bought Herjolfsson's ship, collected a crew of about 35 men, and sailed west following Herjolfsson's route.

Erikson sailed along Greenland's west coast and then turned west across the open sea. After a voyage of some 600 miles, he sighted a land covered by rocks and glaciers. He named the place Helluland, meaning "flat rock land," which most scholars agree is Baffin Island. From Helluland he continued south until he arrived at a land with white beaches and heavily wooded interiors. This place he

This postcard shows Leif Erikson aboard a Viking ship. Viking vessels were fast and sleek and could easily handle voyages across the Atlantic. These versatile ships did not need a harbor and could land on beaches or riverbanks.

named Markland ("wood land"); scholars believe this corresponds to Labrador, Canada. Not satisfied with the timber there, Erikson left Markland and headed southeast for two days, at which point he came to an island a short distance from the mainland, probably present-day Newfoundland. The area was rich with pastureland and forest and the weather was relatively warm, so Erikson decided to stop there for the winter.

Erikson and his party built homes there and he ordered his crew to explore the surrounding territory. When one of his crew did not return from one such side expedition, Erikson ordered a search party. When they found him, he told of wild grapes he had found farther inland. Erikson thus dubbed the area Vinland, or "wine land," but modern scholars are unsure of its location. Because of the cold climate of Newfoundland today, many believe that the crewmember might have traveled as far south as present-day Cape Cod, where grapes are grown even today. Others believe that Newfoundland may have been warmer in Erikson's time and therefore conducive to growing grapes.

Return to Greenland. Both sagas agree that the following spring Erikson loaded his ship with timber and grapes and set sail to return to Greenland. Along the way he encountered a wrecked trading ship and rescued its crew. The grateful sailors rewarded him by giving him their entire cargo. It was from this episode that he earned the nickname "Leif the Lucky."

One of the mysteries of Erikson's voyage is the exact location of his North American landing. In 1963 an archaeological* expedition came across the ruins of Viking-type homes in a place called L'Anse aux Meadows in northern Newfoundland. Since the terrain of that region matches Erikson's description, most scholars now accept this as the site of his brief stay in North America. In 1977, L'Anse aux Meadows was declared a National Historic site.

*archaeological of or relating to archaeology, the scientific study of past human life and activities, usually by excavating ruins

THE FORSTERS

Johann Reinhold Forster
1729–1798
NATURAL PHILOSOPHY,
GEOGRAPHY

Georg Adam Forster
1754–1794
NATURAL PHILOSOPHY,
GEOGRAPHY

*oceanography study of oceans

*ethnography branch of anthropology dealing with the scientific description of different cultures

Johann Reinhold Forster and his son Georg Adam were among the leading natural philosophers of their time. Johann's research and writings influenced the work of many later scientists, while Georg's accounts of his scientific journeys created a strong interest in literary travel books among the German public.

Born in Dirschau (now Tczew), Poland, Johann Forster began his career as a pastor in a town near the German city of Danzig. Here he began to maintain a correspondence with many prominent scientists. In 1765 the Russian government hired Johann to make a survey of a portion of the lower Volga River. Georg, Johann's 11-year-old son, accompanied him on this trip. After the survey, Johann found that he was unable to advance professionally in Russia and he lost his pastorate. The Forsters then moved to England where Johann became a tutor at the Dissenter's Academy in Warrington, Lancashire. Georg later joined him as an assistant teacher at the academy.

Johann quickly earned a reputation for his writings on zoology, ornithology (the study of birds) and ichthyology (the study of fish). He also published works on mineralogy (study of the properties of minerals), insects, and botany, and translated the account of the voyage of the French explorer Louis-Antoine de BOUGAINVILLE. In 1772, the Forsters, by that time reputed as "gentlemen skilled in Natural history and Botany," were invited to join the expedition of Captain James COOK to search for the mythical southern continent. The expedition sailed through the Antarctic Ocean as well as much of the Pacific.

In 1775, when Johann and Georg returned to England, they released a small work describing the botanical sights they had seen during the voyage. Two years later Georg published his first major solo work, *A Voyage Around the World,* and the following year Johann published a more scholarly work called *Observations Made During a Voyage Round the World.* Johann's book was an influential and in-depth study of the sciences of geography, oceanography*, and ethnography* based on his experiences on the expedition. Georg's work, which was less scholarly and more popular, established the style of travel writing that was later popularized by Alexander von HUMBOLDT.

In the late 1770s, the Forsters returned to Germany, where both accepted professorial posts. Johann continued to publish on zoological topics and edited a journal that introduced important scientific work to the public. In 1780 he became a professor of natural history and mineralogy at Halle. Georg began an extensive correspondence with leading scientists throughout Europe and also edited and published works in scholarly journals. He also published several works on botany based on his discoveries on the Cook expedition. These became the basis for later works on the subject by other scientists.

Later in life, Georg became increasingly interested in social history and politics. While serving as librarian at the University of Mainz, Germany, he became involved with the French administration that governed the city at the time. In 1793 he was named the German deputy to the National Convention in Paris. He traveled to France in March

1793, but fell ill and died the following January. His father outlived him by four years before passing away in the German city of Halle.

John Franklin spent a lifetime at sea, traveling to such far-flung places as the Mediterranean, Australia, and the Arctic Circle. He is best known for his final expedition, when he disappeared during his search for the Northwest Passage*. The expeditions' disappearance led to one of the greatest search missions in history. It took nearly 15 years before the fate of Franklin and his crew was revealed.

Early Career. Franklin was born in Lincolnshire, England. He joined the Royal Navy when he was just 14 and participated in the battle against France at Copenhagen, Denmark. Shortly thereafter he became a member of the crew aboard the *Investigator,* a vessel that was assigned to map the western coast of Australia under the command of the English navigator Matthew Flinders. However, the ship began to give way before the job was complete and Flinders and his crew were forced to abandon the mission. Franklin suffered a shipwreck and hostile attacks by pirates on his return journey to England. He arrived home in 1804.

In the years that followed, Franklin participated in several naval engagements, including the battles at Trafalgar in 1805 and at New Orleans in 1815. When the Napoleonic Wars ended in 1815 he was put on inactive duty with half pay. Three years later he returned to the field of exploration as part of an expedition attempting to sail to the North Pole. However, the ships became stuck in heavy ice and the effort was abandoned after three weeks at sea.

Exploring Canada. Around that time the English crown decided to concentrate its efforts to find a Northwest Passage connecting the Atlantic and Pacific Oceans. The navy decided that this task would be easier to accomplish if they had some knowledge of the northern coast of Canada. To this end, on May 23, 1819, Franklin led a party to explore and map the Canadian coast.

Unfortunately, problems dogged the expedition almost from the start. Franklin was forced to rely on the Canadian fur traders to supply him with transportation, supplies, labor, and accommodation. However, the fur traders were engaged in a bitter trade war and were unable to help Franklin to the extent he desired. He made very slow progress toward the Canadian coast, establishing his base camp at an unknown territory north of the Great Slave Lake in northwestern Canada the following summer. On July 14, 1821, he finally set out for the northern coast, but the treacherous weather and the lack of adequate supplies and equipment forced him to turn back at Kent Peninsula. Little of his mission was complete and about half of his men were dead. Franklin and the rest of his crew barely made it back to the base camp and they were spared starvation only because of help from the local Indians. He spent another year in Canada before returning to England.

John
FRANKLIN
1786–1847
MARINE EXPLORATION

Northwest Passage water route connecting the Atlantic and Pacific Oceans through the Arctic islands of northern Canada

Cause of Death: Lead or Ice?

The final chapter of the story of Franklin's expedition remained unwritten until the 1980s. A Canadian archaeologist studied tissue remains from the crew and found that many of them had suffered lead poisoning. The foods that Franklin's party carried were sealed in lead tins. The archaeologist reckoned that the seals might have been defective, allowing the lead to leak into the food. Consuming the tainted food probably led to weakness among the crew and as a result, impaired their judgment. This may well have played a major part in the crew's fate.

---

*frigate small warship

Within a year of his return to England, Franklin began to plan a second expedition. This time he planned to take along enough supplies and men to free him from dependence on the fur traders. On February 16, 1825, the party set out from England and would enjoy greater success than the earlier voyage. The expedition quickly reached Great Bear Lake in northwestern Canada, where they established a new base camp, Fort Franklin. On June 22, 1826, Franklin and his men set out to map the region. With little difficulty they sailed as far as the Mackenzie Delta, where the group then separated into two. Franklin went west to explore the coast to the Bering Strait, but he had to turn back at Return Reef, Alaska, because of bad weather. The other team explored the coast as far east as the Coppermine River. The mission was a great success—Franklin and his men mapped more than 1,200 miles of coast from central Canada to Alaska. The party returned to England in 1827, and Franklin received a knighthood that same year.

For the next three years, Franklin commanded the *Rainbow*, a frigate* in the Mediterranean, and in 1836 he was appointed lieutenant governor of Van Diemen's Land (present-day Tasmania). He tried to institute reforms on the island and reduce its role as a prison colony, but both the British government and the local settlers opposed his plans. Six years later a disappointed Franklin resigned his post and sailed back to England.

A Fateful Voyage. By this time, the Royal Navy had again become interested in finding the Northwest Passage and Franklin was invited to plan and command the expedition. In May 1845, he again set sail for Canada with two ships, *Erebus* and *Terror*, and a crew of 128 men. On July 26, a whaling vessel sighted the ships in Baffin Bay off Canada's northeast coast. It was the last time the crew would be seen alive. Because such journeys took a great deal of time, there was little concern for the safety of the expedition until two years had passed without any news of their fate.

In 1848 the navy launched the first of nearly 40 search efforts to locate Franklin and his crew. Three separate search parties were sent— one approaching from the Atlantic, one from the Pacific, and one searching overland through northern Canada. However, the area to be searched was immense, and the plan for Franklin's expedition gave little hint as to where the lost party might be found. Two of the parties returned after a year, while the other waited almost five years to see if Franklin appeared before they gave up.

Eight navy ships and four private vessels resumed the search in 1850. In August, the *Intrepid* found evidence that Franklin had spent the winter on Beechey Island, several hundred miles north of Canada's coast. However, there were no clues to indicate what happened to the party after that. Despite extensively combing the many islands north of Canada, none of the ships found any more signs of the party's fate. By 1851 most of the vessels had abandoned the hunt.

In 1852 a Royal Navy expedition left England to make one final attempt, but ice forced them to abandon two of their ships and return to

England empty-handed. During the time that this expedition was stuck in the ice, an explorer not involved with the search finally unlocked the secret of Franklin's fate. Dr. John Rae was in northern Canada mapping the only unexplored part of the North American coast when he encountered an Inuit* tribe. Members of that tribe told him of a party of Europeans they had seen years before. They said the men in the party were so weak that they fell down dead as they walked along. The Inuit also sold Rae some items that belonged to the expedition.

Despite Rae's findings, the navy would not reopen its investigation. Franklin's wife then paid for a private search effort, and in 1859 a crew reached King William Island where the Inuit had last seen Franklin's party. There they located some remains of the party as well as two notes that said the ships became stuck in ice in September 1846. Franklin died in June 1847 and in April the following year, the survivors attempted to walk to civilization. Lacking provisions, they resorted to cannibalism but eventually all died of starvation.

*Inuit people of the Canadian Arctic and Greenland, sometimes called Eskimo

---

On April 12, 1961, Yuri Gagarin made history by becoming the first person to travel into space and orbit earth. Gagarin's flight lasted 108 minutes, during which he made a single orbit of earth.

Gagarin was born on March 9, 1934, on a collective farm in the city of Gzhatsk, outside Moscow. He studied at technical and vocational schools before enrolling in an industrial college at age 17. He graduated with a degree as a qualified metalworker, but soon discovered an interest in flying. After earning a pilot's license, he entered the Soviet Air Force in 1957. Gagarin's superiors soon recognized his outstanding ability and made him a test pilot, flying experimental aircraft of various types.

Gagarin later volunteered for the Soviet space program and was chosen as one of the first 20 people to be trained as cosmonauts*. He showed the same abilities in cosmonaut training as he did while a test pilot. On April 9, 1961, he learned that he would make the first manned spaceflight. Three days later he blasted off into the history books.

The *Vostok 1* blasted off at 9:07 A.M. Moscow time and reached a maximum altitude of 187 miles above the earth. Fourteen minutes later Gagarin reported that "separation from the carrier rocket" was complete. He then began to test his food and water samples to see if they would have an effect on the weightlessness that he was experiencing; he reported no side effects. Throughout the flight, he maintained "continuous communication with Earth in different channels by telephone and telegraph." At 10:15 A.M., when Gagarin was above Africa, the spacecraft turned around and fired its retro-rockets, which slowed it down for re-entry into earth's atmosphere. Plummeting at a speed of 17,000 miles per hour, he ejected from the craft about four miles above the earth (*Vostok* was not designed to withstand the impact with the ground). The Soviets informed the International Aeronautical Federation (FAI) of the flight so it could be recorded as a

Yuri Alekseyevich GAGARIN

1934–1968

SPACE EXPLORATION

Yuri Gagarin, shown here in full cosmonaut gear, was hailed a hero in Russia after his successful space mission. Many sites in Russia were renamed in his honor and his legacy lives on in space as well—a crater on the moon was named in his honor.

*cosmonaut astronaut from the Soviet or Russian space program

world record. However, they omitted the fact about Gagarin's ejection, because the federation required that a pilot finish a flight in the aircraft to set an official record.

Hailed as hero in the Soviet Union and around the world, Gagarin received many honors. Streets and cities throughout the Soviet Union were renamed in his honor, as was his hometown of Gzhatsk. Surprisingly, however, he never returned to space. He spent the rest of his life training cosmonauts and continuing his career as a test pilot. Gagarin died in 1968 while test-piloting a two-seater jet plane.

Vasco da
GAMA
ca. 1460–1524
NAVIGATION

The Portuguese navigator Vasco da Gama commanded the first European fleet to reach India by voyaging around the southern tip of Africa. Gama's historic voyage changed Europeans' view of world geography and began an era of Portuguese trade, conquest, and colonization in eastern Africa and Asia. His success, however, was merely the final step in a long series of explorations undertaken by Portuguese mariners since the early 1400s.

The Portuguese Navigators

In the early 1400s, Portugal, a small Roman Catholic country on the Atlantic coast of southwestern Europe, began an organized program of exploration—the first large-scale undertaking in an era of discovery that eventually carried Europeans throughout the world. Since that time, decades before Gama sailed around Africa into the Indian Ocean, Portuguese seafarers had been exploring the unknown Atlantic waters as they worked their way along the west coast of Africa.

Prince Henry. Portuguese maritime exploration began under Henry (1394–1460), a prince of Portugal's royal family whom later British historians called Henry the Navigator. Henry was a sponsor or patron of exploration who planned and paid for the voyages of the men who sailed while in his service.

*caravan large group of people traveling together across a desert or other dangerous region

When Henry was governor of Ceuta, a city in Morocco that the Portuguese had captured, he became aware that the Muslims of North Africa carried on a caravan* trade in gold and ivory with regions south of the Sahara. Henry then became curious about the geography of Africa. His curiosity was inspired by more than a love of knowledge, however; he was eager to find routes that would give the Portuguese direct access to the trade goods of Africa and Asia, bypassing the middlemen.

In 1420, when Henry became governor of the Algarve region in southern Portugal, he established an academy of exploration at the coastal city of Sagres. Henry encouraged mariners, shipbuilders, cartographers (mapmakers), astronomers, and makers of navigational instruments to visit the city, share their knowledge, and combine their skills in new enterprises. Under Henry's patronage, Portuguese shipbuilders developed the caravel, a small ship equipped with triangular sails, which could be steered into the direction from which the wind was blowing. Such a vessel was a necessity on long voyages of exploration that sometimes required travel over great distances despite unfavorable winds. The caravel became the principal vessel of European seaborne exploration and was used by Christopher COLUMBUS and many other navigators. It remained in use well into the 1600s.

Exploring the African Coast. As early as 1418, Henry sent his best seamen into the Atlantic Ocean southwest of Portugal. These navigators located the Madeira island group off the coast of Morocco. Although Italian seafarers had visited the islands in the 1300s, Portugal claimed them, and they remain Portuguese territory even today.

A few years later Henry sent out ships to explore the Atlantic coast of Morocco. The voyages he sponsored became more ambitious as each captain sought to reach a point farther along the African coast than the one before him had reached. As time went on, Henry began to hope that his navigators would find a route not just to the gold-producing regions of sub-Saharan* Africa but eventually to the southern edge of the African continent and beyond it to Asia.

In 1434, in a milestone voyage, one of Henry's mariners became the first European known to sail past Cape Bojador, a point on the Atlantic coast south of Morocco. Until that time, sailors had been afraid to venture past the cape because of superstitions about the dangers that lay beyond it. Seven years later one of Henry's caravels returned from the African coast carrying gold and slaves, proving that the voyages could be profitable. The trade in slaves grew rapidly, and by 1448 Henry had established Europe's first overseas trading post on Arguin Island off the African coast. Its purpose was to acquire captives. Shortly thereafter, two of Henry's captains pushed the limit of exploration farther south, reaching the mouths of the Senegal and Gambia Rivers.

The voyages continued after the 1440s, but the pace of exploration slowed, and Henry began to concentrate on developing trade relations with Portugal's colonies. Scholars believe that the farthest point that Portuguese navigators reached during Henry's lifetime was present-day Sierra Leone. Mariners sponsored by Henry also discovered the Azores and Cape Verde island groups, which are still part of Portugal.

Bartolomeu Dias Reaches the Cape. After Henry's death, trade with the markets along the African coast continued under King John II, who came to the throne in 1481. John ordered new voyages of exploration along the coast. He equipped his navigators with carved stone pillars called *padrõe* to set up in the new lands they encountered; the purpose of these pillars was to claim the lands for Portugal.

The year after John became king, his mariner Diogo Cão journeyed even farther along the African coast. Cão reached the mouth of the Congo River and kept pushing southward. He set up a *padrõe* on the coast of present-day Angola, and believing that he was close to the southern limit of Africa, returned to Portugal.

King John next became determined to find and control a route to the Indies (the European name for India and the lands east of it). He

*sub-Saharan referring to the region south of the Sahara

sent explorers to search for an overland route through Egypt and Ethiopia into the Red Sea, which was known to be connected to the Indian Ocean. He also sent Bartolomeu Dias to complete the task that Cão had begun. Dias left Portugal in August 1487 with three ships and orders to locate the limits of Africa.

Dias sailed past Cão's southernmost pillar, continued along the coast for hundreds of miles, and passed the desert coast of present-day Namibia. In January 1488 he began to sail away from the coast to avoid storms. After sailing out of sight of land for a few days, Dias turned back to the east expecting to find the coastline, but he encountered only empty sea. He did not see land until he turned north and found that the coastline ran east and then slightly north. From these facts, Dias correctly concluded that he had rounded the southern end of Africa, the Cape of Good Hope, albeit without seeing it.

Dias reached a point near the mouth of the Great Fish River in South Africa, and at that point the crew and the other captains urged a return to Portugal. The fleet retraced its route, and Dias arrived in Portugal in December 1488 to announce that he had proved it was possible to sail around Africa into the Indian Ocean. Dias had also shown that the geography of PTOLEMY, a scientist and mapmaker of the ancient world, was incorrect. Ptolemy had portrayed the Indian Ocean as a landlocked sea, enclosed by an African continent that stretched far to the east. This cartographic error persisted for centuries, until Dias disproved it.

At first Dias called the southern tip of the continent the Cape of Storms, but either King John or Dias himself changed the name to Cape of Good Hope because its discovery offered good prospects for trade with the Indies. On the cape and at other points, Dias had erected *padrões* to mark his arrival there. One of them was found in 1938 on an island not far from the Great Fish River, a silent memorial to Portugal's golden age of seagoing exploration.

The Voyages of Vasco da Gama

For some time after Dias's return, King John waited to hear from the explorers he had sent to locate a Red Sea route. One of them, Pêro da Covilhã, eventually sent word that he had reached India from the Red Sea. He reported that Arabs in the region surrounding the Red Sea and along the east coast of Africa regularly sailed to the Indies.

While the king was waiting, Columbus made his historical voyage across the Atlantic Ocean, opening what at first appeared to be a westward route to the Indies for Spain. This made the Portuguese monarch more eager to secure a sea route for the empire. After John died in 1495, his successor, King Manuel I, decided that the time had come to send a fleet to the Indies along the route that Dias had discovered. Vasco da Gama would command the expedition.

First Voyage to India. Gama was born in Sines, a town on Portugal's southwestern coast. His father, Estevão da Gama, was the commander

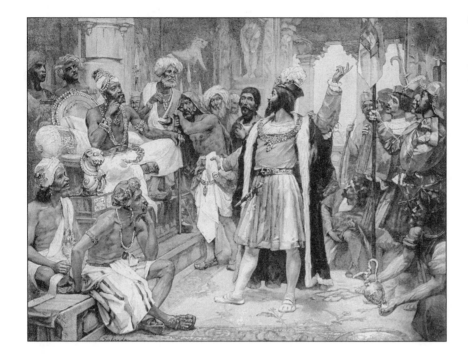

In this engraving made from a painting by Galgado, Vasco de Gama is shown presenting a letter from the King of Portugal to the ruler of Calicut.

of a fortress there and served as an official in the royal court. King John II wanted Estevão da Gama to lead the expedition that would go beyond Dias's cape, but both the king and Estevão died before that expedition got underway. Manuel chose Vasco da Gama, who had served Portugal by defending its colonies on the West African coast from French attacks and by seizing French ships off the Algarve coast, to take his father's place as head of the expedition to India.

In July 1497 Gama set sail from Lisbon with four ships and about 150 men. He carried a supply of *padrões* and recruited interpreters who spoke Arabic and several African languages. Dias accompanied the expedition for a time in his own ship, bound for service at a Portuguese fort on the coast of present-day Ghana in West Africa.

Gama's fleet spent a week in the Cape Verde Islands. When it resumed sailing, Gama did not stay close to the African coast. Instead, he set his course in a wide semicircle, bearing far out into the South Atlantic Ocean before veering southeast to approach the Cape of Good Hope. In this way he avoided the strong winds and water currents that push northward along Africa's shores.

On November 7, 1497, Gama reached St. Helena Bay on the coast of present-day South Africa. Winds delayed his progress, but several weeks later Gama rounded the Cape of Good Hope. In mid-December he passed the farthest point that Dias had reached, and on Christmas Day, the fleet landed on the African coast. Gama named the place Natal, from the Portuguese word for "birth," in honor of Christ's birthday. The region is now the province of Kwazulu-Natal, South Africa.

Proceeding northward, erecting *padrõe* as they went, Gama and his crew reached the coast of Mozambique on January 25. They halted there for about a month to make repairs to their ships and to allow the

An Epic Hero

Almost 50 years after Gama's death, he became the hero of the Portuguese national epic. Luis Vaz de Camões was a well-educated but poor aristocrat who spent years as a soldier of fortune in Asia. When he returned to Portugal, he published *Os Lusíadas* (from Lusitania, an old Roman word for Portugal), a long poem about Vasco da Gama's discovery of the sea route to India. Camões raises the story to the level of myth by portraying the gods of ancient Greece as watching over Gama. With sections that glorify Portugal's early history and predict its future glories, *Os Lusíadas* is a stirring expression of national pride.

crew to regain their strength. Many of Gama's men were suffering from scurvy, a vitamin-deficiency disease caused by a lack of fresh fruit and vegetables in the diet.

On March 2, Gama reached Mozambique Island and found that Muslims, who regularly did business with Arab traders who crossed the Indian Ocean, inhabited the region. Gama had reached a stretch of coastline that for hundreds of years had been part of a network of commerce linking Arabia, India, and East Africa. Arabs from the north had introduced Islam and the Arabic language, and people of Arab or mixed Arab and African ancestry ruled small kingdoms along the coast and on the offshore islands. At the island of Mozambique and elsewhere along the coast, however, Gama's expedition met hostility from Arabs who viewed the Europeans as a threat to their control of trade.

In April, Gama's fleet landed at Mombasa and Malindi, both in present-day Kenya. At Malindi, Gama recruited a local pilot to help navigate the route to Calicut, a major center of trade on the southwest coast of India. After a 23-day crossing of the Arabian Sea, an arm of the Indian Ocean, Gama landed in Calicut and planted a *padrõe*. His goal was to trade for the most prized goods of the Indies: spices, silks, gemstones, gold, and pearls. Yet the goods he had brought to trade were the same items that the Portuguese used for barter along the West African coast, mostly glass beads and tin balls. These cheap trinkets failed to dazzle the merchants of India, and Gama could do little more with them than purchase food for his men. Moreover, Gama failed to convince the local Hindu ruler *(zamorin)* to sign a formal treaty with Portugal that would provide for future trade.

By the end of August, the relations between the Hindu ruler and the Europeans had become hostile and Gama decided to leave Calicut. Sailing against the wind, the fleet took three months to cross the Arabian Sea to Malindi. So many men perished of scurvy on this leg of the trip that Gama burned one of his ships and combined the survivors into two crews for the trip home (he had already destroyed one, a supply ship emptied of much of its cargo, on the outward voyage). In September 1499 Gama arrived in Lisbon.

In commercial terms, Gama's expedition was a failure. Instead of cargo holds bulging with treasure, he brought home only small amounts of spices. Still, King Manuel I, pleased that Gama had staked Portugal's claim to a sea route to India, rewarded the explorer with estates, a pension, and the title Dom, similar to the knighthood.

Later Voyages. The king immediately sent a large fleet to Calicut with orders to establish trade. The commander of this mission was Pedro Álvares Cabral with Bartolomeu Dias as captain of one of the expedition's 13 ships. Cabral swung west into the South Atlantic as Gama had done, and one day he sighted land in the west. The fleet landed on the coast of Brazil in South America and claimed the land for Portugal before returning across the Atlantic to sail around the Cape of Good Hope. Sadly, Dias never traveled to India along the route he had pioneered. He was lost at sea near the cape.

Cabral reached Calicut, where he settled a group of Portuguese and established a trading post before returning to Portugal. Later, however, the news reached Lisbon that the Hindus and Muslims of Calicut had attacked and killed the Portuguese. Manuel ordered a fleet of 20 ships to set out immediately to punish Calicut and to demonstrate Portugal's might to all the powers around the Indian Ocean. The king named Gama to command the fleet and gave him the title Admiral of India. The expedition left Portugal in 1502.

On his way to India, Gama stopped at the East African ports of Sofala (in present-day Mozambique) and Kilwa (in present-day Tanzania), forcing the local rulers to pledge their loyalty to King Manuel. He then ambushed an Arab ship, seized its cargo, and burned the vessel and all its crew and passengers—several hundred people, including women and children. With the help of an Indian ruler who was an enemy of the ruler of Calicut, Gama besieged the trading center, bombed its port, destroyed ships in its harbor, and again forced local rulers to make alliances and treaties. Having proved Portugal's ability to dominate the Indian Ocean and its coasts, Gama returned to Portugal in 1503 with a large and immensely valuable cargo of spices.

Gama then retired from public life for a time. Some accounts suggest that he felt he deserved a richer reward than he had received. In addition, he had difficulty gaining control of the estates Manuel had granted him after his first voyage. Later, however, Gama did receive more honors and a larger income—the king made him Count of Vidigueira in 1519. Gama married, raised a family, and occasionally advised the king on matters concerning India.

In 1524 King John III, Manuel's successor, named Gama viceroy of India, awarding him the power to rule in the king's name over the territory that Portugal claimed in Asia. Gama sailed to Goa, a settlement in western India that had become the center of Portuguese activity since his last voyage to that country. Finding the colony in disarray, he immediately began a program of reform, but illness soon struck him. He died in Cochin, a city on India's southwest coast, and was buried there. Fifteen years later the Portuguese brought his remains back to his homeland for reburial.

Gama is rightly regarded as one of the most influential figures of the European age of exploration. His legacy was more than a record of successful and adventurous voyaging—it was also the string of territorial claims he had made in Portugal's name.

The American astronaut and senator, John Glenn, can claim to have spent a lifetime in space. As one of the original seven astronauts, Glenn became the first American to orbit the earth. Thirty-six years later, as a retired U.S. senator, he returned to orbit aboard the space shuttle to study the similarities between the body's adaptation to weightlessness and the aging process.

John Herschel, Jr.
GLENN

born 1921

SPACE EXPLORATION

Glenn was born in Cambridge, Ohio, and grew up in the town of New Concord. After graduating from New Concord High (now John Glenn High), he enrolled in Muskingum College to study engineering. He left school in 1942 to become a Marine Corps fighter pilot in World War II (1939–1945). As a combat pilot he flew more than 150 missions and earned 6 Distinguished Flying Crosses and many other decorations.

After the Second World and Korean Wars, Glenn became a test pilot. In 1957 he set a record by flying from New York to Los Angeles in less than three and one-half hours. The following year he was selected as one of the original seven astronauts for the Mercury space program. At age 38 he was the oldest member of the group. Glenn served as backup pilot for the first two manned American space flights, which did not orbit the earth. He was then chosen to be the first American to make an orbital flight.

On February 20, 1962, Glenn took off in the spacecraft *Friendship 7*, which he later said "was so small you didn't climb into it, you put it on." His flight lasted about an hour and a half and circled the earth three times before returning to earth. Near the completion of the first orbit, the spacecraft, which was being guided automatically, began to swing to the right. Glenn took control and steered it manually, earning the distinction as the first person to actively pilot a spacecraft for an extended period.

Glenn's flight made him a national hero. In fact, he was so popular that President John F. Kennedy refused to let him return to space for fear of losing such a prominent figure in a future flight. Glenn resumed his Marine Corps career and retired in 1965. He later worked as an executive for a beverage company, but was not yet ready to give up his public life. In 1970 he ran unsuccessfully for the U.S. Senate, but four years later he was elected Democratic senator from Ohio. He has since been reelected three times, and in 1984 he made an unsuccessful bid for the presidency.

Although it had been more than 30 years since his only space flight, Glenn never lost the "space bug." In 1995, when he noticed that some of the physiological* changes that occur during the aging process were similar to those that occur during weightlessness, he persuaded NASA to include him on a mission in the space shuttle. Three years later, at age 77, Glenn became the oldest person in space. He spent nine days as the subject of an experiment to compare the effects of the two processes on the human body.

*physiological of or relating to physiology, the science that deals with the functions of living organisms and their parts

John Paul GOODE

1862–1932

GEOGRAPHY

John Paul Goode was a founder of the field of economic geography and a gifted speaker who helped popularize geography. He is best known, however, for the most widely used atlas in the United States, which today bears his name.

Goode was born in Stewartville, Minnesota, and grew up on rugged farmland. He always prided himself on the fact that he had to work hard to earn his way through school. After graduating from the

University of Minnesota with a bachelor's degree in science, he taught natural science at the Minnesota State Normal at Moorhead (now Moorhead State University). During summers he attended graduate classes at Harvard University and the University of Chicago. He eventually began to attend graduate school full-time and received his doctorate from the University of Pennsylvania in 1901.

Two years later Goode joined the faculty of the University of Chicago, where he developed courses in economic geography. He was quickly recognized as an expert in the field, and in 1908 the Chicago Harbor Commission sent him to Europe to study that continent's major ports. At this time he was also active in many professional associations; he was named president of the Geographic Society of Chicago in 1904, and the same year he helped to found the Association of American Geographers (AAG).

In 1907 Goode presented a pioneering paper at the annual meeting of the AAG, discussing the interaction between living organisms and the physical environment. During his presentation Goode talked about how geography affects human culture and coined the term *human ecology* to refer to this area of study. Prominent geographers enthusiastically adopted this idea and developed it in the years that followed.

Despite his successes in geography, Goode's real interest was in cartography, or mapmaking. He taught the first cartography course ever offered in the United States. He was particularly critical of the projection* developed by Gerardus MERCATOR, the standard map view used for years. He designed new projections that more accurately reflected the true size and shape of areas depicted on maps. In 1923 he published a school atlas, which became an immediate success. The atlas's name was later changed to *Goode's World Atlas,* and has since become a fixture in classrooms and homes throughout the United States.

Goode was as talented a speaker as he was a geographer and mapmaker, and his many lectures opened up the world of geography to the American public. He accompanied his lectures with slides of maps and graphs illuminated by a lantern. A measure of his popularity is the fact that he delivered more than 70 lectures in 1926 alone. Goode was so overwhelmed with requests to speak that he eventually had to hire an outside firm to manage his speaking engagements. The money he made from his lectures even allowed him to pay for a leave of absence from his teaching duties. He died in Little Point Sable, Michigan, at age 69.

*projection method of arranging three-dimensional geographic data on a two-dimensional map

---

Born in Kharkov in the Ukraine, Jean Gottmann's parents enjoyed their son for only two years before they were killed. The toddler was taken to Paris by an uncle who made it possible for him to grow up in an atmosphere of intellectuals—well-educated, talkative, and fairly prosperous Russians. Gottmann attended the best schools, traveled widely, and studied the two subjects that interested him most: geography and history.

Jean
GOTTMANN
1915–1994
GEOGRAPHY

In 1940, when Gottmann was in his early 20s, the Nazis occupied France. Having completed much of his studies by that time, he fled from Paris to Montpelier and later, via the Iberian Peninsula, to the United States. There he worked at Princeton and Johns Hopkins Universities until the end of World War II in 1945.

After the war, Gottmann took a job in the office of the minister of the national economy in Paris and became involved in planning the postwar reconstruction of France. He later entered academic life and published many books on the geography of metropolitan areas. Gottmann's views were widely accepted, and in 1956 he was invited to America to study the urban problems that were emerging there.

His initial project in the United States was concerned with the stretch of cities along the Atlantic seaboard, from Boston to Washington, D.C., a region he called megalopolis (from the Greek, meaning "very large city"). For five years he studied the BosWash megalopolis (so named because of the Boston to Washington, D.C., region), and in 1961 he published his findings. The work, aptly titled *Megalopolis,* brought him international acclaim and was considered "a monumental achievement and ranks as one of the most important single geographical ideas of the mid-twentieth century."

According to Gottmann, the megalopolis "provides the whole . . . with so many essential services, of the sort a community used to obtain in its 'downtown' section, that it may well deserve the nickname of 'Main Street of the nation.'" He acknowledged that there are still "twilight" areas of farms, woods, and semirural sections between the cities "that matter little to the continuity of Megalopolis." He believed that the foundation of any megalopolis is its economic activity, which fuels the transportation, commuting, and communication links between the cities.

Gottmann believed: "We must abandon the idea of the city as a tightly settled and organized unit in which people, activities, and riches are crowded into a very small area clearly separated from its nonurban surroundings." Instead, he considered the distinct cities; their suburban, greener outskirts; and other communities as parts of one whole—the megalopolis.

In addition to his work in America, Gottmann also studied and lectured on the urban problems of Belgium, Israel, Italy, the Netherlands, Switzerland, Great Britain, Japan, and Central and South America. In 1968 he was appointed professor of geography at Oxford University. Gottmann received honorary degrees from universities in the United States and awards from academic organizations in England and France.

Arnold Henri GUYOT

1807–1884

GEOGRAPHY, GEOLOGY, METEOROLOGY

Born in Boudevilliers, Switzerland, Guyot studied at the University of Neuchâtel, where he satisfied his interest in nature by collecting plants and insects. At age 18, he traveled to Karlsruhe, Germany, to continue his education. There he met many prominent scientists. Guyot later went to Berlin to study theology*. Later he chose science as his lifework, and in 1835 he completed his dissertation on the natural classification of lakes.

Some of Arnold Guyot's teaching and research materials are on display at Princeton University. They include 46 cloth wall hangings that he used during class and handwritten labels of glacial stones he collected. A glacial boulder, named after him and donated by some former students, also stands in the university grounds.

*theology study of religion

Shortly thereafter, Guyot moved to Paris, where he accepted an offer to tutor the sons of the Count de Pourtalès-Gorgier. Guyot knew that the position would afford him the opportunity to travel throughout Europe and to renew his acquaintance with his scientist friends. During one of these visits, he had an opportunity to spend six weeks in the Alps. He spent the time taking notes on the glacial moraines (sediment left by glaciers), the effects of the moving ice on rocks and the terrain, and their effects on the landscape in general.

In 1839 Guyot received an invitation to teach history and physical geography at the University of Neuchâtel. In the years that followed, he *naturalist one who studies objects in their natural settings

became increasingly interested in the structure and movement of glaciers and was guided in his work by Louis Agassiz, who was both a naturalist* and a geologist. Word of Guyot's studies and research soon became international and he was invited to teach and advance his own studies at various universities. In 1848 he accepted an appointment to teach physical geography at the Lowell Technological Institute in Boston, Massachusetts. He also developed new and more productive teaching methods at the request of the Massachusetts Board of Education. For many years, the textbooks Guyot wrote and produced for that state were used in schools throughout the United States.

In 1854 Guyot accepted a full professorship to teach physical geography and geology at the College of New Jersey (now Princeton University). There he founded the Princeton Museum of Natural History and developed new concepts of teaching geography based on field trips. He also became involved in a project to develop a weather forecast system for the Smithsonian Institution. Guyot selected 50 sites along the Atlantic seaboard considered suitable for meteorological* observations, and he equipped them with the latest instruments. Along with students he had selected from Princeton, he spent several summers taking measurements along the coast, at sites from Maine to Georgia. This undertaking was the first step in forming a national weather forecasting system that is now one of the best in the world.

*meteorological referring to meteorology, the science that deals with the atmosphere, especially the weather and weather predictions

Another field in which Guyot's achievements became prominent is oceanic geography. He identified the "seamount," an undersea, flat-topped mountain that is inherently volcanic in origin but distinctive in its formation. These oceanic mesas (plateaus) were later named *guyots* in honor of the geographer. Additionally, there are three mountains, one crater on the moon, and a glacier in Alaska that bear Guyot's name.

Guyot's writings include *Earth and Man, or Lectures on Comparative Physical Geography in Its Relation to the History of Mankind,* which became a highly successful textbook of the same name. Among other books and articles that he wrote are the remarkable meteorological and physical tables that were commissioned and published by the Smithsonian Institution. Guyot died in Princeton at the age of 76.

Richard HAKLUYT

1552–1616

GEOGRAPHY, HISTORY, ADVOCACY OF ENGLISH OVERSEAS EXPANSION

Richard Hakluyt never traveled farther than Paris, yet he was one of the most vocal advocates of exploration. He promoted and chronicled England's quest to colonize and expand its horizons overseas. His best-known publication, *The Principall Navigations, Voiages and Discoveries of the English Nation,* discusses almost everything that is known today about early English exploration in North America.

Hakluyt was born in London into a wealthy family. His father died when he was only five and a cousin, a lawyer with a passion for geography, raised him. Hakluyt was surrounded by family, friends, and associates who were geographers, explorers, and successful merchants and who created an atmosphere that inspired him to study geography.

This title page for the first volume of Richard Hakluyt's history of English exploration was printed in 1598.

THE
PRINCIPAL NAVI-
GATIONS, VOIAGES,
TRAFFIQVES AND DISCO-
ueries of the English Nation, made by Sea
or ouer-land, to the remote and fartheſt di-
ſtant quarters of the Earth, at any time within
the compaſſe of theſe 1500. yeeres: Deuided
into three ſeuerall Volumes, according to the
poſitions of the Regions, whereunto
they were directed.

This firſt Volume containing the woorthy Diſcoueries,
&c. of the Engliſh toward the North and Northeaſt by ſea,
as of *Lapland*, *Scrikfinia*, *Corelia*, the Baie of S. *Nicolas*, the Iſles of *Col-
goieue*, *Vaigatz*, and *Noua Zembla*, toward the great riuer *Ob*,
with the mighty Empire of *Ruſſia*, the *Caſpian* ſea, *Georgia*, *Armenia*, *Media*, *Perſia*, *Boghar* in *Bactria*,
and diuers kingdoms of *Tartaria*:

Together with many notable monuments and teſtimo-
nies of the ancient forren trades, and of the warrelike and
other ſhipping of this realme of *England* in former ages.

*VVhereunto is annexed alſo a briefe Commentarie of the true
ſtate of Iſland, and of the Northren Seas and
lands ſituate that way.*

*And laſtly, the memorable defeate of the Spaniſh huge
Armada, Anno 1588. and the famous victorie
atchieued at the citie of Cadiz, 1596.
are deſcribed.*

By RICHARD HAKLVYT *Maſter of*
Artes, and ſometime Student of Chriſt-
Church in Oxford.

Imprinted at London by GEORGE
BISHOP, RALPH NEWBERIE
and ROBERT BARKER.
1598.

Title-page of Hakluyt's "Voyages" 1598

Hakluyt, Richard

*cosmography science that describes the world or the universe

*maritime of or relating to navigation or commerce on the sea

*Northeast Passage water route along the northern coast of the Eurasian landmass, lying mainly off northern Russian Siberia

*Northwest Passage water route connecting the Atlantic and Pacific Oceans through the Arctic islands of northern Canada

*East India Company English trading company chartered in 1600 to enhance England's political and economic power in east and southeast Asia and India

*diplomatic of or relating to diplomacy, the practice of conducting official relations between nations

*circumnavigate to travel completely around the world

His cousin also introduced him to marine exploration and overseas expansion and supplied him with books and maps on cosmography*.

Hakluyt studied at Westminster School, London, and Christ Church, Oxford. He graduated in 1577 with an M.A. and became an authority on maritime* affairs. He taught at Oxford, lecturing on geography and exploration, and spent a great deal of time reading about current voyages and discoveries. He also continued to expand his network of professional acquaintances and met with highly regarded sailors, sea captains, and merchants of the time.

In 1579 Hakluyt published a pamphlet in which he recommended that England take control of the Strait of Magellan and so command "the gate of entry into the treasure of both the East and the West Indies." The pamphlet was timely in that it came at a time when England was determined to find the Northeast* and Northwest Passages* and to sail completely around the world. He supported the colonization of North America and the search for the Northwest Passage, especially because Spain and Portugal already possessed rich empires in Asia and America.

Around 1580 Hakluyt commissioned the translation of the voyage notebooks of such foreign explorers as John and Sebastian CABOT and Jacques CARTIER. He used these works as propaganda for English enterprise and as intelligence about regions already explored. Three years later Hakluyt traveled to Paris where he worked as a type of intelligence officer and learned about France, Spain and Portugal's trading methods, and their general experiences in North America.

He returned to London in 1589 and published the first edition of *The Principall Navigations, Voiages and Discoveries of the English Nation,* in which he spelled out his vision of England's goals for exploration and professed that geography was the "right eye" of history. When the three-volume, second edition was reissued between 1598 and 1600, it was highly acclaimed as the prose epic of the modern English nation. The work was the most scholarly and comprehensive piece of geographical literature to date.

Hakluyt not only recorded and advocated England's expansion but also participated in those projects. Two times he came close to sailing to North America, but others went instead. In 1599, he was hired as a consultant for the East India Company* and his involvement increased the income of the company greatly. Hakluyt also collected and published the accounts of many explorers, but his *Voiages and Discoveries* remained a valuable historical document because of its accounts of daring adventures interwoven with diplomatic* and economic papers. Some of the English explorers whose voyages were the subject of his books include Francis Drake, who circumnavigated* the world and explored the coast of California; Richard Chancellor, who made one of the first attempts to find the Northeast Passage; and John Hawkins, who was one of the first English slave traders and the architect of the Elizabethan navy.

Hakluyt died in London at age 64 and was buried in Westminster Abbey. The Hakluyt Society, which was founded in London in 1846, carries on Hakluyt's work by publishing records of voyages and travel.

One of Britain's most accomplished contemporary geographers, David Harvey is best known for his early work concerning the philosophy and methods of geography. His more recent work focuses on the issues of cultural change; globalization*; and the interactions among politics, economics, and geography.

David W.
HARVEY
born 1935
GEOGRAPHY

Early Life and Studies. Harvey was born in Kent, England, and was educated at local schools. Around age 11, he began to avidly read books about the world beyond England's shores, developing an early interest in geography. The romance and adventure of faraway places instilled in him a fascination for the subject that later blossomed into a distinguished career. A few years later, Harvey came across some historical maps of Britain that fired his interest in how landscapes had changed during the course of history.

Harvey pursued other interests as well, providing important, if unconventional, influences on his later career. One of these was his habit of taking bicycle tours through the Kent countryside. He credits these rides with developing his appreciation for landscapes. Harvey's riding and reading instilled in him a wanderlust that expressed itself as an urge to run away from home. He later said, "I think all good geographers try to run away from home!"

In 1954 Harvey entered Cambridge University with the intention of studying English, but he soon found that his English courses consisted more of reading critics' comments about literature than reading the works of literature themselves. He switched his major to geography, eventually receiving a Ph.D. in that field. After leaving school Harvey took a position as lecturer in geography at the University of Bristol, the university with the best geography program in Great Britain.

From England to America. During his early career, Harvey focused on problems of the philosophy and methodology of geography. His first published work, *Explanation of Geography,* dealt with these issues. Critically acclaimed by his colleagues, the book established Harvey's reputation as one of the leading thinkers in the field. The book was published in 1969, the same year that Harvey moved to Johns Hopkins University in Baltimore, Maryland. Harvey had married an American and had grown weary of traveling back and forth across the Atlantic. Although leaving Bristol was a difficult decision, he was attracted by the Johns Hopkins geography program, which concentrated on environmental engineering and urban problems.

Around this time Harvey became interested in urban development and the issues of poverty and racism in American cities. In 1973 he published a book on this theme, titled *Social Justice and the City.* Later Harvey also examined how economic change and urbanization affect each other, particularly in developed capitalist countries. Many books came out of these studies, including *The Limits of Capital, The Urbanisation of Capital,* and *Consciousness and The Urban Experience.*

Recent Work. In 1987 Harvey received a tempting offer from Oxford University—the much sought-after post of Halford MACKINDER Profes-

*globalization becoming universal; referring to the development of worldwide patterns of economic relations between nations

sor of Geography. (Mackinder is credited with establishing geography as an academic discipline in British universities.) Harvey accepted the offer and returned to England that year. His acceptance coincided with another shift in his interests—he began to study issues of cultural change as they relate to environmental problems.

The culmination of Harvey's work in this area was his 1989 book, *The Condition of Postmodernity*. The *London Independent* called it one of the 50 most important works of nonfiction published since 1945. In 1993 Harvey returned to Johns Hopkins, and three years later he released *Justice, Nature, and the Geography of Difference,* in which he took a detailed look into environmental issues.

In recent years Harvey has intensified his focus on environmental justice and how to deal with environmental issues in a progressive manner, such as exploring alternative approaches to urbanization. He has also delved more deeply into the subject of globalization and the problems of uneven geographic development in a world that is becoming increasingly interconnected. Harvey is currently working on *Spaces of Hope,* in which he examines alternative forms of social and geographical organization.

Awards and Honors. Harvey has been honored with a wide range of awards and honorary degrees. He was a Guggenheim Fellowship winner in 1976 and received the Royal Geographical Society of London's Gill Memorial Prize four years earlier. In 1980 the Association of American Geographers (AAG) presented Harvey with the association's Outstanding Contributor Award. His other awards include the Anders Retzius Gold Medal from the Swedish Society of Anthropology* and Geography, the Vautrin Lud International Prize for Geography, and the Patron's Medal of the Royal Geographical Society of London. He has also received honorary degrees from universities in Argentina and Denmark.

Perhaps the greatest tribute to Harvey's work is the success of the schools and students with which he has been associated. Johns Hopkins University boasts one of the foremost geography programs in the United States, and many of his former students hold faculty positions in prominent universities in the United States and in Great Britain.

*anthropology study of human beings, especially in relation to origins and physical and cultural characteristics

---

Sven Anders
HEDIN

1865–1952

EXPLORATION OF CENTRAL
ASIA, GEOGRAPHY

*archaeology scientific study of past human life and activities, usually by excavating ruins

Sven Anders Hedin of Sweden spent years exploring Tibet, western China, and other parts of Central Asia that seemed forbiddingly remote and exotic to the rest of the world. He mapped mountain ranges, discovered the ruins of lost cities, and gathered geological specimens. Hedin's travels, which culminated in a massive expedition that lasted almost eight years, resulted in important contributions to geography, geology, and archaeology*.

Early Journeys. Hedin was born in Stockholm, Sweden, where he attended high school. As a child he enjoyed books about adventure, and he admired the courage and adventurousness of such explorers as David LIVINGSTONE, who is famous for his African journeys.

Hedin's own adventures began when he was about 20 years old. A Swedish engineer working in the oil fields in the city of Baku, on the Caspian Sea in Central Asia, hired Hedin to tutor his children. After just six months in Baku, Hedin had learned to speak Russian and Persian and had saved enough money to set off on a horseback journey through Persia (present-day Iran). Afterward he returned to Stockholm and published an illustrated account of his travels. In 1888 he obtained his bachelor's degree from the University of Uppsala, and the following year he began advanced study in geography in Berlin, Germany. Ferdinand von RICHTHOFEN, an expert in Asian geography and geology, supervised Hedin's work and inspired his interest in Central Asia.

In 1890 Hedin interrupted his studies for a year to serve as an interpreter on a Swedish diplomatic* mission to Persia. He then journeyed through northern Persia, ventured into Russian territory in Central Asia, and crossed several mountains in the Pamir region to reach Kashgar, a city in western China on the old caravan* trade route known as the Silk Road. In 1892 Hedin returned to Berlin to complete his studies and write about his recent travels.

After his graduation he launched his career as a scientific explorer, beginning a series of expeditions into Central Asia. On the first of these trips, which lasted from 1894 to 1897, he explored the Taklamakan, a desert region in western China. According to Chinese chronicles and local folklore, the region contained the ruins of rich communities buried under the sands. The desert crossing was dangerous—the expedition ran out of water, several members of the group perished, and Hedin barely managed to save himself and his guide by finding a stream with some water.

Having survived the Taklamakan, Hedin pushed across northern Tibet and part of Mongolia on his way to the capital of China, Peking. He published a popular account of this journey in 1898 and the scientific results, including a set of maps, two years later. Throughout his career Hedin would share his discoveries with the general public as well as with geographers and geologists. Popular books such as *Across the Gobi Desert, The Conquest of Tibet,* and *My Life as an Explorer* recounted his adventures and introduced people to the regions he found so fascinating, while scholars turned to his other works, massive volumes such as *Scientific Results of a Journey in Central Asia.*

Hedin's second expedition, from 1899 to 1902, took him through northern Tibet. Unable to reach that country's capital, Lhasa, which was then closed to foreigners, Hedin mapped a range he called Trans-Himalaya, north of the Himalayas. During his next journey, from 1906 to 1908, he studied a salt desert in eastern Persia, continued his survey of the Trans-Himalaya, and located the sources of three of southern Asia's major rivers: the Indus, Brahmaputra, and Sutlej.

On all of these expeditions, Hedin traveled without European companions, but he did not travel alone. He took along local guides, servants, and camel drivers. Hedin himself carried out all the scientific work of the expeditions, however, taking compass bearings and making maps of his route, sketching the landscapes through which he

*diplomatic of or relating to diplomacy, the practice of conducting official relations between nations

*caravan large group of people traveling together across a desert or other dangerous region

The courageous, generous, and witty Sven Hedin quickly gained the respect and admiration of the people he encountered on his journeys.

passed, and gathering rock samples for pioneering studies of Central Asian and Tibetan geology.

The Sino-Swedish Expedition. World War I (1914–1918) interrupted Hedin's field trips, but in the mid-1920s he resumed his exploration of western and northern China. In contrast to the solitary and self-directed nature of his earlier trips, the next phase of his career grew into a large and complex operation involving dozens of scientists.

This phase of Hedin's career was originally financed by Lufthansa, a German airline that wanted to establish an air route across the deserts of Central Asia from China to Berlin. At its request Hedin led a group of meteorologists* into Central Asia to establish weather stations along the route. For political reasons, however, Lufthansa had to withdraw its sponsorship after about a year and a half, but Hedin was able to continue his work and broaden its scope. The Swedish government paid for supplies and for a staff of research scientists who worked under Hedin's guidance from 1928 through 1935. During the final two years of this period, the expedition also received funding from the Chinese government. In return, Hedin supervised a survey of possible routes for a highway from Peking through western China. Because the eight-year research project included both Swedish and Chinese scientists and was funded by both governments, it is known as the Sino-Swedish Expedition (*Sino* means "relating to China").

One highlight of the expedition was the study of ruined cities, including a centuries-old outpost of the Chinese empire in the middle of the Gobi Desert in Central Asia. Hedin and his group found about 10,000 bamboo manuscripts that shed much light on the organization of early Chinese colonies along the ancient caravan routes.

Between 1952 and 1959, the U.S. Army Map Service published the expedition's surveys, which covered the region from Kashgar to the Gobi Desert, as *Sven Hedin Central Asia Atlas*. The mission produced an enormous amount of data on Central Asian fossils, plants, geology, archaeology, cultures, and geography. The data, published in more than 50 volumes between 1937 and 1971, set a standard for modern geographic research, in which all aspects of a region are studied together.

His Legacy. Hedin combined the qualities of a great explorer, writer, and artist; his physical endurance, willpower, patience, and apparently reckless courage often aided him through seemingly hopeless situations. He was the last of the classical explorers of the nineteenth century, but as leader of the Sino-Swedish Expedition, he became one of the most active representatives of the modern trend in geographic research. He devoted the years after the war to preparing material from the Sino-Swedish Expedition for publication. Hedin died in Stockholm at age 87, leaving his estate to the Sven Hedin Foundation, which is sponsored by Sweden's Royal Academy of Science.

meteorologist one who practices meteorology, the science that deals with the atmosphere, especially the weather and weather predictions

Mapping the Past

During his 1899–1902 expedition into Central Asia, Hedin 1,000 miles of the course of the Tarim River in western China and northern Tibet. He showed that the river had changed course dramatically in historical time. Before the A.D. 300s, the Tarim flowed into a large lake called Lop Nor. Around 330, however, it shifted course to the southeast, forming a new lake, Kara Koshun. Hedin mapped the river's dried-out former course and found the ruins of a town where it had once emptied into Lop Nor. The Chinese had founded the town around 260 on a trade route. When the river shifted, so did the route, and the town was abandoned to the desert sands.

A skilled navigator and one of history's foremost African-American explorers, Matthew Henson was a member of the first expedition to reach the North Pole. Along with Robert PEARY and four Inuit* men, Henson arrived at the world's northernmost point. This accomplishment, however, earned Henson more respect from future generations of historians and travelers than it did during his own time because he was an African-American.

Matthew Henson was born in Charles County, Maryland. Orphaned as a young boy, he moved in with relatives in Washington, D.C. At the age of 12, he joined the crew of a merchant ship as a cabin boy and quickly became an adept seaman. Recognizing Henson's intellectual talents and curiosity, the ship's captain taught him mathematics and navigation.

After about five years at sea, Henson returned to Washington, where he met Peary, a naval engineer and avid explorer who had recently returned from a voyage to Greenland. Impressed with Henson's skills, Peary employed him as a valet (personal assistant) for his 1888 expedition to Nicaragua. Like the sea captain before him, Peary recognized the extent of Henson's capabilities and quickly increased his responsibilities. He asked Henson to serve as navigator when necessary and made good use of Henson's mechanical skills and his knowledge of carpentry. In 1891, when Peary took a leave of absence from the United States Navy to further explore Greenland, he asked Henson to join his expedition. Henson eagerly accepted.

During the next 15 years, Henson and Peary undertook six journeys to the Arctic. These expeditions, sponsored by the Philadelphia Academy of Natural Sciences and the American Museum of Natural History, among others, resulted in new scientific and geographical knowledge. Although Henson had had no previous experience in polar exploration, he quickly grew accustomed to the cold, the dangers of travel across the ice, and the frequent lack of food. Indeed, Henson soon became something of an expert on Arctic survival.

Part of Henson's expertise came from close observation of Inuit ways. Although many earlier explorers believed that the Inuit had little to offer, Henson recognized that they had thrived in the polar cold for generations. He studied and adopted traditional Inuit survival skills, such as hunting, caring for sled dogs, and building sledges, or load-bearing sleds.

The six voyages were generally successful, but Peary had one last goal: to reach the North Pole itself. In 1909 he and Henson prepared themselves for the journey, which had had little, if any, scientific intent; the sole purpose was to reach the pole. Henson took primary charge of the equipment and, from the base camp near Ellesmere Island in Canada, began pushing a trail north across the frozen Arctic Ocean.

The voyage required a relay of helpers who would travel part of the way to the pole, then return to base camp after carrying supplies to a specified point. Not all team members traveled the whole distance. Peary chose Henson as one of the few who would travel to the pole because "I can't make it there without him."

Matthew
HENSON

1866–1955

POLAR EXPLORATION

Matthew Henson was a master dog driver and mechanic, physically strong, popular among the Inuit, and attuned to the Inuit language.

*Inuit people of the Canadian Arctic and Greenland, sometimes called Eskimo

Conditions were difficult that Arctic spring. Leads, or stretches of open water, appeared unexpectedly, threatening to swallow men, dogs, and equipment. Henson once fell into a lead, and with the help of an Inuit team member, narrowly escaped. They encountered steep ridges of ice that they crossed by pushing the sledges up and over the mounds. Still, the group made surprisingly good time. Henson, Peary, and the four Inuit men covered the last 174 miles in just 5 days, arriving at the North Pole just over a month after leaving Ellesmere.

Reaching the pole marked the end of Matthew Henson's explorations. In 1912 he published an autobiography, *A Negro Explorer at the North Pole,* and served as a customs clerk for the remainder of his working life. For much of this time, he was generally ignored by polar historians and the media, who focused their attentions on Peary. In the late 1930s, his accomplishments were finally recognized and he was honored by the Explorers' Club of New York. He received other honors including personal congratulations from President Dwight D. Eisenhower and the Congressional medal awarded to all the members of the Peary expedition. Henson died in New York City at the age of 88.

HERODOTUS OF HALICARNASSUS

ca. 484 B.C.–ca. 425 B.C.

GEOGRAPHY

Herodotus wrote one of the first important history books of the ancient Western world, a lengthy account of the wars between Greece and Persia (present-day Iran). Although he was mainly concerned with narrating historical events, he was also a geographer. His book contains much information about the physical characteristics, peoples, and cultures of various lands. Some of Herodotus's knowledge was acquired through direct experience—he traveled widely, although his journeys were cautious and fairly comfortable, not epics of hardship and adventure.

Details about Herodotus's life are few. He was probably born in Halicarnassus, a Greek colony in Asia Minor, now known as Turkey. He is thought to have lived for a time in Athens, the foremost Greek city of the time, where he is said to have met Sophocles, an important playwright. He then lived in Thurii, an Athenian colony in southern Italy. His work appears to have been published in Greece by 425 B.C.

Herodotus devoted many years of his life to travel. In addition to Greece and Italy, he visited Egypt and Libya, parts of Asia Minor, Mesopotamia (present-day Iraq), and the region of southwestern Russia then called Scythia. Scholars believe, however, that he did not travel to Persia, although his book contains much information about that land and other countries that came under its rule. Herodotus often relied on accounts and descriptions from other people, and where he did not speak the local language, he depended on interpreters to obtain answers to his questions. As a result, not all of the information he gathered was accurate. But Herodotus also had strengths as a researcher: his freedom from prejudice against non-Greeks, his questioning of some of the wilder stories he heard, and his willingness to present different versions of an event. "My business is to record what people say," he wrote, "but I am by no means bound to believe it."

The *History* falls into two broad parts. The first part, divided into five books, describes the origin, growth, and organization of the Persian Empire, including regions under Persian rule, such as Asia Minor and Egypt. For example, the fourth book is about Scythia, which the Persians invaded but never fully conquered, and the Persian attack on Greek colonies in Libya. The second part of the *History* consists of four books and covers the period during which Herodotus lived. It deals with relations between the Persian Empire and the Greeks beginning in 499 B.C., when Greek cities in Asia Minor revolted against Persian rule, with emphasis on the 480–479 war between the two powers.

In the manner of a true storyteller, Herodotus wove entertaining anecdotes, conversations, and speeches by famous figures into his narrative. Herodotus's style was highly influential—throughout ancient times other writers would adopt his method of writing history. Despite Herodotus's fanciful additions and his inaccuracies, modern scholars and historians value the *History* as a source of information about an important stage in Greek history and about the larger world of which ancient Greece was only a part.

Alfred HETTNER
1859–1941
GEOGRAPHY

The German geographer Alfred Hettner is best known for his efforts to place geography on a scientific foundation similar to those that underlie such experimental sciences as biology and chemistry. He also helped develop and popularize geography in Germany.

Hettner was born in Dresden, Germany, into a large family. An exceptional student, he passed secondary school with an "outstanding" rating and entered the University of Halle in 1877. After only a year at Halle, he transferred to the University of Bonn and later to the University of Strasbourg, where he earned his Ph.D. in geography in 1881. His thesis was titled "The Climate of Chile and West Patagonia."

The following year Hettner was hired as a private tutor to the children of the British Ambassador to Colombia. In March 1883, shortly after Hettner arrived in South America, the ambassador decided that he disliked the position and returned to England. Before leaving, however, he gave Hettner a large sum of money, which Hettner used to travel in South America and in the United States. He returned to Germany in 1884, and four years later he published an account of his journeys, *Travels in the Colombian Andes*. Unable to resist the lure of South America, Hettner returned in 1888, this time to work with the famous German ethnologist* Adolf Bastran.

Hettner and Bastran spent more than two years collecting specimens for Berlin's Ethnological Museum. Hettner also wrote several letters to a colleague in Germany, reporting on the progress of his work. The letters were published in the *Proceedings of the Geographical Society in Berlin*. The trip was hard on Hettner's health. He suffered from leg problems that had lifelong effects on his ability to walk.

*ethnologist one who practices ethnology, the scientific study of the physical and cultural differences between human races

Returning to Germany in 1891, Hettner spent the next six years teaching at the University of Leipzig. He also served as editor of the *Geographische Zeitschrift,* an annual journal of geography. Hoping to use the journal to popularize the field, Hettner said that it "will serve first of all scientific research, but . . . contain no specialized work which can only be understood by specialists and is of interest only to them. Rather, it will deal only with basic questions . . . in generally comprehensible and entirely fluent presentation."

By 1897 Hettner had resumed his travels, this time journeying through Russia. This trip resulted in *European Russia,* which was translated into Russian and released in several editions. During the years that followed, Hettner undertook trips to Egypt, Algeria, Tunisia, and Asia. Between expeditions, he also taught at the University of Heidelberg, a job he accepted in 1899, and founded the city's Geographical Institute.

Hettner, who had been concerned mainly with the political problems of the world until that time, began to devote his attention to political geography (branch of geography concerned with the borders, governments, and populations of nations). The outbreak of World War I in 1914 increased his interest in this subject, and he wrote several books, including *England's World Dominance and the War,* published in 1915, and *The Peace and Germany's Future,* published in 1917. In 1916 he started a series called *Theatres of the War.*

After the war Hettner began to concentrate on regional studies. In 1923 he reworked his old materials on Europe and added studies of non-European regions as well. He typically began by focusing on a continent as a whole and gradually looking at smaller and smaller regions within it. His guiding principle was the conviction that geography was about the spatial arrangement of things in the landscape. He was the leading advocate of the chorological (spatial) principle.

In 1933, when the Nazis gained power in Germany, things became difficult for Hettner. The government classified Hettner as a "quarter-Jew," and he was not permitted to publish in Germany. Many of his works were published shortly after World War II (1939–1945), but Hettner, who died in 1941, did not live to see them in print.

Hettner's honors and awards include the American Geographical Society's Collum Gold Medal "for regional studies that are admirably proportioned and informed with experience as explorer, editor, and teacher," and honorary membership in the Geographical Society in Dresden, Germany. Many of his students were also outstanding scholars in the field. Eleven became professional geographers and others received professorships in related fields such as geology.

TSANG, *Hsüan*

See Xuan Zang.

Alexander von Humboldt was one of the most accomplished natural scientists of his day. His investigations covered a range of topics including mineralogy*, mining, botany, geomagnetism*, and chemistry. However, his greatest efforts were in the field of geography; in fact, many scholars consider him one of the founders of modern geography.

Early Career. The son of a high-ranking army officer, Humboldt was born in Berlin, Germany. His brother was an accomplished statesman and scholar who founded the University of Berlin. Humboldt studied at several German universities, acquiring an education in economics, mining, geology, and botany. As a student he became a supporter of the ideals of the French Revolution, visiting Paris in 1790, shortly before the anniversary of the famous storming of the Bastille.

After completing his studies in 1792, Humboldt joined the Prussian* mining service. He invented safety lamps for miners and a rescue-breathing device for miners trapped underground and facing the threat of asphyxiation (choking from the lack of oxygen). He tested these inventions himself, often under dangerous conditions. Humboldt also used his own money to open a training school for miners. In addition to mining work he conducted investigations into botany and physiology*.

During the years that followed, Humboldt traveled extensively for the mining service, touring mines in central Europe and making a trip through the Swiss and French Alps. This trip stimulated his interest in geomagnetism, a topic that fascinated him for the rest of his life. Humboldt also formed a desire to put together a comprehensive theory of nature based largely on earth sciences, but his duties as a government official gave him little time to do so. However, when his mother died in 1796 she left him an inheritance that enabled him to resign his post in the mining service and pursue his scientific interests.

The following year Humboldt went to the city of Jena, Austria, to conduct scientific experiments on animals and plants. There he learned the techniques for making geodetic* and geophysical* measurements and for taking astronomical bearings (compass readings). For the next two years Humboldt traveled to different parts of Europe to carry out scientific investigations. He conducted experiments on the chemical composition of air, took measurements of the degrees of latitude, and did geographic and botanical research in France and Spain.

Exploring America. In March 1799, with permission from the Spanish government, Humboldt and his companion, the French botanist Aimé Bonpland, began a tour of Spain's American colonies. They arrived in present-day Venezuela in July and spent the next five years exploring Venezuela, Colombia, Peru, Ecuador, Cuba, and Mexico. Humboldt and Bonpland made observations, sketches, measurements, and descriptions of everything they encountered. Humboldt compiled maps and collected information about magnetism, minerals, geology, climate, weather, animal life, plant life, and the cultures of the peoples he met.

Humboldt canoed up the Orinoco River and showed that it is connected to the Amazon. In Ecuador he climbed Mount Chimbora-

Friedrich Wilhelm Heinrich Alexander von
HUMBOLDT
1769–1859
GEOGRAPHY, NATURAL SCIENCE

*mineralogy study of the properties of minerals

*geomagnetism study of the earth's magnetic field

*Prussian of or relating to Prussia, a country that existed from the 1400s until 1947 in the area of present-day eastern and central Europe

*physiology science that deals with the functions of living organisms and their parts

*geodetic having to do with the study of the size and shape of the earth

*geophysical of or relating to the structure and physical characteristics of the earth

Humboldt, Friedrich Wilhelm Heinrich Alexander von

The Humboldt Current, a 550-mile-wide, cold-water current that flows off the coasts of Peru and Chile, was named after Alexander von Humboldt, who in 1802 took measurements that showed the coldness of the current in relation to the surrounding air and sea.

*orography scientific study of mountains and mountain ranges

*meteorology science that deals with the atmosphere, especially the weather and weather predictions

*humanitarian one who is concerned with human welfare and social reform

*anti-Semitism hostility or discrimination against Jews

zo, reaching an altitude of more than 20,000 feet without oxygen, ropes, or any modern mountaineering equipment. He set a world mountain climbing record that stood for almost 30 years. Although he failed to reach the summit, his trip has been called "the scientific discovery of America."

Humboldt spent the last part of the journey in Mexico, where he closely studied the history, politics, and economics of the country. He also investigated the relationship between climate and vegetation as well as that between altitude and fertility. He examined connections between geography, economics, and social conditions. His later writings on Mexico and Cuba were the first works to study geography in terms of science, politics, and economics.

Before returning to Europe, Humboldt stopped in Philadelphia and Washington, D.C., where he met President Thomas Jefferson. Although impressed by the freedom and energy of the new nation, Humboldt was distressed to see its people so devoted to making money above all else. He was also disappointed that Americans were indifferent to slavery, which he considered one of the great evils of the world.

Later Years. Humboldt returned to Paris in 1804 and began to prepare a report of his travels for publication. He developed climatology (study of climates) as a separate science, founded the fields of plant geology and orography*, and introduced concepts in meteorology* and geography. Humboldt wished to take a trip to Asia, but his five-year journey had left him bankrupt, forcing him to take a government post in 1827.

Using the Prussian court's ties to Russia, Humboldt arranged a scientific trip to Siberia. The Russian government sponsored the expedition and Humboldt embarked on a 9,000-mile journey during which he suggested that meteorological and geomagnetic stations be set up to make measurements over larger areas. Using methods of comparative geology that he developed, he accurately predicted the existence of diamonds in the Ural Mountains.

Humboldt spent the last decades of his life between Paris and Berlin. During this time he prepared *Kosmos,* a popular exploration of the entire physical world from simple plants and animals to the creation of galaxies. The work was a great success and went a long way toward making science interesting and approachable for the layperson. In the work, Humboldt credited every scientist who he felt contributed to his knowledge. The book cites more than 9,000 sources and serves as an important reference work for the history of science.

In addition to his scientific achievements, Humboldt devoted much of his life to humanitarian* causes such as fighting slavery and anti-Semitism*. He also inspired and financially assisted a whole generation of young scientists. Although he made few great discoveries, the extent of his scientific vision and his services to humanity make him one of the outstanding figures of his time.

IBN BATTŪTA

1304–ca. 1368

GEOGRAPHY, TRAVEL

Abu Abdallah Muhammad Ibn Battūta, a North African traveler, journeyed through many parts of the medieval* Islamic world. Although modern scholars debate whether he actually visited all the places he claimed to have seen, his account of his many years of travel is both a record of an extraordinary life and a useful source of information about various realms and cultures in Asia and Africa during the 1300s.

An Extended Pilgrimage. Ibn Battūta was born in Tangier, in the North African country of Morocco. He was a Berber, a member of the region's original population. The Berbers had accepted Islam when invading Arabs brought it to the region centuries earlier; many of Ibn Battūta's ancestors had been *qadis,* Muslim judges.

As was the tradition in his family, Ibn Battūta was educated in Islamic literature and law. When he was 21, he left Tangier to take the pilgrimage* to Mecca, the birthplace of Islam, that every Muslim hopes to complete in his or her lifetime. When young scholars made this pilgrimage, they frequently spent a year or two along the way studying with learned teachers or mystics*. But Ibn Battūta went farther and stayed away longer than most. He returned to Morocco after 25 years, having visited, or claiming to have visited, much of the world known to Muslims of his day.

Ibn Battūta made his way across North Africa from Tangier to Egypt. Unlike many who traveled because they had to get from one place to another, he found that he enjoyed travel for its own sake. Seeing new places and ways of life delighted him. He decided to journey throughout the world and "never to travel any road a second time."

During the early part of his travels, he benefited from the aid that Muslim communities traditionally provided for visiting students and scholars. As his reputation as a traveler and a *qadi* grew, he received hospitality and generous gifts from the rulers of many lands and often held official positions in the places that he visited. Eventually Ibn Battūta supported a large group of servants, followers, wives, and mistresses, many of whom accompanied him in his travels.

From Egypt he journeyed to Syria and then on to Mecca to complete the pilgrimage. His course from Mecca, however, is not easy to follow. Ibn Battūta's dating of his travels contains many inaccuracies, and when he later recounted his experiences, he did not always discuss countries in the order in which he had visited them. It is clear, however, that he went from Mecca to Mesopotamia (present-day Iraq) and Persia (present-day Iran). He spent three years, from 1327 to 1330, in Mecca and the Arabian holy city of Medina and then voyaged by ship through the Red Sea and into the Indian Ocean. Africa's east coast was dotted with Muslim ports and trade centers, and Ibn Battūta visited many of these, traveling as far south as Kilwa in present-day Tanzania. In 1332, on his return to Mecca, he passed through southern Persia and Arabia and crossed the Persian Gulf.

Thereafter Ibn Battūta decided to go to Delhi, India, then ruled by a Muslim sultan* who was said to be generous to visiting scholars. His route to India was long and circuitous. First he went to Anatolia (pre-

*medieval referring to the European Middle Ages, a period from about A.D. 500 to 1500

*pilgrimage journey of religious devotion, usually to a sacred site

*mystic follower of a spiritual way of life involving the direct communication with God

See the routes taken by Ibn Battūta in the "Maps" section.

*sultan king of a Muslim state

95

Ibn Battūta

In this engraving by Dumouza, Ibn Battūta is shown in Egypt. Ibn Battūta traveled more than 75,000 miles and wrote a famous book about his journeys through North Africa and Arabia.

sent-day Turkey), where he was welcomed by local rulers and religious societies. He traveled extensively in Anatolia. His account of his travels there contains valuable information about the politics, customs, and social organization of the region, which at the time was divided into many small states. He then pushed across the Black Sea to Crimea and the northern Caucasus (region between the Black and Azov Seas) until he reached Saray, the capital of the last Mongol emperor, on the lower Volga River in present-day southern Russia. From Saray he claimed to have traveled north to Bulgary or Bulghar, a city on the Volga, but this assertion has been disproved. Modern historians are more inclined to believe his description of a trip to Constantinople, the city on the Black

Sea that is now Istanbul, Turkey. In Ibn Battūta's day it was the capital of the fading Byzantine empire, a Christian realm. His colorful account of the city appears accurate.

From Constantinople, Ibn Battūta traveled across the Russian steppes* and returned to Saray, where he joined a caravan* for the journey east through Central Asia. On his way he visited the ancient trade route towns of Samarkand, Bukhara, and Balkh, and then made his way south through Afghanistan and Pakistan to Delhi. There he entered the service of the sultan, whom he vividly portrayed in his writings as both generous and frighteningly cruel. A few years later, in the early 1340s, on his way to China as the sultan's ambassador, Ibn Battūta was shipwrecked. He spent several years as a *qadi* in the Maldive Islands of the Indian Ocean and then became involved in war, politics, and travel in various parts of India before resuming his journey to China—a trip that may not really have occurred.

*steppe arid land found in regions of extreme temperatures

*caravan large group of people traveling together across a desert or other dangerous region

In the late 1340s, Ibn Battūta set out to return home. He traveled through Sumatra and Malabar and crossed the Persian Gulf. He then journeyed through Syria and Egypt and made another pilgrimage to Mecca, returning to Morocco in 1353. During these travels, which lasted more than 25 years, he journeyed more than 75,000 miles; visited all Muslim countries and some non-Muslim ones; met at least 60 rulers, governors, and other officials; and met or visited more than 2,000 other people, all of whom he mentions by name in his writings.

Later Journeys and the Rihla. Ibn Battūta did not rest for long in his homeland. He left almost at once for a tour of Spain, which was then occupied by the Moors, Muslims from North Africa. Afterward, at the command of the sultan of Morocco, Ibn Battūta traveled to the Muslim kingdoms of West Africa, south of the Sahara. He spent a year at the court of Mali, a powerful empire, and visited such sites as the trading center Timbuktu near the Niger River.

After his return to Morocco from West Africa, Ibn Battūta recounted his experiences to a scribe* and court official named Ibn Juzayy, who compiled them into a book called the *Rihla* (Travels). Little else is known of Ibn Battūta's life. During his last years, he served as a *qadi* in a Moroccan town and was later buried in Tangier.

*scribe person of a learned class who serves as a writer, editor, or teacher

Although he did not discover or explore unknown lands, Ibn Battūta made a significant contribution to geographic knowledge. The *Rihla* contains many details about what has sometimes been called human geography: the economies, customs, and interrelationships of peoples and cultures. Historians and scholars of Islam value the *Rihla's* insights into the inner workings of the medieval Islamic world, which consisted of a highly diverse group of peoples united in a single faith that reached from Spain to Southeast Asia. Ibn Battūta probably saw more of the world than almost anyone of his era. His description of it reveals the zest with which this superb traveler encountered new sights and new people wherever he went.

Between 1958 and 2000, the Hakluyt Society of London, which publishes records of voyages, travels, and geographical discovery, republished Ibn Battūta's account of his travels in five volumes.

IBN MAJID

ca. 1432–unknown

NAVIGATION, GEOGRAPHY

*medieval referring to the European Middle Ages, a period from about A.D. 500 to 1500

*sheikdom state ruled by a sheik, an Arab chieftain

Shihab al-Din Ahmad Ibn Majid, who called himself "The Lion of the Sea," was a master navigator, a seafarer who was highly skilled in plotting a route to a desired destination. The medieval* Arab world produced many excellent navigators, but historians consider Ibn Majid foremost among them. The handbooks he wrote about sailing and navigation, and about the Red Sea and the Indian Ocean, are valuable geographical and historical documents.

Life. Ibn Majid was born in Julfar, today known as Ras al Khaimah, a sheikdom* on the Arabian Peninsula that is part of the United Arab Emirates. He inherited a tradition of skilled seamanship—his grandfather and father were *mu'allim,* "masters of navigation," considered experts in the art of guiding ships through the treacherous waters of the Red Sea. Although little is known about Ibn Majid's life, his writings reveal that he was well educated. He was familiar with the works of many Muslim geographers, astronomers, and navigators, as well as those of ancient Greek scholars such as the geographer PTOLEMY.

According to tradition, Ibn Majid played a part in the historic voyage of Portuguese explorer Vasco da GAMA, the first European to reach India by sailing around Africa. European accounts of that voyage say that when Gama reached the east coast of Africa, he found an Arab navigator who piloted him across the Indian Ocean to India. Some European versions name Ibn Majid as that pilot. An Arab historian named Qutb al-Din al-Nahrwali also wrote that Ibn Majid had helped Gama reach India by giving him the navigational directions he needed to cross the Indian Ocean. Ibn Majid was certainly aware of the activities of the Portuguese explorer; in his book *Al-Sufaliyya* (The Poem of Sofala) he records Gama's voyage around Africa, his trip to India, his return to Portugal, and a later Portuguese expedition to India.

Some modern researchers, however, question whether Ibn Majid was directly involved in the Portuguese venture or had any contact with Gama. In A.D. 2000 the ruler of Sharjah, one of the states in the United Arab Emirates, published a book in which he argued that it was not Ibn Majid but a Christian Indian pilot who guided Gama to India. Because Gama's voyage brought disaster and decline to the Arab and Muslim powers around the Indian Ocean, Muslim scholars may be particularly eager to show that Gama did not receive help from the most famous Arab navigator. As yet, Ibn Majid's role in Gama's voyage has not been proved one way or the other.

Writings. Ibn Majid wrote at least 38 works in prose or poetry. Of these, 25 have survived. They cover a wide range of topics, including astronomy; the use of birds as guides to land; other signs that indicate that land is near; calendars; sea routes of the Indian Ocean and the latitude of harbors; the Red Sea; the coastal regions of Asia and Africa (this book reveals that Ibn Majid knew more about the Indian Ocean than about the Mediterranean Sea or the Caspian Sea); and what he called the "ten large islands" of the Indian Ocean (Arabia, Madagascar, Sumatra, Java, Taiwan, Ceylon, Zanzibar, Bahrain, Ibn Gawan, and Socotra). A modern scholar has called Ibn Majid the first writer on nautical* science and has said that, apart from errors in latitude, his guide to sailing the Red Sea has never been equaled.

Of all of Ibn Majid's works, *Kitab al-Fawa'id* (The Benefits and Principles of Oceanography*), dated 1490, was most valuable to navigators. In it, he gathered all the navigational knowledge of his time, both theory and practical guidance. Although some sources have claimed that Ibn Majid invented the navigational compass, *Kitab al-Fawa'id* makes it clear that he did not. He did claim, however, to have begun the practice of attaching a needle to a case containing the magnetic instrument—something that made it easier for navigators to read the compass. He also boasted that Arab compasses were superior to those used by Egyptian or North African navigators.

Ibn Majid's writings show how geographers of his time and place pictured the world. The geographers knew of the writings of Ptolemy, who had described Africa's southern coast as extending eastward all the way to Asia, making the Indian Ocean a landlocked sea. Most medieval Arab maps follow this pattern, showing the Indian Ocean surrounded by a great southern landmass, with a channel connecting it to the Pacific Ocean but none linking it to the Atlantic. The Arab geographer Al-Biruni, however, had suggested that a channel, called *al-madkhal* ("the place of entry"), linked the Indian Ocean and the Atlantic, perhaps running through the middle of Africa. Ibn Majid believed that this theory was correct. The voyage of the Portuguese from the Atlantic into the Indian Ocean, he felt, had proved that *al-madkhal* existed.

The fame of Ibn Majid, based on his own exploits and on his writings, lasted long after his death. Seamen referred to him by respectful titles and recited chapters from the Qur'an, the Muslim holy book, in his memory before setting out to sea. The British explorer Richard BURTON, sailing from the Arabian port of Aden in 1854, saw sailors praying in Ibn Majid's memory.

*nautical of or relating to ships or seamanship

*oceanography study of oceans

al-IDRISI

1100–1166

GEOGRAPHY, CARTOGRAPHY

The Arab traveler, geographer, and cartographer* al-Idrisi produced one of the most important world maps of the medieval* period. He combined the knowledge of the ancient Greeks and early Arab geographers and astronomers with his firsthand observations to produce an overview map of Europe, Asia, and North Africa.

Little is known about al-Idrisi's early life. He was born in Ceuta, Morocco, into the Idrisi clan, Arabs who traced their descent from the prophet Muhammad, founder of the Islamic religion. Al-Idrisi was edu-

*cartographer one who practices cartography, or mapmaking

*medieval referring to the European Middle Ages, a period from about A.D. 500 to 1500

*Norman referring to the Normans, people originally of Scandinavian descent who settled on the west coast of France and who established a kingdom in Sicily

cated in Córdoba, Spain, a major center of learning, and began traveling at an early age, visiting Asia Minor (present-day Turkey) at the age of 16. He later toured the southern coast of France, visited England, and journeyed widely in Morocco and in Spain, which was then occupied by Arabs from North Africa.

In 1138 al-Idrisi received a communication from Roger II, king of the Norman* kingdom of Sicily, in which Roger invited al-Idrisi to live at his court in the city of Palermo. According to tradition, the king said that if al-Idrisi remained among Muslims, members of rival royal families would try to kill him, but that he would be safe among the Normans. Some historians suggest that information about al-Idrisi is scarce in Arab records because Muslims regarded him as a traitor for spending years among the Norman Christians.

The Normans were keen to promote the arts and sciences, and Sicily, the political center of their kingdom, was a meeting ground of Arab and European cultures. There al-Idrisi worked with Christian scholars on a project envisioned by King Roger: a world map and a work of geography that would present detailed information on the regions of the world. Al-Idrisi drew from numerous sources; his basic picture of Europe, Africa, and Asia was based on the one developed nearly 1,000 years earlier by the Greek geographer PTOLEMY, but he also drew on the work of Arab scientists. Much of the descriptive information was new—Roger sent observers to different nations to gather and record information for al-Idrisi's work.

His labors resulted in a splendid world map and an accompanying geographic text with smaller maps. The world map, which showed mountains, seas, rivers, and towns, was a planisphere, or disk-shaped map, made of silver. This impressive object has since been lost, but the accompanying geographic text contains maps that probably reproduce sections of the planisphere. Al-Idrisi divided the world into the seven climate zones recognized by geographers of the time. Each of the zones is parallel to the equator and is subdivided into ten sections. When joined together, the 70 sectional maps reveal a total picture of the world as known to the Arabs and Normans.

The text also includes an enormous amount of information about the physical features, populations, and social, economic, and political conditions of many lands. Both the mapping and the information are more accurate for Europe, the Mediterranean region, and the Middle East than they are for other places. Although the map contains many errors, it is a source of rich and varied details and is the finest example of Arab-Norman scientific collaboration. It was used in Europe as a textbook for centuries and was later translated into many European languages.

Al-Idrisi wrote other scientific works, including a description of medicinal drugs made from plants and at least one more geographical encyclopedia. After many years in Sicily he returned to Ceuta, where he died.

Preston Everett James ranks as one of the most influential American geographers of the mid-1900s. He was also an outstanding teacher and the author of many important textbooks and scholarly articles. In addition to his academic achievements, James served as a Latin American expert for the Office of Strategic Services (OSS), the predecessor of the modern Central Intelligence Agency (CIA), during World War II.

James was born in Brookline, Massachusetts, to wealthy parents who placed a great emphasis on education. James's academic talents were evident from an early age; he won a medal for outstanding achievement when he graduated from his college preparatory school. In 1916 he enrolled at Harvard University where he planned to study English, but a course in physiography* changed his mind about the direction of his studies, and he switched his major to geography.

James graduated from Harvard in 1920 with a B.S. in geology, and the following year he received a master's degree in climatology (the study of climates). He then entered Clark University in Worcester because Wallace Atwood, the professor whose physiography course had caused James to change his major, was the director of the graduate school of geography. Atwood required his students to specialize in a particular region of the world, and James chose Latin America.

To fulfill the requirements for his Ph.D., James undertook an extensive field trip to Latin America. The fieldwork led not only to his doctoral dissertation, but also to several articles that were published in prominent journals in the field. After earning his Ph.D. in 1923, James took a teaching post at the University of Michigan. During the years that followed, he published three textbooks in his field and conducted research in Central and South America, Canada, Portugal, France, and England.

When the United States entered World War II (1939–1945), James was called to join the research and analysis branch of the Office of Strategic Services in Washington, D.C. He served as Chief of the Latin American Division and later as Chief of the Geographic Division in the Europe-Africa section of the OSS. At this time he also published his most famous textbook, *Latin America,* which was long considered the best regional geography text in English. It remained popular for more than 40 years after its initial publication in 1942.

After the war James joined the faculty at Syracuse University in New York. He spent the next 23 years there, publishing 16 books and some 70 journal articles. From 1950 to 1968 he served as chairman of the Department of Geography at Syracuse, retiring in 1969. The following year he was named to the honorary position of professor emeritus and he remained active in his academic activities, publishing four books between 1978 and 1981.

During his long career, James was an active member of the Association of American Geographers (AAG). He served as secretary of the organization from 1936 to 1941 and as its president in 1951. He also served as honorary president in 1966. The Geographical Society of the former Soviet Union also elected James as an honorary member. James held positions in other prestigious organizations, including the Nation-

Preston Everett
JAMES

1899–1986

GEOGRAPHY

*physiography physical geography

al Research Council, the Council for Latin American Affairs, the Division of Geology and Geography, and the Commission on Geography of the Pan-American Institute of Geography and History.

James was also the recipient of several awards, including the Distinguished Service Award from the National Council for Geographic Education and the Medal of Geography and History from the Pan American Institute. Other geographic societies that honored him include the American Geographical Society, the Geographic Society of Chicago, and the Royal Geographic Society of Great Britain. James won the National Council for Geographic Education Master Teacher Award and received honorary degrees from four universities.

Toward the end of his life, James suffered from macular degeneration, a disease that progressively destroys one's eyesight. Still he continued his writing, aided by his wife, who read his mail and helped prepare revisions of his books. He continued to publish until the final years of his life. One of his colleagues summed up James's importance to the field of geography by stating that, during his lifetime, "his total impact [has been] second to none."

JONES AND PICCARD

Brian Jones
born 1949
HOT-AIR BALLOONING

Bertrand Piccard
born 1958
HOT-AIR BALLOONING

In 1999 the British engineer Brian Jones and the Swiss psychiatrist Bertrand Piccard won what *Time* magazine called "the last world-spanning contest of our era" when they made the first circumnavigation, or trip around the world, in a hot-air balloon. For more than 200 years before the historic flight of Jones and Piccard, people had been ascending in balloons to explore the world above the earth's surface.

Background on Balloons. A balloon is a bag filled with a substance that is lighter than ordinary air, such as helium, hydrogen, or heated air. When filled with one of these substances, the balloon, unless tied to the ground (tethered), will rise into the air. If the balloon is large enough, it can carry a basket or passenger compartment, called a gondola, which hangs below the bag. A balloon travels with the wind, unlike a dirigible, a lighter-than-air craft that has a motor and can be steered in any direction. Balloonists, however, can direct their craft to some extent by raising or dropping it to levels of the atmosphere where the winds are blowing in a favorable direction.

Two Frenchmen, the brothers Joseph-Michel and Jacques-Étienne Montgolfier, invented ballooning in 1783. The first passengers to ascend in one of their hot-air balloons were a duck, a rooster, and a sheep. That same year a scientist named Pilatre de Rozier ascended in a tethered Montgolfier balloon and then, with another passenger, rode for 20 minutes over the rooftops of Paris in an untethered balloon. Two years later, de Rozier died during an attempt to fly across the English Channel when his balloon, consisting of a hydrogen bag tied to a hot-air bag, exploded. Later in 1785 a two-man French and American team made the first balloon crossing of the channel.

Having won the so-called Great Balloon Race, Bertrand Piccard and Brian Jones returned to Geneva where they were welcomed as heroes. They shared a $1 million cash award offered by a brewing company.

Napoleon Bonaparte made the first known military use of balloons in 1794, when he sent observers to spy on enemy troops. From then until World War II (1939–1945), balloons carried observers and messengers or were used to drop bombs during conflicts. Balloons have also been used for research purposes, carrying scientists or scientific instruments high into the atmosphere. Auguste Piccard, a Swiss-born physicist, made a landmark scientific balloon flight in 1932, rising to an altitude of 52,498 feet to study cosmic rays in the stratosphere, or upper atmosphere. He ascended in a cabin that was pressurized to protect him from the effects of the ultra-thin atmosphere at that height.

Throughout the 1900s, balloonists set new records. A 1935 flight climbed 72,395 feet, setting the stage for high-altitude aviation and space travel. Twenty-five years later, the U.S. Air Force captain Joe Kittinger made a parachute jump from a balloon at an altitude of 102,800 feet—a record that still stands. The first balloon crossing of the Atlantic Ocean occurred in 1978; the Pacific crossing took place three years later. In 1991 the Swedish balloonist Per Lindstrand and the English businessman Richard Branson set a distance record, flying 6,700 miles from Japan to the Canadian Arctic in 46 hours.

Circumnavigation by Balloon. In 1981 balloonists began to attempt to fly around the world in a hot-air balloon. Lindstrand and Branson were among those who made repeated attempts as was the American millionaire Steve Fossett, who tried five times to circumnavigate in a balloon but fell short of his goal each time. Fossett called the feat "one of the great explorations." By the late 1990s, the event had become an annual race for a few well-funded adventurers and their crews.

Bertrand Piccard, the grandson of the man who had made the first stratospheric balloon flight, had twice tried and failed to fly around the world in a balloon. On March 1, 1999, Piccard and the engineer and experienced pilot Brian Jones launched the *Breitling Orbiter 3* from the snow-capped mountains of Chateau-d'Oex in Switzerland. Their craft was a 180-foot-tall Rozier-style balloon carried aloft by a combination of helium and hot air. It carried a 10- by 16-foot pressurized cabin equipped with high-technology navigation and communications equipment.

The *Orbiter 3* traveled south across the Mediterranean Sea. Once the balloon was over the Sahara, its pilots picked up a rapid atmospheric current that carried them east toward India and China. On the long stretch of flight over the Pacific Ocean, the balloon lost contact with its ground-based mission control for four days. Despite technical difficulties and the physical exhaustion experienced by both pilots, the *Orbiter 3* continued its voyage across Mexico and caught a swift-moving current over the Atlantic. Passing over the North African nation of Mauritania, the balloon crossed the longitude of its launch site—Piccard and Jones's trip around the world was complete. Exhilarated by their triumph, the pilots continued across the Sahara for a second time, landing in Egypt on March 21, 1999. They had been airborne for 19 days and 21 hours and had covered a distance of 29,055 miles.

Future balloon feats will likely include circumnavigations in the southern hemisphere or over the poles, but the honor of making the first circumnavigation rests with Piccard and Jones.

Mary Henrietta KINGSLEY

1862–1900

EXPLORATION OF AFRICA

The English traveler Mary Henrietta Kingsley undertook several journeys in western Africa, passing through regions that had been claimed by various European powers. Kingsley's lectures and the witty, entertaining books she wrote about her experiences attracted much attention in Great Britain. Although her travels included exciting incidents such as crocodile attacks and cannibal encounters, her explorations remain interesting for other reasons. Kingsley was one of very few white women who traveled alone in Africa in the 1800s, and she was one of the most open-minded European travelers of her time. Her writing reflects deep respect for African people and their cultures. In addition, the fish specimens she collected during her travels were a valuable addition to the knowledge of the zoology of West Africa.

Background and Education. Kingsley was born in London. Her uncle Charles Kingsley was a famous author and clergyman, so highly regarded by Britain's royal family that he tutored the Prince of Wales, heir to the throne. Mary and her younger brother, however, had little connection with the socially prominent factions of the Kingsley clan.

Kingsley's father liked to travel and spent long periods away from home as a companion physician to wealthy travelers. Interested in science and in other cultures, he collected plants, animals, and artifacts*

artifact tool, artwork, utensil, weapon, or other object made by humans

from around the world, although he completed no scientific work. Unfortunately for Mary Kingsley, he also left his wife and children fairly short of money. Mary did much of the work around the house and took care of her brother and her mother, who was often ill. She received little education, although she longed for it. "I cried at not being taught things," she later recalled. Kingsley did, however, read the books in her father's library, educating herself and absorbing many of her father's interests. Books about travel and exploration held special fascination for her.

In the early 1880s, Kingsley's father retired from traveling and moved the family to Cambridge so that her brother could go to university. The move widened Kingsley's world as well. She met and was inspired by scholars, students, and writers, and she tried to help her father write a book about his experiences and observations. The book was never completed, and both of Kingsley's parents died in 1892.

Later that year she began her own travels. Although she spoke of gathering information to complete her father's unfinished manuscript, she ultimately traveled to fulfill her own dreams of seeing the world and making a contribution to geography or science.

First Journeys. With limited funds and no experience as a traveler, Kingsley chose a good destination for her first trip: the Canary Islands, off the West African coast of Morocco. The islands had been European colonies and trading ports for hundreds of years, and familiar elements blended with exotic African ones in their nature and culture.

The Canary Islands voyage introduced Kingsley to sea travel and to adventures such as volcano watching and open-air camping. She also met traders who conducted business along the West African coast, bartering cloth, knives, and other trade goods for ivory and rubber gathered by the local Africans. Kingsley visited that coast on a trading vessel and learned that some traders traveled alone on foot or by canoe through the inland districts. All such traders were men, but Kingsley believed that she could use their methods to finance her own travels in the region.

Kingsley put her plan into practice in 1893, when she spent months traveling through various West African territories, from the Portuguese colony of Angola in the south to Nigeria in the north. At the mouth of the Congo River, she gathered specimens of fish and beetles. In the Belgian Congo colony she witnessed with distress the suffering that epidemics* and a brutal colonial administration were bringing to the Africans. Kingsley found that traveling as a trader not only paid for the trip but also put her on good terms with the African people she met. She later told a lecture audience,

when you first appear among people who have never seen anything like you before, they naturally regard you as a devil; but when you want to buy or sell with them, they recognize there is something human and reasonable about you.

Second Trip to Africa. Kingsley returned to England in 1894, and by the end of that year, she had set off on another journey to West Africa.

Kingsley always dressed as a Victorian lady, whether she was traveling by canoe along a river or journeying through the forests and swamps of Africa.

*epidemic outbreak of disease

Fish and Fetish

Mary Kingsley did not travel solely for pleasure. She wanted her African journeys to have scientific importance. "Fish and fetish" were Kingsley's two areas of research. She used the term *fish* to refer to her study of freshwater fish in West Africa. She gathered specimens for the British Museum in London, which provided her with professional collecting equipment. Among her finds were several new species—one, *Ctenopoma kingsleyae,* was named after her. The term *fetish* referred to objects that the Africans believed to be sacred or magical and to their religious beliefs. Kingsley acquired examples of such objects and made extensive notes on West African religion and law.

*missionary person who works to convert nonbelievers to his or her faith

This trip would last a year and would become the subject of many lectures and articles and two books by Kingsley.

She began by exploring the mangrove swamps of the Niger River delta, reporting on the solemn beauty of the region and on its aggressive crocodiles. She next made a canoe trip through little-known country on the Ogowé River in what is now Gabon, then pushed across 200 miles of forest and swamp to another river, the Rembwé. Along the way Kingsley passed through the territory of the Fang, a group whom she called the Fan because she feared their real name might sound too threatening—especially because they were rumored to be cannibals. Kingsley discovered evidence of cannibal practices but got along very well with the Fang, whose energy and independence she admired. Before returning to England, Kingsley stopped in the German colony of Cameroon to climb the highest peak in western Africa, Mt. Cameroon (13,353 feet). She completed the arduous climb with great difficulty, becoming the first European woman to do so, but was disappointed when she reached the top because clouds blocked the view.

Returning to London, Kingsley, a prolific writer, wrote two books about her journey: *Travels in West Africa* and *West African Studies,* published in 1897 and 1899. In these and other writings about her experiences, Kingsley often criticized the colonial administrators and missionaries* she had seen at work in Africa. She disliked the fact that most Europeans felt superior to the black African people, and she especially disapproved of the missionaries' efforts to wipe out traditional African beliefs and practices and replace them with Christianity and what she called "second-hand rubbishy white culture." Most readers of Kingsley's day could not accept such opinions, but modern readers are likely to admire her freedom from prejudice.

In 1900 Mary Kingsley made her final journey to Africa. She went to South Africa, where the British were at war with the Boers, colonists of Dutch ancestry. While serving as a nurse in a hospital for Boer prisoners of war, Kingsley became ill and died at age 37. She was buried at sea off the coast of Africa, as she had wished.

Petr Alekseevich
KROPOTKIN

1842–1921

GEOGRAPHY

Petr Kropotkin's main claim to fame is his contribution to the theory of glaciation, in which he confirmed that huge masses of ice called glaciers once covered large parts of Europe and Asia. In addition to his work with glaciers, he contributed significantly to the study of Russian geography. Science was not Kropotkin's only passion; he was also one of the leaders of the anarchist movement that advocated the abolition of all forms of government. His revolutionary ideas would land him in jail more than once.

Early Career. Born in Moscow, Kropotkin was the son of a Russian general and landowner. As a young man he attended the exclusive School of Pages in St. Petersburg before enlisting in the Cossack Army in the Amur region of Siberia. As a Cossack officer he hoped to study Siberia and participate in its development. In 1863, he took part in his first scientific expedition in southeastern Siberia and Manchuria when he accompanied a barge carrying provisions to Cossack outposts along the Amur River. The following year, while scouting a new route to the Amur through northern Manchuria, he came across a region of inactive volcanoes among the Greater Khingan Mountains.

During the summer of 1865, Kropotkin journeyed to the Eastern Sayan Mountain Range and climbed the Tunkinskiye Goltsy Mountains, a part of the Sayan range. Atop these dome-shaped mountains, he found clear evidence of glacial activity. On the same expedition he found volcanic craters and rocks near the Dzhanbulak River (a tributary of the Oka River in south central Russia). His report on the area provided new data on the geography of eastern Siberia.

Major Expeditions. In 1866, as a member of the Siberian section of the Russian Geographic Society, Kropotkin headed an extensive tour of Siberia's Vitim and Olekma Rivers. This would prove to be one of his most productive scientific expeditions. The group traveled in boats downstream along the Lena River to the village of Krestovaya. From there they mounted pack horses and followed a complex route through basins and rapids to the Tsipa River. The expedition crossed several smaller rivers and climbed mountains in the Olekmo-Charskoye Nagorye uplands and several hills in the Vitim plateau.

During the trip Kropotkin gathered sufficient evidence to support his previous conclusions about glaciation in the area. Many signs pointed to the existence of glaciers there in the past—the smooth surfaces of many of the mountains, the discovery of marine fossils in sands high above the present level of the rivers, and boulders marked by horizontal grooves.

Kropotkin was the first to observe that the eastern Siberian climate had once been moist enough for the formation of glaciers. Later scientists found traces of previous glaciation near Lake Baikal in southern Siberia. More recently, over 30 existing glaciers have been found in the nearby Kodar Mountains. On this trip Kropotkin also defined and gave detailed descriptions of four separate geographical regions in the areas he traveled. The expedition also inspired him to study the physical geography of the mountains and mountain ranges in the region. He concluded that erosion played a major part in forming the landscape of eastern Siberia.

Kropotkin quickly realized that because he lacked a formal education in natural sciences, his studies would not be taken very seriously. Consequently, after he returned from the Olekma expedition, he enrolled in St. Petersburg University to study physics and mathematics. The following year he was named secretary of the Russian Geographical Society's physical geography section.

In 1871, Kropotkin undertook his most important scientific expedition. The Russian Geographical Society sent him to Sweden and Finland to study glaciers. Kropotkin's report completely overturned existing ideas in the field. Until that time, most scientists felt that the huge boulders found scattered randomly about northern Europe were carried to their present locations by floating packs of ice. Kropotkin, how-

Peaceful Prophet of Violence

Kropotkin's anarchist ideas were often at odds with his other moral convictions. For example, he believed that cooperation, not competition, was the main factor in the evolution of species and societies. He staunchly opposed prisons, calling them "schools of crime" that only served to harden the imprisoned individuals. Kropotkin maintained that, in an ideal world, understanding and moral pressure would be sufficient to deal with antisocial acts. In stark opposition, however, he firmly believed that violence was justified in the struggle for freedom. It was these views that caused the leaders of the countries in which he lived to consider him a dangerous revolutionary.

ever, showed that their positions were the result of glacial activity. He asserted that massive glaciers, as much as 10,000 feet thick, once covered northern Europe and Asia, and that over time, they crawled along the land, regardless of the landscape. Most scholars credit him with formulating the first accurate theory of glaciation.

Revolutionary. During the early 1870s, Kropotkin became increasingly interested in studying social problems. He observed the life of common people in Imperial Russia and began to adopt revolutionary ideas. He became an anarchist and advocated the overthrow of all forms of government. In 1874 the Russian government arrested him for his views and imprisoned him in the Peter and Paul Fortress in St. Petersburg. However, two years later he escaped and made his way to Scotland.

After a brief period in Edinburgh, Kropotkin moved to Switzerland in 1877 where he founded an anarchist newspaper. Four years later he was expelled from Switzerland for his political activity and settled in France. In 1883 he was again arrested for his anarchist activity and sentenced to five years in jail. Three years later, however, the French government pardoned him and he moved to Great Britain. He spent the next 30 years of his life there.

While in Britain, Kropotkin continued to publish anarchist literature, but he also remained involved in scientific activities. The *Encyclopedia Britannica* hired him to write its entries on Russian geography and he contributed a section on Asiatic Russia to the revision of Élisée RECLUS's textbook, *General Geography*. From 1892 to 1901 he was a scientific reviewer for the English magazine *Nineteenth Century*.

In 1912, on Kropotkin's seventieth birthday, the Royal Geographic Society of London honored his contributions to science. Although he was being honored by the British, he was still a marked man in his homeland. Five years later, however, the Russian Revolution erupted and the monarchy was overthrown. The new Communist* government embraced the anarchist ideals that Kropotkin had championed and invited the talented geographer to return home. He died four years later in Moscow. His memory is honored in the names of a mountain range and two towns in Russia.

*Communist of or referring to communism, the system in which land, goods, and the means of production are owned by the state or community rather than by individuals

LEO THE AFRICAN

ca. 1485–ca. 1554

GEOGRAPHY, ASTRONOMY

Leo the African, also known as Leo Africanus, is best known for *Della descrittione dell' Africa* (Description of Africa), one of the earliest treatises about the geography of North Africa. Before the publication of this work there was very little written knowledge about African geography. Leo's *Descrittione* became the basis for many maps of Africa and the Mediterranean.

Leo was born Al-Hasan ibn Muhammad al-Wazzan al-Zayyati al-Gharnati in Granada, Spain. In 1492, when the king of Spain expelled all Muslims from the country, Leo and his family moved to Fez, Morocco, where he received his education. At age 22, Leo embarked on the first of four journeys across Africa that would form the basis for his work. On this trip he traveled across the Sahara to the Middle East, visiting the great city of Constantinople. Then the capital of the powerful Ottoman Empire, the city is now Turkey's largest city, Istanbul.

Leo's second trip, around 1510, took him south of Morocco to the fabled city of Timbuktu in the present-day African nation of Mali. Some two years later he again traveled to Timbuktu, then headed west to Egypt along the southern border of the Sahara. On his final trip, from 1515 to 1518, he went to Constantinople as an ambassador from Morocco to the Ottoman Court. During that period he took several trips to Egypt, journeying up the Nile River as far as the falls at Aswan. Some records state that Leo also traveled to Arabia, Armenia, and Persia at this time, but scholars doubt the authenticity of these stories.

In 1518, when Leo was sailing off the coast of Libya, he was captured by Italian pirates, who took him to Rome and presented him as a slave to Pope Leo X. When the Pope realized his slave was an educated and well-traveled man he granted him freedom. He also instructed three bishops to teach Leo about Christianity. In 1520 the former Muslim converted and was renamed after the pope. Leo wrote his masterwork during his time in Italy.

The *Descrittione* is divided into nine books. The first is a general discussion of Africa and its people, and the next five contain detailed descriptions of North Africa. The seventh book covers the areas bordering the southern Sahara, particularly the upper Niger River. Little was known of these areas prior to the publication of Leo's work. Book eight is about Egypt, and the final book discusses the animals, plants, minerals, and rivers of the African continent. In addition to its excellent descriptions of African life, the work also gives the distances in miles between the various places that Leo visited.

Pope Leo never lived to see the book he commissioned, which first appeared in print in 1526—five years after his death. Three years after completing the *Descrittione,* Leo returned to the African city of Tunis. Some scholars suggest that he also reconverted to Islam, but there is no evidence of this. Leo spent the remainder of his life in Tunis.

LEWIS AND CLARK

Meriwether Lewis
1774–1809
NORTH AMERICAN EXPLORATION

William Clark
1770–1838
NORTH AMERICAN EXPLORATION

Meriwether Lewis and William Clark led the first large expedition organized and paid for by the United States government. Their journey, which was the first documented crossing of North America by Americans, met its political, economic, and scientific goals.

Jefferson Plans an Expedition

Thomas Jefferson, the third president of the United States, was the mind behind the expedition. When Jefferson became president in 1801, the nation was less than 20 years old. Like many other Americans of his time, he was deeply interested in what lay beyond the Mississippi River, which at the time marked the country's western border.

Looking Westward. Ever since the first British colonists landed on the Atlantic coast in the 1600s, Americans had been looking westward.

A Shoshone Heroine

During the winter of 1804–1805, Lewis and Clark hired Toussaint Charbonneau, a French-Canadian trader, as a guide for the next stage of their westward journey. His Native American wife, Sacagawea, accompanied the Corps of Discovery and proved to be a valuable assistant. On the present-day border of Idaho the expedition met the Shoshone people. Sacagawea was a Shoshone, and her brother was a chieftain among that people. She interpreted for the explorers and her people and she helped convince the Shoshone to provide horses and guides. Sacagawea worked as hard and performed as well as any member of the Corps of Discovery—all while caring for her baby son.

See the route of the Lewis and Clark expedition in the "Maps" section.

The ocean marked the fixed eastern boundary of their territory, but they kept expanding the western limits, pushing the settled area of the colonies farther inland. By the time the Revolutionary War broke out in the 1770s, settlers had worked their way across the Appalachian Mountains and had entered the Ohio River valley. The war ended when Britain agreed to turn over to the new United States its territory south of Canada and east of the Mississippi. Before long, settlements such as St. Louis emerged on the east bank of the river, and Americans again looked west toward what was then Spanish territory.

Spain had claimed all of western North America south of Canada and west of the Mississippi. However, because the Spanish government had done little to colonize this vast region, it could not prevent foreigners from wandering about the territory. Fur traders and Indian agents moved south into the region from Canada, and a few Americans had ventured a short distance beyond the Mississippi.

The West Coast. On the other side of the continent, the Pacific coast had been visited by ships of many nations since the 1500s. In 1792, a Boston sea captain named Robert Gray sailed into the mouth of a mighty river that flows from the western interior into the Pacific Ocean. He named it Columbia River, which today marks the border between the states of Washington and Oregon. Gray's visit aroused American interest in the Pacific Northwest as did the explorations of Alexander MACKENZIE, a Scotsman who worked for a British fur-trading company in Canada. The year after Gray reached the Columbia River, Mackenzie journeyed west from northern Alberta across the Rocky Mountains to the Pacific coast of the present-day Canadian province of British Columbia. In 1801 Mackenzie published a report of his travels in *Voyages from Montreal*. Some people in the United States, including President Jefferson, were eager for Americans to make a similar crossing of the continent. Curiosity and concern about the West increased further in 1802, when Americans learned that Spain had given France the Louisiana Territory, the region that lay between the Mississippi and the summit of the Rocky Mountains.

Lewis and Clark

In early 1803 Jefferson told the U.S. Congress that he wanted to send explorers west of the Mississippi. He communicated this idea secretly in order to avoid angering Spain. A few months later, in one of history's biggest land deals, Jefferson arranged for the United States to buy the Louisiana Territory from France. The purchase of this territory made it possible for Americans to venture west of the Mississippi River—at least as far as the Rockies.

Jefferson next began to organize the expedition into the Louisiana Territory even before the purchase was final. He chose his friend and personal secretary, a young army captain named Meriwether Lewis, as the mission's commander.

Lewis and Clark. Born near Charlottesville, Virginia, Lewis was not only eager to lead the expedition but was also well suited to do so. He was physically fit, educated, and knowledgeable about natural history*. After joining the army in 1794, he served for six years on the western frontier—he was familiar with wilderness life and travel and with some aspects of Native American culture. To better prepare himself for travel across an unexplored region, Lewis learned the basics of navigation from Jefferson and from scientists in Philadelphia.

As preparations got under way, Jefferson and Lewis agreed that the expedition was important enough to warrant a second officer, someone to share the command with Lewis and to take charge if something happened to him. They agreed on Lieutenant William Clark, an officer under whom Lewis had briefly served early in his military career and the younger brother of George Rogers Clark, a hero of the Revolutionary War.

Like Lewis, Clark was born in Virginia, but his family had moved to the Kentucky frontier when he was still a boy. Clark joined the Kentucky militia* at age 19 and later became an officer in the U.S. Army. Tall and muscular, he had extensive frontier experience; he was a wilderness veteran who had served in campaigns against the Native Americans and had spied on Spanish activity along the Mississippi.

Jefferson offered to promote Clark to captain, so that his rank would be equal to Lewis's, if he joined the expedition. Lewis wrote to Clark, offering him a co-captaincy of the expedition, ". . . your situation if joined with me in this mission will in all respects be precisely such as my own." Clark responded, "My friend I assure you no man lives with whome I would perfur to undertake Such a Trip & as your self." Disappointingly, Clark was promoted only to the rank of second lieutenant. Throughout the trip, however, Lewis addressed him as captain and all the members of the expedition treated Lewis and Clark as equals. Relations between the two men remained harmonious, and no quarrels over leadership marred the journey.

natural history systematic study of nature and natural objects in their original settings

militia group of civilians trained and authorized to act as troops in a defense emergency

The Corps of Discovery

The expedition that began to take shape in 1803 was officially called the Corps of Volunteers on an Expedition of North Western Discovery. Expedition member Sergeant Patrick Gass later published his journal and used the phrase "Corps of Discovery," by which the expedition has become known.

Goals of the Expedition. Jefferson set forth the expedition's goals. The explorers were to observe, record, and when possible collect samples of the wildlife, plants, minerals, and other features of the west. Improving geographic knowledge was a key part of their mission as well. Like many geographers of the day, Jefferson believed that the Northwest Passage existed somewhere in North America and that it would offer an easy water route through the continent, or at least its western part, into the Pacific Ocean. He believed that such a passage would also offer an excellent trade route to Asia. Robert Gray's visit to the mouth of the Columbia River had raised hopes that he might have found the Pacific end of the passage, and Jefferson wanted Lewis and Clark to locate the inland part of the passage, if it existed. The explorers were instructed to go not just to the Rocky Mountains, the official boundary of U.S. territory, but all the way to the Pacific, and to map the terrain as they journeyed through it.

The expedition also had economic and political goals. The explorers were to identify a route to the known riches of the Pacific Northwest, such as sea otter pelts, and perhaps discover other valuable resources. They were also to establish political relationships with the Native American groups they met and to inform them that the Louisiana Territory had become part of the United States.

Finally, Jefferson hoped that the expedition would demonstrate to the world that Americans were interested in the northwestern part of the continent, where Britain was already challenging Spain's territorial claim. The west also seemed a likely rich source of fur, and Jefferson wanted Americans to have a share in that profitable trade, which otherwise might fall to the British.

The Route. The expedition began to take form in October 1803, when Lewis and Clark met on the Ohio River in present-day Indiana. With more than a dozen men and several boats, the two captains moved down the river to the Mississippi. Clark oversaw the building of a winter camp near St. Louis, and there the leaders and their crew spent several months recruiting and training additional expedition members and packing and sorting supplies.

The two men also reviewed their plans for the journey. They proposed to travel by boat up the Missouri River, which flows into the Mississippi from the northwest. Lewis and Clark both hoped that the river would prove to be navigable all the way to its headwater*, which they believed lay somewhere near the eastern slopes of the Rockies. They then planned to carry their canoes across the mountains, on the far side of which they expected to find the headwaters of the Columbia River. From there they planned to float down the river until they reached the Pacific Ocean.

*headwater source of a stream or river

Down the River to Mandan Country. On May 14, 1804, the Corps of Discovery left its winter camp near St. Louis and, as Clark wrote in his journal, "proceeded on under a jentle brease up the Missouri" in a 55-foot boat and two canoes. The expedition consisted of 29 members who would travel the entire journey and 15 temporary escorts who would help during the first stage of the journey. Among the core members were George Drouillard, who was part Native American, and York, Clark's African-American slave.

The first part of the journey was across somewhat familiar territory. Trappers and frontiersmen had visited the hospitable Mandan country in present-day North Dakota, and some French-Canadian traders lived among the Mandan Sioux people. These early stages were not

This drawing by Alfred Russell shows Sacagawea with members of the Lewis and Clark expedition. As a guide and Shoshone interpreter, Sacagawea played an important part in the expedition's success.

without adventure, however, especially for Lewis. On one occasion he nearly fell to his death while climbing a cliff to carve his name into a sandstone wall—he saved himself by jabbing his knife into a crevice in the rock. On another occasion he tasted an ore sample that poisoned him, but he medicated himself back to health. Along the way, the captains met with Native American leaders to tell them of the transfer of the land to the United States government. Lewis often handled this duty, which generally went smoothly, although the Teton Sioux of South Dakota, who favored the British, were hostile to the Americans. As the journey progressed, Clark assumed the role of the cartographer (mapmaker) of the expedition. Both captains kept journals and gathered samples of plants, animals, minerals, and Native American goods.

In October 1804 the travelers reached the Mandan country and built a winter camp called Fort Mandan. They spent the next five months there, during which time Lewis and Clark oversaw the building of canoes for the onward journey and prepared their notes and samples to be sent back to St. Louis in the spring. Clark drew a new map of the area between the Mississippi and Missouri Rivers. It was based not just on the expedition's observations but also on information he had gathered by talking with Indians and traders. At the end of the winter, the 15 escorts turned back to St. Louis, carrying with them natural-history samples and reports to be forwarded to Jefferson.

Up and Over the Rockies. In April 1805 the core members of the expedition headed upstream. Lewis and Clark employed a French-Canadian interpreter named Toussaint Charbonneau, who brought along his Shoshone wife, Sacagawea. Sacagawea would help Lewis and Clark win the friendship of the Shoshone people and also serve as an

*portage to carry boats of goods over land from one body of water to another

interpreter. A few weeks later the travelers portaged* their canoes for 18 miles to get around the Great Falls of the Missouri. Clark, who during the entire trip had carefully measured the distances and directions of travel and then mapped the route between major landmarks, did an especially thorough job of surveying and measuring this landmark. His maps often included notes on plant and animal life.

Above the falls, the explorers followed one branch of the Missouri up into the Rocky Mountains. Supplies were growing short, and they hoped to cross the mountains and reach the Columbia River before winter set in. They climbed steadily onward, and on August 12 they reached the continental divide, the line along the Rocky Mountain range that divides westward-flowing streams from eastward-flowing ones. They expected to see the terrain ahead descending toward plains, with the Columbia River to serve as a highway through them. Instead, they saw a wilderness of peaks stretching before them in all directions. They had entered west-central Idaho, one of the most mountainous regions of North America, and the Bitterroot Mountains lay between them and the water route to the Pacific. It was impossible to carry canoes through this tangle of mountains.

Fortunately for the weary travelers, the local Shoshone Indians provided food, guides, and especially horses for the difficult 50-day, 300-mile journey through the Bitterroots. Once the Corps reached the Clearwater River on the western side of the mountains, they received more help from the Nez Percé, who helped them build new canoes. In these vessels the expedition continued westward down the Clearwater. When that river emptied into the Snake River, they followed the Snake until it merged with the Columbia. Clark wrote on November 7, 1805, "Great joy in camp. We are now in view of the ocean."

The Fate of Meriwether Lewis

Lewis was always moody and prone to depression, and he was known to drink alcohol to excess. After the expedition, President Jefferson made him governor of Upper Louisiana, but Lewis delayed taking up his responsibilities, causing tensions in his relationship with Jefferson. When Lewis finally assumed his post, he only held the appointment for a year and a half. He then headed to Washington, D.C., to meet with heads of government. On the way he attempted suicide several times, and at a Tennessee tavern he died of two gunshot wounds. Rumors of murder swirled about the sad event, but most historians agree that Lewis's death was a suicide. President Jefferson and Clark both said it was suicide.

The Return. The long journey was only half over, however. The Corps of Discovery had to survive the winter on the Pacific coast and return to St. Louis the following spring. The captains selected a site on the Oregon coast, near present-day Astoria, and ordered the men to build Fort Clatsop, named for a Native American group that lived in the area. To Lewis and Clark's disappointment, because no ships visited the Columbia mouth while they were there, they had to abandon the possibility of returning to the United States by ship. They spent the entire winter in the chilly, rain-lashed fort.

In March 1806 Lewis and Clark began to retrace their path, paddling up the Columbia and Snake Rivers. Again with the help of Nez Percé guides, the party crossed the continental divide at a point slightly north of the pass they had used on the outward journey. At this point, the expedition split into two groups.

Clark led one group south to explore the Yellowstone River, which he followed east until it joined the Missouri not far from Fort Mandan. Lewis led the other group north to explore the Marias River, then traveled back along the main branch of the Missouri, reversing their outward journey. During this time Clark's party suffered some setbacks when a small band of Native Americans stole horses from them. Minor conflicts with the Blackfoot also vexed Lewis's party, but a greater trouble was the gunshot wound that Lewis suffered in the "thye"—one of his men shot him by accident. The two groups reunited as planned at the mouth of the Yellowstone, and after a stop in Mandan country, they floated down the Missouri, reaching St. Louis on September 23, 1806. Lewis and Clark and their men had been gone for almost two and a half years, and some had thought them dead.

A Wealth of Information. The Lewis and Clark expedition was a tremendous success. In a letter to President Jefferson, Lewis wrote, "In obedience to your orders we have penetrated the continent of North America to the Pacific Ocean, and sufficiently explored the interior of the country to affirm with confidence that we have discovered the most practicable rout which does exist across the continent by means of the navigable branches of the Missouri and Columbia Rivers."

The captains had also unearthed a wealth of natural-history information and specimens, greatly increasing the scientific knowledge of the continent. They also formed relationships with and gathered information about many Native American peoples. In his report to Jefferson about the route from the Mississippi to the Pacific, Lewis spelled out the obstacles but also pointed out that the mountainous country that they had crossed contained abundant wildlife and game. In particular, the expedition's accounts made it clear that the western rivers and lakes were teeming with beaver—within a few years, fur trappers and traders were combing the Rockies.

Some of the expedition's most important achievements were cartographic. Lewis and Clark had located several passes through the mountains and had gathered an abundance of other geographic information. Clark combined all the information into the first reliable map of the northern part of the American West, which was published in 1814 along with the expedition's official report. Explorers, traders, and settlers migrating westward would use his map for years to come.

Both Lewis and Clark received land grants and government posts as rewards for their service. Lewis, however, died only three years after the expedition's return, while Clark went on to serve as governor of the Missouri Territory and then superintendent of Indian Affairs. Clark died in St. Louis at age 68.

David Livingstone extensively explored central and southern Africa, unearthing much new information about the continent. He was also the first European to cross Africa. Although he experienced as many failures as he did successes during his journeys, Livingstone's courage and determination inspired future generations of British explorers.

Early Life and Career

Livingstone was the son of a Scottish tea salesman and evangelist* who handed out religious materials to his customers. His mother was a

David
LIVINGSTONE
1813–1873

EXPLORATION OF AFRICA

*evangelist one who preaches the Christian gospel

The School of Hard Knocks

Livingstone's formal schooling consisted of a short stint in night school; he was entirely self-taught. He worked daily from 6 A.M. to 8 P.M. at a cotton mill, attended two hours of night school, and then read when he got home. After the night school closed he took his books to the factory where he worked. According to his memoirs, he would place the book on part of the machine he operated, "so that I could catch sentence after sentence as I went by." In this way he taught himself Latin, Greek, and mathematics.

*missionary person who works to convert nonbelievers to his or her faith

*theology study of religion

*indigenous referring to the original inhabitants of a region

devout Presbyterian. The religious environment of Livingstone's youth influenced his later decision to become a missionary*.

Early Life and Studies. Livingstone was one of seven children, and grew up in poverty in Blantyre, a town near Glasgow, Scotland. At age ten he was forced to go to work to help support his family. As a result, he received no formal schooling as a child. However, he taught himself classics and mathematics well enough to later gain admittance to the University of Glasgow, where he studied Greek and theology*.

When Livingstone was 21, several British and American churches sent out a request for medical missionaries to serve in China. Inspired by the call, Livingstone intensified his studies and added medicine to his list of subjects to master. In 1838 the London Missionary Society accepted his application to prepare for the ministry. Two years later he was not only ordained as a minister but he also received a medical degree from the Faculty of Physicians and Surgeons at Glasgow.

Livingstone was to be disappointed in his first attempts at missionary work—the start of the first Opium War (1839–1842) between Britain and China ended his hopes of going to Asia. Shortly thereafter, Livingstone met the Scottish missionary Robert Moffat, who was known for his work in southern Africa. Moffat convinced Livingstone to choose Africa as the site of his missionary activities.

Arrival in Africa. In late 1840, Livingstone left for Cape Town, arriving there on March 14, 1841. A month later he reached Algoa Bay and from there he set out for Kuruman, a mission station established by Moffat some 700 miles north of Cape Town. The journey took ten weeks by oxcart. Livingstone became restless at Kuruman, and in 1843 he traveled 250 miles north to Mabotsa where he founded his own mission station.

By this time, Livingstone's activities had taken him farther into the Kalahari Desert than any other European had traveled. He became familiar with the languages and cultures of the peoples he met and he recruited indigenous* people as "native agents" to help spread the gospel. In 1844, on his way to set up a mission, Livingstone was attacked by a lion. His left arm was injured and he never regained full use of it.

Livingstone returned to Kuruman to recover from his injuries. During this time he married Moffat's daughter Mary. When Livingstone was again healthy, he and Mary went back to Mabotsa. But while there he quarreled with a fellow missionary and decided to strike out alone once again. In 1847 he established a new station at Kolobeng on the eastern border of the Kalahari. Within two years he would again be on the move.

Crossing the Continent

In 1849 Livingstone decided to preach to the Makololo people, who lived north of Kolobeng. At this time the Boers (British and the Dutch settlers) were engaged in a struggle for control of the region and Livingstone hoped that the presence of missionaries would prevent the Boers from taking that control.

Initial Explorations. Livingstone financed his mission by recruiting the support of a wealthy English game hunter named William Colton Oswell and one of the hunter's friends, Mungo Murray. Livingstone and the two Englishmen set out on June 1, 1849, with 80 oxen, 20 horses, 30 to 40 men, and an African guide, Ramotobi. The trip was very difficult, and several times the party ran out of water. They survived only because Ramotobi knew where to dig for water. On July 4 they reached the Zouga River (now the Botletle) and followed it for 280 miles, reaching Lake Ngami on August 1. However, the local chief refused to provide guides that would enable the Europeans to continue the 200-mile trip to where the Makololo lived, and the party had to return to Kolobeng.

The following year Livingstone set out to reach the Makololo, this time with his pregnant wife and their three children. Unfortunately, he was again forced to turn back when animals ravaged by tsetse flies that carried sleeping sickness, and malaria-carrying mosquitoes attacked the expedition. Two of his children fell ill with malaria and Mary gave birth to a girl who died of malaria six weeks later.

Despite these hardships, Livingstone took his family and Oswell on another trip in 1851. This expedition was as difficult as the previous one. The group, led by an inexperienced guide who eventually deserted, lost its way several times and at one point, went without water for four days. Livingstone wrote, "The less there was water, the more thirsty the little rogues became," referring to his children. When they finally found a water source, it was infested with tsetse flies that killed 43 of their oxen. Pressing on, the group reached Makololo country. In June 1851, while scouting the region for a site for a mission, Livingstone and his party came across the Zambezi River, becoming the first Europeans to discover that the river flowed that far into Africa.

After reaching the Zambezi, Livingstone "suddenly announced his intention of going down to the west coast," Oswell wrote. They were about 1,800 miles from the coast. However, Livingstone decided to first send his family home to England to spare them from "exposure to this unhealthy region." They headed back to Cape Town and in April 1852 they reached the coast. Mary and the children boarded a ship for London.

Coast-to-Coast. Livingstone returned to Kolobeng the following year, only to find that Boer raiders had destroyed the mission in an effort to drive out the missionaries. Undeterred, he continued on to Makololo country where Chief Sekelutu guided him up the Zambezi to find a site for a new mission. In November 1853 they reached the Makololo capital at Linyanti, where Sekelutu gave Livingstone 27 porters and guides to continue his trip. In February 1854, after traveling through the land of the Barotse people and around Lake Dilolo, Livingstone reached the Kasai, a tributary of the Congo River, which flows to the west coast.

Through his lectures on African culture and the evils of slave trade and his contributions to the geographical knowledge of central and southern Africa, David Livingstone helped spark great public interest in the continent.

Despite suffering from malaria the entire trip, Livingstone continued west along the river. A local chief once tried to force him to sell some of his men into slavery in return for food, but Livingstone refused. Finally, in May 1854, the expedition reached the coastal city of Luanda after a journey of some 1,500 miles. Livingstone had not found a satisfactory site to establish a mission. The group stayed in Luanda for four months before returning to the Zambezi.

When Livingstone reached Linyanti after a yearlong journey, he was suffering from malaria and rheumatic fever. He stayed there long enough to recover his strength before leaving again. Accompanied by Sekelutu and a bigger party than he had traveling west, Livingstone set out east on the Zambezi. Within a few weeks, he reached the magnificent waterfall the Africans called *Mosi-Ao-Tunya,* or "smoke that thunders." Livingstone renamed it Victoria Falls in honor of the English queen, claiming, "It had never before been seen by European eyes; but scenes so lovely must have been gazed upon by angels in their flight."

The party continued east and at the end of November 1855, they entered territory controlled by enemies of the Makololo. In the months that followed, they encountered many hostile groups and were forced to take detours away from the river. The detours caused them to lose time and caused their food supplies to run low. They avoided starvation only because they met a Portuguese scouting party from a nearby military outpost, who refilled their supplies. On May 20, 1856, when Livingstone and his men reached the port of Quelimane in present-day Mozambique, they became the first Europeans to travel across Africa.

When Livingstone's feat became public knowledge, the Royal Navy escorted him back to England. The British government named him Consul for the East Coast of Africa and gave him a cash reward, several assistants, and a steamship, *Ma-Robert,* to continue his explorations. However, the London Missionary Society felt that Livingstone's explorations were unrelated to missionary work, so he resigned from the society. By May 1858 Livingstone had returned to Africa.

Final Journeys

Livingstone planned to take the *Ma-Robert* up the Zambezi to find a water route to the interior. However, rapids and waterfalls upstream made the Zambezi impassable. He tried unsuccessfully two more times. On his third trip, he found Lake Nyasa (Lake Malawi) and one of the busiest slave routes in east Africa, but no good inland waterway.

Disappointment and Frustration. The following year Livingstone again went to Makololo country, where he found Sekelutu on his deathbed and the kingdom in turmoil. Livingstone returned to the coast and helped some newly arrived missionaries establish two new missions. However, these were eventually abandoned. In late 1861 he returned to explore Lake Nyasa. The following year, Mary joined Livingstone at Quelimane, but she died within three months of her arrival.

See the routes taken by Livingstone in his travels in the "Maps" section.

A despondent Livingstone made one last unsuccessful effort to find a water route to the interior. By this time all of his companions had died or had returned to England, and in July 1863 the government recalled Livingstone as well. Finding that the public was no longer interested in his latest adventures, he retired to a country estate. Before long, however, the Royal Geographical Society asked him to lead an expedition to seek the source of the Nile River. The English explorers Richard BURTON and John Hanning Speke had just returned from East Africa but each had a different opinion on the river's source. Speke believed that Lake Victoria was the river's source, but Burton, Livingstone, and others disagreed. Livingstone accepted the challenge and in 1866 undertook his last voyage of exploration in Africa.

Death in Africa. Livingstone was convinced that the Nile arose in a small lake in Tanganyika (now Tanzania) that the local people called Bangweulu. He assembled a party of 60 porters in Zanzibar and headed for Lake Nyasa, arriving there on August 8, 1866. From there they headed to Lake Tanganyika, which Livingstone believed would lead them to Bangweulu. However, the party was hit with a string of bad luck. A porter broke a crucial navigational instrument, another deserted with Livingstone's medicine chest, and by January 1867 the entire party had come down with fever. Livingstone, who was suffering from rheumatic fever, wrote, "I feel as if I had now received sentence of death."

Their luck changed when a party of Arab traders found and rescued the group and took them to Lake Mweru around November 1867. Livingstone then took four men and began his search for Bangweulu. They found the lake on July 18, 1868, but realized that it was not the Nile's source. Livingstone and his men were weary and they decided to travel to the town of Ujiji to join the Arabs who had earlier saved them. They reached Ujiji in March 1869, but found that their supplies had been stolen.

Livingstone was suffering from pneumonia and for the next year he traveled little. In March 1871 he again went out to explore but he never found any firm clues as to the source of the Nile. He returned to Ujiji, penniless and without food. Just when things looked the bleakest, he was found by Henry Morton STANLEY, an American journalist whose newspaper had sent him to look for Livingstone. "Dr. Livingstone, I presume," said Stanley when he found Livingstone, a remark that became famous in the history of exploration.

Stanley had brought with him greatly needed food and medicines with which he nursed Livingstone back to health. Soon the two men set out to explore Lake Tanganyika. Shortly thereafter Stanley left for the coast, but Livingstone remained to explore farther inland. In August 1872 he began explorations around the lake but he soon lost his way. Suffering from dysentery and severely bleeding hemorrhoids (mass of enlarged veins near the anus or rectum), he became so weak he could not walk. He wrote, "It is not all pleasure, this exploration." On the morning of May 1, 1873, his companions found him dead, kneeling beside his cot where he had said his prayers the night before.

Livingstone's companions cut out his vital organs and embalmed his body in raw salt. They then wrapped it in cloth and carried it to a trading town where they met an English expedition that was looking for the explorer. Livingstone's body was returned to England for a public funeral, after which he was buried in London's Westminster Abbey.

His Writings and Legacy. Livingstone recorded the details of his journeys in *Missionary Travels and Researches in South Africa, Narrative of an Expedition to the Zambesi and Its Tributaries, and of the Discoveries of the Lakes Sherwa and Nyassa, 1858–1864,* and *Last Journals of David Livingstone in Central Africa, from 1865 to His Death.* These works sold hundreds of thousands of copies and became a great influence on future explorers. In his three decades of travel and missionary work in Africa, Livingstone unearthed a complex body of geographic, social, cultural, medical, and technical knowledge about the region. He also believed that Africa could advance into the modern world on its own merit, inspiring a brand of African nationalism.

Shannon Wells LUCID

born 1943

SPACE EXPLORATION

Only the second American woman in space, Shannon Lucid is considered one of the nation's most accomplished astronauts. A veteran of many space shuttle missions, she has logged more hours in space than any American female astronaut. She also holds the record for the most hours in orbit by any non-Russian, and has recorded more flight hours in orbit than any woman in the world.

The daughter of American missionaries, Lucid was born in Shanghai, China, during World War II (1939–1945). At the time, Japanese forces were occupying China, and Lucid spent her early childhood in a Japanese detention camp. The family was eventually released as part of a prisoner exchange, and in 1949 they returned to the United States and settled in Bethany, Oklahoma.

Lucid enrolled at the University of Oklahoma and earned a B.S. in chemistry in 1963. She later received a master's degree and Ph.D. in biochemistry from the same institution. In 1974, after her graduation, she took a research position at the Oklahoma Medical Research Foundation and remained there until 1978, when she was one of the six women chosen that year for NASA's astronaut training program.

In 1985 Lucid undertook her first space mission. She spent seven days aboard a space shuttle during which she assisted the crew in deploying communications satellites and performing various experiments in X-ray astronomy and biomedicine. Four years later she returned to orbit on a five-day mission during which she helped launch the Galileo probe, which explored Jupiter. On this mission Lucid and other astronauts conducted research on radiation and lightning and a student experiment on growing ice crystals in space.

Between 1991 and 1993, Lucid was assigned to two more shuttle flights. During these missions she helped conduct various experiments that greatly increased knowledge of the physiology* of humans and

physiology science that deals with the functions of living organisms and their parts

animals in space as well as on earth. On one of these voyages she set the record as America's most experienced female astronaut.

Perhaps the culmination of Lucid's career was her fifth mission. On March 22, 1996, Lucid took off in the space shuttle *Atlantis,* which carried her to the Russian Space Station, *Mir.* She spent 188 days aboard the station, setting a duration record for a single mission by any American astronaut. The station orbited earth more than 3,000 times, traveling more than 75 million miles. Later she said that life aboard *Mir* was comparable to "living in a camper in the back of your pickup with your kids . . . when it's raining and no one can get out."

Lucid was scheduled to leave the station seven weeks earlier, but was delayed due to mechanical problems with the shuttle that was to pick her up, as well as bad weather during the next shuttle launch. She returned to earth in October and scientists conducted various studies to determine the effects of weightlessness (caused by the lack of gravity) on the human body. After returning to earth, Lucid was awarded the United States Congressional Space Medal of Honor and Russia's Order of Friendship. The latter is the highest civilian honor that country awards to noncitizens.

A fur trader and explorer, Alexander Mackenzie traced the course of a river in northern Canada that today bears his name. On a journey in 1793 he reached the Pacific Ocean, becoming the first European to cross the North American continent north of Mexico.

Early Life and Career. Mackenzie was born on the Isle of Lewis, in the Hebrides, Scotland. He received a good education. When he was still a child, he moved to New York with his widowed father and two aunts. In 1776 he moved again, this time to Montreal, Canada, where he was hired as a clerk in a small trading company. Shortly after Mackenzie joined the firm, it was absorbed by a larger concern, the North West Company. In 1785 the company sent Mackenzie to the Athabasca region of the present-day province of Alberta. Two years later he became a partner in the firm, and the following year he took charge of the Athabasca region. Mackenzie used a trading post on Lake Athabasca called Fort Chipewyan as a base from which he directed the company's fur trade in northwestern Canada. It was from here that he launched his celebrated expeditions of discovery.

The Disappointment River. From fellow trader Peter Pond, Mackenzie had heard of a river in northwestern Canada that led to the Pacific. Based on this information Mackenzie decided to lead an expedition west in search of the Northwest Passage*. On June 3, 1789, he left Fort Chipewyan with a group of voyageurs*, Indians, and their wives, and an Indian guide named "English Chief." The party headed north until they reached the Great Slave Lake in northwestern Canada. There they found the west-flowing river that Pond had spoken of and decided to follow its course. The expedition traveled northwest along the river,

Alexander
MACKENZIE

1762–1820

EXPLORATION OF CANADA

*Northwest Passage water route connecting the Atlantic and Pacific Oceans through the Arctic islands of northern Canada

*voyageur expert French-Canadian canoeists and guides in the North American wilderness in the 1700s and 1800s

covering a distance of about 1,100 miles until they reached the river's mouth on July 13, 1789. When Mackenzie saw large pieces of ice floating in the salty water, he realized that he had reached the Arctic Ocean and that he had failed to discover the Northwest Passage. He returned to Fort Chipewyan, recognizing that Pond had been mistaken. In a letter to his cousin, he called the river that he had traveled along "River Disappointment." It was later renamed Mackenzie River.

Dissatisfied with his mapping and navigational skills, Mackenzie traveled to England to study astronomy and cartography (mapmaking) in 1791. When he returned to Canada, he was armed with new instruments and sharpened skills, with which he began to plan his next expedition.

To the Pacific. In the spring of 1793, Mackenzie decided to again seek the route to the Pacific Ocean, which the indigenous* people called "the stinking lake." On May 9, he again set out with 7 voyageurs, 2 young Indian guides, a dog, and a 25-foot-long birch bark canoe. Heading west, Mackenzie and his party followed the Peace River to the Parsnip River and from there portaged* to the Fraser River, which Mackenzie mistakenly believed to be the Columbia River.

Mackenzie and his men traveled down the Fraser until they reached a place where a trading post named Alexandria was later built. There, Indians advised him to turn back because the river downstream was filled with rapids and waterfalls, so Mackenzie retraced his steps. Although still far from the coast, he refused to give up. The party loaded their supplies into packs weighing almost 90 pounds each and walked the rest of the way. They crossed mountain passes and streams and passed down the Bella Coola River in an Indian canoe. There they encountered trouble in the form of threats from hostile Indians, and at one point they lost their canoe.

Two weeks later the expedition reached the Pacific Ocean at Dean Channel, British Columbia. No other white explorer would reach the Pacific overland until LEWIS AND CLARK 12 years later. Here Mackenzie painted an inscription on a rock, "Alex Mackenzie from Canada by land 22d July 1793." The inscription can be seen in a park on the site today. The trip back was incredibly quick but exhausting, and by August 24, Mackenzie had returned to his base at Fort Chipewyan.

Later Life. In 1799 Mackenzie traveled to London, England, where he compiled a record of his travels. The work, *Voyage From Montreal on the River of St. Lawrence, Through the Continent of North America, to the Frozen and Pacific Oceans, in the years 1789 and 1793,* was published two years later. The work was highly influential, spurring President Jefferson to sponsor Lewis and Clark's expedition.

The following year, Mackenzie received the knighthood from King George III and returned to Canada to join the XY Company, rivals to the North West Company. He settled in Montreal and served four years in the Lower Canada Assembly (1804–1808) before retiring to an estate in Scotland in 1812. Eight years later he died on his way home from seeing a doctor in Edinburgh.

*indigenous referring to the original inhabitants of a region

*portage to carry boats or goods overland from one body of water to another

Alexander Mackenzie undertook many courageous expeditions, but it was not until eight years after his last journey, when his account of his journey was published, that the world learned of his adventures.

His Legacy. Interestingly, both of Mackenzie's journeys failed in their primary objectives. Rather than locating the Northwest Passage, his trip to the Arctic Ocean confirmed that the passage likely did not exist. His second trip was also disappointing, albeit from a commercial standpoint. The North West Company was expanding its fur trade in the Athabasca region and had hoped Mackenzie would find rivers to make it easier for them to ship furs to the east. However, Mackenzie discovered no major rivers there, and he also showed that the terrain in western Canada was too rugged for an overland route. Still, Mackenzie's missions added to the body of knowledge about the lands and peoples of northern Canada and filled in large sections of the map of that region.

The English geographer and educator Halford Mackinder is credited with establishing the discipline of geography in British universities. His insightful political writings anticipated developments such as the rise of the North Atlantic Treaty Organization (NATO), a military alliance between North American and European countries.

Halford John MACKINDER

1861–1947

GEOGRAPHY, POLITICS

Studies and Academic Achievements. Mackinder was born in the town of Gainsborough in eastern England. He entered Oxford University in 1880 to study natural sciences and later history, geology, and law. At that time geography was not a separate subject in British universities. After graduating in 1885, Mackinder became a geography lecturer at Oxford's extension service, which provided education to those who could not afford the university. His teaching focused on what he called "the new geography," in which he sought to establish the relationship between the sciences and the humanities. Mackinder's lectures at the extension were very popular, prompting the Royal Geographical Society in London to ask him to give a speech to its members. In 1887 the society convinced Oxford to appoint Mackinder the first reader, or lecturer, in geography at a British university.

Five years later, Mackinder was named principal of the newly established Oxford University Extension College at Reading, a city near London. Shortly thereafter he became a part-time lecturer at the London School of Economics. In 1899 Mackinder had two impressive accomplishments—he led an expedition to East Africa, becoming the first to reach the summit of Mount Kenya; and he became the first director of the Oxford School of Geography, which was opened by the Royal Geographical Society and Oxford University.

Important Writings. In the early 1900s Mackinder wrote two of his most influential works. In his book *Britain and the British Seas*, he presented his ideas about "the new geography" in coherent and engaging language. The work is considered an important milestone in British geographical writing. His other work, a paper titled "The Geographical Pivot of History," examines the importance of eastern Europe and Asia in maintaining the balance of world power. Mackinder argued that Asia and eastern Europe had become the strategic "pivot areas" or "heartlands" of the world. According to Mackinder, whoever controlled the "heartland" would control the world.

Mackinder elaborated on these ideas in a book called *Democratic Ideals and Reality,* published in 1919 after World War I. He suggested that Britain and the United States should act as a balance against nations trying to control the "heartland." He also favored the creation of smaller states between Germany and Russia, which occurred as a result of the peace treaty ending the war.

The book contains other astute observations. Mackinder supported regional organizations of minor powers and warned that if Germany descended into chaos, a dictator would emerge. These things came to pass in the years after the book was written. Mackinder also published a theory that western Europe and North America could combine to offset the power of any country that controlled the "heartland"—an idea that occurred with the formation of NATO after World War II (1939–1945).

Mackinder also led an active life in politics. In 1910 he was elected to the British Parliament, where he was a strong supporter of imperialism*. He was named British High Commissioner to Russia, and he tried, without success, to organize the forces fighting against the Bolsheviks (Russian revolutionaries). He was knighted for his efforts, but he lost his Parliament seat in 1922. Thereafter he served as chairman of the Imperial Shipping and the Imperial Economic Committees. Mackinder received awards from both the Royal and the American Geographical Societies honoring his life's work. He died at the age of 86 in Dorset.

*imperialism policy of extending the national power by gaining territory and economic and political control over other areas

Ferdinand MAGELLAN
ca. 1480–1521
NAVIGATION

Ferdinand Magellan commanded the first voyage around the world (circumnavigation), but the explorer himself died before the voyage was complete. Magellan achieved two milestones in the history of geography and exploration: he discovered the long-sought sea route from the Atlantic Ocean to the Pacific Ocean, and he led the first expedition to make a documented crossing of the Pacific, the world's largest body of water. Magellan's historic voyage resulted in a new era of geographic knowledge, the expansion of the spice trade with Southeast Asia, and the Spanish colonization of the Philippines.

His Background. Magellan was born around 1480 in Sabrosa, Portugal. His name was originally Fernão de Magalhães, but was later changed to Fernando de Magallanes in Spanish and Ferdinand Magellan in English.

The tradition of Portuguese maritime* exploration was more than a century old at the time of Magellan's birth. For many years ships from Portugal had been exploring the waters off Africa's western coast, seeking a sea route from Europe to Asia around Africa. Magellan was still a young boy when Bartolomeu Dias sailed around the Cape of

*maritime of or relating to navigation or commerce on the sea

Good Hope at the southern tip of Africa, opening a Portuguese sea route to the Indian Ocean. Ten years later, Vasco da GAMA led an expedition to India along the route that Dias had pioneered.

Sandwiched between Dias's triumph and Gama's was Christopher COLUMBUS's voyage to the Americas; Columbus sailed for Spain. Like Portugal, Spain sought a sea route to the Indies (the European name for India and the lands east of it). With the Portuguese claiming the eastern route around Africa, Columbus turned west to reach the Indies. The fact that he landed in America and not the Indies did not prevent the mariners of many nations from following in his path, hoping to find a passage to India by sailing through or around the new western lands that Columbus had located. The world-changing voyages of Dias, Columbus, Gama, and others formed the background of Magellan's boyhood.

Born into a noble family, Magellan served as a page, or attendant, at the court of the Portuguese queen during his teens. In 1505 he joined the Portuguese viceroy* Francisco de Almeida's fleet, whose mission was to establish Portuguese superiority over Muslim powers in Africa and India. In the years that followed, Magellan took part in Portuguese military actions in eastern Africa, India, and Malacca (in present-day Malaysia).

*viceroy governor of a province or colony, ruling as the representative of a king or queen

To the Spice Islands. Francisco Serrão, a shipmate and comrade of Magellan's, traveled east from Malacca to the group of Indonesian islands called the Moluccas. These were also known as the Spice Islands because they were a source of cloves and the other spices that, along with silks, pearls, and gems, attracted Europeans to the markets of Asia. Some sources say that Magellan accompanied Serrão to the Moluccas, but this claim cannot be proved. Serrão, however, is known to have remained in Ternate, one of the islands of the Moluccas, where he became friendly with a local ruler. In a letter to Magellan, he described the wealth of the islands.

By 1513 Magellan had returned to Portugal. He joined briefly in a Portuguese attack on Morocco in North Africa, but a dispute over his conduct during the war caused the Portuguese king Manuel to become displeased with him. The king refused to increase Magellan's monthly income. He also refused to authorize or pay for an expedition that Magellan wanted to lead to the Moluccas.

Frustrated and disappointed, Magellan decided to look for another patron. He moved to Seville, Spain, where he gained the attention of the Spanish king Charles I, who was also Emperor Charles V of the Holy Roman Empire. There was no doubt that India, Malacca, and at least some of the Moluccas lay within the portion of the world then claimed by Portugal. However, with the help of Rui Faleiro, a Portuguese astronomer who had also moved to Spain, Magellan argued that the Moluccas stretched so far eastward that some of the islands were outside Portugal's territory. He claimed that according to the Treaty of Tordesillas that Spain and Portugal had signed in 1494, some of the islands lay in the part of the world that fell under Spain's control.

The Treaty of Tordesillas

When Portugal and Spain began to explore different routes to Asia, it was unclear who would own new lands found along the way. The two nations asked the pope to settle the question. The pope proposed the terms of what became the Treaty of Tordesillas, which Spain and Portugal signed in 1494, dividing the yet-undiscovered parts of the world between them. Portugal received claims to everything east of a north-south line through the Atlantic. Everything west of the line went to Spain. Brazil, which lay east of the line, fell under the Portuguese. The rest of South America and the islands in the Pacific including the Philippines became Spanish territory.

---

*strait narrow waterway that runs between two landmasses and links two bodies of water

Like Columbus, Magellan proposed to sail west to reach the distant east. He would avoid the Portuguese waters around Africa and the Indian Ocean and instead seek a passage through the Americas into the South Sea, the ocean that Spanish explorer Vasco Núñez de BALBOA had seen west of Panama in Central America. Magellan was sure that once he reached the South Sea he could simply sail across it to the Indies.

Charles agreed to sponsor Magellan's expedition, which was outfitted in Seville. Portuguese agents tried to sabotage the preparations, but their efforts to keep Magellan from sailing for Spain failed. Magellan said farewell to the Spanish woman he had married several years earlier and to his infant son, and on September 20, 1519, his fleet of five ships and about 270 men sailed from the port of Sanlúcar de Barrameda into the Atlantic. The expedition's first goal was to reach Brazil because Magellan believed that the passage he sought, referred to in his agreement with King Charles as "the strait*," would be found in the southern part of the American lands.

The Strait of Magellan. Even before the expedition crossed the Atlantic Ocean, it ran into trouble. First it was slowed by a lack of winds, and then storms battered the ships. Moreover, Cartagena, one of several Spanish captains in the group who resented taking orders from a foreigner, led a mutiny against Magellan, but the commander quelled the uprising and imprisoned Cartagena.

Finally, on December 13, the ships reached the bay of present-day Rio de Janeiro, Brazil. After restocking their supplies of water and fresh food, Magellan and his crew sailed down the coast, examining each river mouth and bay in the hope that it would prove to be the strait that would carry them west into the other ocean. Each time, they were disappointed. They traveled for weeks and the strait did not appear, and by March 1520, the southern hemisphere's winter had begun. Because cold weather and storms prevented the fleet from going farther, the men spent the winter months camped at Port St. Julian on the coast of present-day Argentina. During this time, one ship, the *Santiago,* went ahead to scout the coast farther south, but it was wrecked.

The winter also brought a second and larger mutiny, again led by Cartagena, whom Magellan had released from imprisonment. With the help of officers and men who remained loyal, Magellan managed to again put down the mutiny. The commander then executed some of those who had rebelled, including one of the Spanish captains. Magellan also decided to take no further chances with the ringleader. He marooned Cartagena, leaving him behind on the desolate shore when the fleet again set sail on August 24, 1520, at the onset of spring.

After several months of probing the coast, Magellan and his men finally located a passage that appeared to lead west. This winding waterway, between the tip of the South American continent and a large island off the southern coast, is now called the Strait of Magellan. As the ships passed through the strait, the Portuguese travelers noticed

Indian campfires in the distance and named the place Tierra del Fuego (Land of Fire). The island south of the strait still bears that name.

While Magellan and the other captains were picking their way through the strait, finding the right passage among a maze of channels, one of the Spanish captains deserted, taking his ship, the *San Antonio*, back to Spain. Unfortunately for Magellan and the others on the three ships that remained in the fleet, the deserting vessel held a large share of the expedition's food stores.

The *Trinidad*, the *Concepción*, and the *Victoria* continued through the strait, taking more than a month to travel its length. On November 28, the three ships sailed out of its western end into the open sea. South America was now on their right, east of them. Ahead stretched the ocean, and beyond the ocean, Magellan was certain, lay the Indies.

Across the Pacific. Magellan was right in thinking that Asia lay on the far shore of the South Sea, which he renamed Pacific (Peaceful) because its waters were calm during his voyage. His big mistake, however, was in underestimating the size of the earth—and the size of the Pacific. He incorrectly believed that after a few days' sailing west, he would have successfully commanded his fleet to Asia. Despite the shortage of food, the captains and crew set forth, eagerly looking forward to the riches and luxuries of the Indies.

Magellan first set his course north along the coast of Chile, but later steered northwestward into the unknown. Very soon conditions aboard the ships went from bad to dreadful. Supplies of drinking water became foul, and food ran out. The men had to eat moldy flour that had become infested with beetle larvae and fouled with rat droppings. When that ran out, they devoured the rats—a sailor lucky enough to capture one of the beasts could sell it for a handsome sum. The starving men also ate sawdust and gnawed on bits of leather, hoping to dull the pangs of hunger. A number of them died of scurvy, a vitamin-deficiency disease caused by a shortage of fresh fruits and vegetables.

Historians are not certain what course Magellan followed across the Pacific. According to the accounts of Antonio Pigafetta, an Italian member of the expedition who greatly admired the navigator, the men sighted many islands that appeared to be uninhabited. On March 6, 1521, after 99 days without fresh water and food, the fleet made landfall at an island, probably Guam in the Marianas group, and acquired food from the local people. The long Pacific crossing was over.

The Circumnavigation. After stopping for just three days, Magellan moved his fleet on from Guam, continuing to sail west and later south. The explorers soon encountered the island chain that would become known as the Philippines. Magellan stopped at Samar, Cebu, and other islands in the group, attempting to convert the inhabitants to Christianity and to make the local chieftains into loyal allies of Spain.

A few weeks later Magellan became involved in a conflict between two local chieftains and was killed in a fight. The two men who

When Ferdinand Magellan encountered in the Philippines a group of nobles who resisted conversion to Christianity, he challenged them to a duel. In full body armor, he thought himself invincible until a spear through his foot slowed him down, leading ultimately to his death. Magellan never completed the circumnavigation that he had masterminded.

became the expedition's leaders after Magellan's death were themselves killed a few days later, leaving the fleet disorganized and without a leader, nearly halfway around the world from home.

The 108 surviving crew elected the pilot João Lopes Carvalho as their new leader. They boarded the *Trinidad* and the *Victoria,* abandoning the *Concepción,* and sailed south from the Philippines on a quest to reach Magellan's goal, the Moluccas. Carvalho directed them on a wandering course through the East Indies and captured and looted local vessels whenever he encountered them. He remained in command only until September 1521, when two seamen—Gonzalo Gómez de Espinosa and Sebastián del Cano, or Elcano—took control.

Elcano guided the two ships to the Moluccas, but when they arrived there they learned that Serrão, Magellan's friend, had been killed. Moreover, they heard that Portuguese ships were due to arrive in the Moluccas at any time and realized that the men aboard those ships would be most displeased to find the ragged remnants of a Spanish fleet in what they considered Portuguese territory. The Spanish expedition hurriedly left the Moluccas, but not before filling the holds of the two ships with whatever food supplies and spices they could obtain. The food, they hoped, would keep them alive to reach Spain, while the spices might win them their fortunes, or at least the king's goodwill.

Elcano and the *Victoria* left the Spice Islands in December 1521. He decided to sail west across the Indian Ocean and return to the Atlantic by passing around Africa's Cape of Good Hope. The *Trinidad* needed repairs and was not ready to leave the Moluccas until the following April. Espinosa planned to return to Spain by sailing back along the expedition's outward-bound route: across the Pacific to South America, back through the Strait of Magellan, and across the Atlantic. The Portuguese captured Espinosa and his men, however, and those who were not killed were imprisoned. The *Trinidad* never returned to Spain.

Elcano was more fortunate. Although the *Victoria* sailed through Portuguese trade routes in its journey across the Indian Ocean and around the Cape of Good Hope, it was not captured. In September 1522, the ship and 22 men—18 survivors of the original expedition and four Indian captives from South America—sailed into port in Spain. Pigafetta, one of the survivors, wrote that they were "weaker than men have ever been before," but the spices in their ship's hold were worth more than the cost of the entire expedition.

King Charles honored Elcano by adding a globe to the navigator's coat of arms. Accompanying it were the Latin words *Primus circumdedisti me* ("You were first to encircle me"). Although Elcano had completed the circumnavigation, it was Magellan's vision, determination, and leadership that drove the expedition on through the strait and across the unknown ocean. The achievements of Magellan and Elcano together proved to geographers that the world's oceans are connected and that it *is* possible to reach the east by sailing west.

Alejandro Malaspina, a Spanish naval officer, undertook several important voyages of exploration, but he is best known for his investigations of the Pacific Ocean. Malaspina's voyages helped advance Spain's political strength in its colonies in the Pacific Ocean.

Malaspina was born in Mulazzo in Parma, Italy. As a young adult, he traveled to Malta, where he learned to sail. In 1774 he joined the Royal Spanish Navy, and for the next two years he participated in numerous sea battles and earned several promotions. As a junior officer aboard the frigate* *La Astrea,* Malaspina made his first major voyage between 1777 and 1779. The Philippines-bound vessel traveled in both directions by way of the Cape of Good Hope on the southern tip of Africa. After the voyage, Malaspina once again took part in naval warfare and continued his rise through the ranks. He returned to the Philippines for a shorter voyage in the mid-1780s, this time serving as second-in-command on his ship, *Asunción.*

Around this time Malaspina's interests began to shift from warfare to commerce, politics, and science. Cartography (mapmaking), in particular, began to intrigue him, and he spent some time charting parts of the coast of Spain. Between 1786 and 1788, as commander of *La Astrea,* Malaspina also undertook a commercial voyage around the world.

These interests culminated in 1788, when Malaspina proposed a voyage of exploration to the Spanish government. His plan was to visit nearly all the Spanish possessions in Asia and in the Americas, survey and map poorly known stretches of the oceans, claim any new and important discoveries for Spain, and help ensure that Spain still held sway over its distant possessions. Because his proposal had both scientific and political value, the Spanish government financed the voyage and gave him two ships, the *Descubierta* and the *Atrevida.*

On July 30, 1789, Malaspina sailed from the Spanish port of Cádiz and began what would become a five-year voyage. The expedition sailed west to Brazil and then continued south, stopping at Tierra del Fuego and rounding Cape Horn on the southern tip of South America. Moving slowly north along the eastern shores of the Pacific Ocean, Malaspina stopped often to visit Spanish-held ports and to survey the South American coastline.

Following orders from King Charles IV of Spain, he then began an unsuccessful attempt to find a Northwest Passage* across northern North America. From Acapulco, Mexico, he sailed north and explored the Alaskan coastline. An early visitor to the shores of present-day Oregon and Washington, he sent several officers inland to explore the region around Vancouver Island. He sailed as far north as present-day Juneau, Alaska, but turned back when he encountered a glacier that today bears his name. Malaspina left North America and headed west to the Philippines and Australia. Along the way, as before, he surveyed and mapped coastlines and investigated the political and economic conditions in Spanish colonies.

Malaspina then recrossed the Pacific Ocean and sailed home by way of Cape Horn, arriving in Cádiz in September 1794. The voyage

---

Alejandro
MALASPINA

1754–1810

NAVAL EXPLORATION

*frigate small warship

*Northwest Passage water route connecting the Atlantic and Pacific Oceans through the Arctic islands of northern Canada

had lasted just over five years. He was received by the king and was awarded yet another naval promotion; his future seemed bright. However, before Malaspina could publish the scientific data he had gathered from his voyage, he made a political misstep by suggesting that Spain free its American colonies. The idea offended the Spanish government and Malaspina was arrested.

In the ensuing trial, Malaspina was stripped of his naval rank and imprisoned in an isolated castle, where he wrote essays on art and economics. Later exiled to Parma, his birthplace, he died at the age of 55. An account of his five-year voyage was finally published in 1885.

Jacques MARQUETTE

1637–1675

EXPLORATION OF NORTH AMERICA

*missionary person who works to convert nonbelievers to his or her faith

*indigenous referring to the original inhabitants of a region

*strait narrow waterway that runs between two landmasses and links two bodies of water

A missionary* and an explorer, Jacques Marquette was one of the first Europeans to explore the upper Mississippi Valley. Together with the French-Canadian explorer and fur trader Louis Jolliet, Marquette traveled through the American Midwest, recording his impressions of the region in maps and diary entries. His journal provided the Europeans with valuable information about the Mississippi Valley and the Great Lakes region and is the only surviving record of their journey.

Marquette was born in Laon, France. As a young man, he joined the Society of Jesus, a religious order, and spent several years teaching at Jesuit schools in France. In 1665 he expressed to his supervisors his desire to travel to North America and to become a missionary among the Native Americans. This desire became a reality the following year, when Marquette was sent to the town of Trois Rivières in Quebec.

Marquette had a gift for learning languages, and in Quebec, his superiors put him to work studying the language of the Huron. Two years later he was sent to Sault Ste. Marie (now in Ontario), a region populated at the time almost entirely by Native Americans. During the years that followed, Marquette lived at various missions along the shores of the western Great Lakes, converting to Christianity members of the Ottawa, Huron, and other indigenous* groups. He also founded the mission of St. Ignace near the Straits* of Mackinac in Michigan.

While in Sault Ste. Marie, Marquette befriended Louis Jolliet, who had a proposition for Marquette. Jolliet had heard rumors of a great river to the south that was known only to the Native Americans; he wanted to find it, and he asked Marquette to accompany him on the journey. On May 17, 1673, Marquette, Jolliet, and five other Canadians set out from St. Ignace in two bark canoes.

The purpose of the voyage was threefold. Marquette and Jolliet hoped to learn about the geography of the upper Mississippi and the culture of its people. They also believed that the expedition would strengthen France's claim to the region and at the same time weaken England's control. Finally, there was a religious purpose to the expedition; the men hoped to convert all the Native Americans they encountered and to lay the groundwork for future conversions.

The mission headed south from St. Ignace into Lake Michigan and through Green Bay on the western shore of the lake. From there they paddled up Fox River and carried their boats over land to the Wisconsin River, which led directly into the Mississippi. Although the Spanish explorer Hernando de Soto had visited the lower Mississippi almost a century earlier, Marquette and Jolliet's was the first European expedition to visit the upper part of the river.

The voyagers continued south along the Mississippi until its junction with the Arkansas River, where they stopped and turned around. They had established that the river runs into the Gulf of Mexico and not into the Pacific; they also worried that they were getting too close to Spanish territory. Marquette and Jolliet continued north, upstream to the Illinois River, sailed through the Des Plaines, and portaged (carried over land) their boats to the Chicago River. From there they traveled into the southern part of Lake Michigan and back to Green Bay sometime at the end of September.

Marquette spent part of the 5-month, 2,500-mile journey drawing detailed maps and recording his impressions in a journal. He also preached to the Native Americans he met along the way. Marquette found the trip arduous, however, and his health was seriously compromised. He remained at the mission of Saint Francis Xavier near the head of the Green Bay River in Wisconsin for a year to recover from the journey.

In October 1674, Marquette set out to establish a mission among the Illinois Indians farther south. Unfortunately, he left too late in the year, and cold weather forced him to spend the winter near present-day Chicago, short of his destination. The following spring, he completed his journey, but he did not spend much time with the Illinois because his health had again become a concern. Marquette set out to return to his mission at St. Ignace but died along the way near the mouth of a river that today bears his name. Marquette's journal from his journey was later published in the *Jesuit Relations,* annual reports written by French Jesuit missionaries at their stations in New France*.

Counties in the states of Michigan and Wisconsin; a city in Wisconsin; and a Catholic, Jesuit university in Milwaukee, Wisconsin, were renamed in Marquette's honor.

Within two years of his arrival in New France, Jacques Marquette learned six Native American languages.

*New France French colony in North America that included the Great Lakes, the St. Lawrence River valley, and until 1713, Acadia (present-day Nova Scotia)

At various times in his life, George Marsh served as a lawyer, lecturer, politician, diplomat*, newspaper editor, sheep farmer, and mill owner. But his greatest distinction was his role as America's first environmentalist. His masterpiece, *Man and Nature,* was the first work to study the impact of human action on the ecology of the earth.

Early Life and Work. Marsh was born in Woodstock, Vermont, and spent much of his youth in the woods with his father, a U.S. senator,

George Perkins
MARSH

1801–1882

GEOGRAPHY

*diplomat one who conducts official relations and negotiations between nations

who instilled in the youth an interest in nature. As a child Marsh suffered from eye problems that prevented him from reading for long stretches of time. As a result, he often asked people to read to him, developing a magnificent memory from the practice.

Despite his disability, Marsh was an outstanding scholar. He enrolled at Dartmouth College, majoring in law. In 1820, when he graduated from Dartmouth, he opened a law practice, but he continued to study languages, classical literature, soil conservation, and forestry. By age 30 he had become fluent in 20 languages and had written a book on the origins of the English language.

Marsh then worked for a time in Vermont's forest industry, where he first noted the relationship between human activity and environmental change. In an 1847 speech to a local agricultural society he commented on the links between deforestation and soil erosion. He said that the changes he saw "within a single generation, are too striking to have escaped the attention of any observing person. The signs of artificial improvement are mingled with the tokens of improvident waste."

Politician and Ambassador. In 1843 Marsh was elected to the United States Congress. After two terms Marsh was appointed U.S. Ambassador to Turkey by President Zachary Taylor. While in the Middle East, Marsh traveled throughout Egypt and Arabia, where he observed how the Arabs used camels for transportation across the desert, and felt that the animals could be employed in the American southwest. After he returned to the United States, Marsh gave a lecture that inspired the Congress to order 74 camels from the Middle East for use in Texas. However, the army's unfamiliarity with the camel's habits, as well as the outbreak of the Civil War, doomed the experiment to failure.

Marsh was recalled from Turkey in 1852, and for the next nine years he lectured in English and etymology (the study of word origins) at Columbia University and the Lowell Institute. In 1861 President Lincoln named Marsh the country's first ambassador to the newly united kingdom of Italy. He served in that capacity until his death 21 years later.

Man and Nature. In 1864 Marsh published *Man and Nature; or Physical Geography as Modified by Human Action,* which was the first book to suggest that humans were active agents of environmental change. At the time, most scholars argued that the state of the physical environment was completely the result of natural phenomena. No one had seriously considered humans as having a significant impact on the environment.

Marsh also emphasized that human activities have long-term effects, even some that are not immediately apparent. His ideas were enthusiastically received by scientists and the public, and had many practical consequences. Among these were the establishment of the Arbor Day movement, forest reserves, and America's system of national forests. Marsh's work laid the foundation for the environmental movement that emerged in the 1900s.

al-MAS'UDI

ca. 890–ca. 956

GEOGRAPHY, HISTORY

Al-Mas'udi was an Arabic historian and geographer noted for his writings that combined history and geography. Known as the "Herodotus of the Arabs," al-Mas'udi traveled widely and recorded his observations in several works that are early masterpieces of history and geography.

Life and Travels. Al-Mas'udi was born Abu al-Hasan Ali ibn al-Husayn al-Mas'udi in Baghdad (in present-day Iraq) at a time when the city was a center of learning and commerce. Little is known about his life except that he was the descendant of a companion of the prophet Muhammad, the founder of Islam. Al-Mas'udi was a keen student with an excellent memory and strong writing skills. He showed a wide variety of interests ranging from history and geography to sciences and religion.

Al-Mas'udi valued book learning, but he also believed that true knowledge came from traveling to different places and by observing firsthand the people, places, religion, and customs of the peoples. His accounts also contain tales, myths, and legends that he learned from his discussions with men who had traveled to various parts of the world. As a result, it is not always obvious which of the places he described he actually visited. Moreover, the sequence of his travels and the times he visited various countries are not always clear.

Around 915, al-Mas'udi left Baghdad and spent most of the rest of his life traveling in Asia and Africa. His journeys took him to Iran, Syria, Armenia, Arabia, Zanzibar, East Africa, India, Sri Lanka, and possibly to Madagascar. He returned to Baghdad periodically but again resumed his journeys. Near the end of his life, he settled in the town of al-Faustat (present-day Cairo), where he died in about 956.

Scholarly Writings. Al-Mas'udi was a prolific writer; scholars have found evidence of 37 works from his surviving writings and from other sources. One of his earliest works describes the customs of Jews, Christians, Indians, and Iranians as well as the geography and climate of the places he visited. He followed with his 30-volume masterwork, *Reports of the Age.* It contains a comprehensive world history covering politics, social customs, geography, and many other aspects of human activity. Only one copy of a single volume exists today. Al-Mas'udi next wrote *The Book of the Middle,* which scholars consider a supplement to his first work. His early works had little impact on the scholars of his day, perhaps because of their great length.

Al-Mas'udi's best-known work is *The Meadows of Gold and Mines of Precious Stones,* which is a combination of his two previous histories. Unlike the others, it quickly became popular and established al-Mas'udi as one of the leading Arab historians. In fact, one of the great Arab philosophers of history, Ibn Khaldun, later called al-Mas'udi an *imam* (a "leader" or "example") for historians.

The Meadows contains an account of the creation of the world, examines Jewish history, and discusses the history of non-Islamic lands including Greece, Rome, and India. Al-Mas'udi also described how the philosophers of ancient Greece and India explained the origin and shape of the earth and included an Arabic version of the ancient Greek geographer PTOLEMY's writings. In addition to history and geography, *The Meadows* outlines social and religious customs, climate, calendars, and other aspects of these ancient societies. The book also contains a history of Islam beginning with the life of Muhammad and covers the reign of each caliph (Muslim ruler considered the successor of Muhammad) down to al-Mas'udi's lifetime.

Al-Mas'udi's Philosophy. Al-Mas'udi's works are unique because of his philosophy of knowledge. Instead of focusing solely on political events, al-Mas'udi concentrated on economic, religious, and cultural issues as well. His approach to history, unlike that of most Muslim scholars, was secular rather than religious. He refused to follow the example of scholars who forced their ideas to conform to principles set forth in the Muslim holy book, the Qur'an.

He believed that to paint an accurate picture of history, one must seek the primary sources of information. He refused to rely solely on so-called "authoritative" sources and instead traveled widely to seek information firsthand and to learn about faraway places and people from travelers, merchants, peasants, and sailors. Al-Mas'udi adopted this method during an era in which scholars uncritically accepted the authority of ancient sources and considered such knowledge superior to any gained by observation.

For example, he did not adhere to the idea of a great southern continent, proposed by Ptolemy. According to Ptolemy, the Indian Ocean was surrounded on all sides by land except for an opening for the Pacific Ocean to the west. Al-Mas'udi correctly refuted the idea based on the accounts of sailors who had worked in the region. It is just one example of the triumph of al-Mas'udi's approach to the study of geography and to all branches of knowledge.

Matthew Fontaine
MAURY

1806–1873

PHYSICAL GEOGRAPHY, METEOROLOGY, OCEANOGRAPHY

*oceanography study of oceans

A naval officer and scientist, Matthew Fontaine Maury is remembered today as a founder of modern oceanography*. He gathered large amounts of data on ocean depths, currents, and winds that led to an increased understanding of weather and the oceans. Although other scientists often disagreed with Maury's interpretations of data, few denied his overall scientific achievements.

Maury was born near Fredericksburg, Virginia, but he grew up in Tennessee. The son of a planter, he joined the United States Navy at the age of 19. Five years later he became a member of the crew of the *Vincennes,* the first American naval ship to circumnavigate the globe. Later, he undertook a three-year voyage to the western shore of South America. These journeys helped spark Maury's interest in weather, navigation, and the oceans.

His scientific career began in 1836, when he published two articles and a textbook on navigation. Three years later, however, a stagecoach accident caused a physical handicap that left him unable to continue active shipboard duty. Maury remained a naval officer but he served in Washington, D.C., writing vigorously on naval reform and those branches of science he believed could be applied to seafaring. In 1842 he was placed in charge of the navy's Depot of Charts and Instruments—the forerunner of today's Naval Observatory and Hydrographic* Office.

As director of the agency, Maury systematically studied numerous ships' logs for information on currents and winds. He used this valuable data to create charts showing typical wind and current patterns in various oceans. He began to publish his *Wind and Current Charts* and issued copies to naval and merchant captains in exchange for access to their logbooks. Over the years his charts became increasingly accurate, resulting in a series of charts and accompanying sailing directions that presented a climatic picture of the surface winds and currents for all the oceans.

Maury next became involved in measuring the depth of the oceans. Under his direction, U.S. naval ships in the North Atlantic used sound waves to measure ocean depths over a five-year period. Maury expressed the data in chart form, producing the first maps that accurately showed the ocean floor. The first transatlantic telegraph cable was placed according to a route suggested by Maury's charts. His charts of winds, currents, and the ocean floor soon captured the world's attention. His work represented a leap ahead from earlier, less accurate charts, and sea captains found them invaluable in planning and undertaking voyages.

Although his charts added to scientific knowledge of the oceans, Maury's chief aim was the promotion of maritime commerce. The more that mariners knew about the oceans, he reasoned, the easier it would be to send trade ships from one port to another. His work had an effect on international cooperation as well. In 1853, he helped organize an international marine conference. The participants agreed to work toward standardizing observations and measurements at sea, especially where weather conditions were concerned. Maury hoped to extend this kind of cooperation to weather observation on land, but that did not occur until after his death.

Maury's achievements earned him the praise of many prominent scientists but he also received some criticism for his interpretations of oceanographic and meteorological data. He believed, for example, that variations in the wind were due to the earth's magnetism, and that the sea around the North Pole was free of ice. Many scientists of the time doubted these theories, which have since been proven false. Still, Maury received many awards for his work, including decorations from the rulers of Denmark, Portugal, and Russia; honorary degrees from several American universities; and membership in prestigious scientific academies and societies.

In 1861 Maury resigned his naval commission to serve the Confederate Navy. After the war, he tried unsuccessfully to establish a confederate colony in Mexico. He then returned to Virginia, where he wrote several geography textbooks and taught at a military school. Maury died at the age of 67 in Lexington, Virginia.

*hydrographic of or relating to hydrography, the mapping or charting of bodies of water

Donald W.
MEINIG

born 1924

GEOGRAPHY

*diplomat one who conducts official relations and negotiations between nations

One of the leading geographers in the United States, Donald W. Meinig is best known for bringing history into the study of geography—and by the same token, including geographical studies in history. His many influential publications helped establish the concept of historical geography as an important academic discipline in the United States. Inquisitive and hardworking, Meinig became a dedicated researcher and writer who also greatly influenced the general public.

Meinig was born in Palouse, Washington, and was raised outside the town in a rural region he remembers well. He spent his childhood among hills, forests, mountains, and other geographical features that sparked his curiosity about the world around him. "As far back as I can remember," he later wrote, "I was fascinated by that panorama. I wanted to know the names of all those features, I wondered what lay beyond."

Meinig pursued his interest in geography in school. He enjoyed drawing maps and creating imaginary landscapes and countries. After graduating from high school, he took several courses in geography at the University of Washington. World War II (1939–1945) intervened, however, and he left school to serve in the U.S. Army.

Meinig's stint in the military steered him toward a career as a diplomat* and away from geography. After the war he enrolled at Georgetown University, where he pursued a degree in the School of Foreign Service. He graduated in 1948 but chose not to enter the diplomatic corps after all. Instead, Meinig returned to school to study geography with the hope of becoming a professor.

Graduate School. Meinig again enrolled at the University of Washington, this time as a graduate student in geography. He received his master's degree in 1950 and his doctorate three years later. Meinig's career in academia began even before he received his Ph.D.—the University of Utah's geography department hired him as an instructor.

Meinig's experiences in Utah helped shape and define his career as a geographer. At first he wrote and published on a variety of topics, among them Australian agriculture, climate and wheat production of Washington State, and the history of geography. Shortly thereafter, Meinig's focus shifted when he became intrigued by the relationship between history and geography. What he saw and learned in Utah only strengthened that interest.

Meinig noted the influence of the Church of Jesus Christ of Latter-day Saints, commonly known as the Mormon Church, on the residents of Utah. He believed that the Mormons had helped shape the history and the geography of Utah in distinctive ways. This notion became the basis for one of Meinig's most famous publications, a 1965 paper entitled "The Mormon Culture Region: Strategies and Patterns in the Geography of the American West." Adding historical analysis to regional studies became increasingly important to Meinig, and became a hallmark of his work.

In 1959, by then promoted to the rank of associate professor at Utah, Meinig accepted the offer of a position at Syracuse University, in

New York. He remained there for the rest of his academic career, eventually serving as chair of the geography department. In 1968 he published a book about Washington State titled *The Great Columbia Plain: A Historical Geography,* and the following year, he issued what he termed a "cultural geography" of Texas. Meinig focused on the connections between land, history, and culture for the rest of his career.

Meinig saw this connection among disciplines as far from static. "Geography is not just a physical stage for the historical drama," he wrote, "not just a set of facts about areas of the earth." Instead he argued that the landforms and other physical features of a particular region helped define the human societies that lived there. He explored this notion in great detail in *The Shaping of America: A Geographical Perspective on 500 Years of History,* published in 1986. "Geography," he explained, "is a way of making sense of the world."

A frequent guest lecturer at various universities, Meinig has won honors and awards from the American Geographical Society, the Association of American Geographers, and several other organizations. Many of his ideas about geography and its connection with history continue to influence educational theory. Meinig greatly enjoyed his work. "Every place is of interest," he wrote about his life as a geographer. "Every place is full of clues about history and culture, about values, tastes and fashions." To him, geography was always "an inexhaustible source of interest and pleasure."

Gerardus
MERCATOR

1512–1594

GEOGRAPHY, CARTOGRAPHY

theology study of religion

Gerardus Mercator was a man of many talents, an artist who knew mathematics, astronomy, and theology*. His fame, however, rests on his contributions to geography and cartography (mapmaking). Among other achievements, he created a map of the world for seafarers that became the most-used such tool in history.

Mercator was born in Gerhard Kremer in Rupelmonde, Flanders, now part of the nation of Belgium. In 1530 he entered the University of Louvain, also in Belgium, and at that time he adopted the Latin form of his name—Latin was still used throughout Europe as the language of scholarship. At Louvain, Mercator studied philosophy and theology. After graduating he became interested in geography, mathematics, and astronomy, and he studied these subjects informally with Gemma Frisius, a noted scientist of the day. Because the two often visited the workshop of an engraver and metalworker, Mercator became skilled in engraving as well as in calligraphy*. The two arts were essential to cartography in the 1500s, when maps were hand-drawn and lettered. His graceful lettering influenced the style of other mapmakers.

calligraphy art of fine handwriting

Before long Mercator had combined his new interests and skills to create maps. His first production, in 1536, was a globe. The following year he published his first map, which covered the region that is now Israel. He went on to make more globes and maps of the entire world and of regions or countries, including Flanders. He also crafted scientific instruments. During the 1530s and 1540s Mercator traveled fre-

heresy belief that departs from the doctrine of the established or official church

cosmographer one who practices cosmography, the science that describes the world or the universe

quently to gather information for his maps, married, and began raising a family. In 1544 the authorities in Louvain imprisoned him, along with 42 other people, on charges of heresy*. With the support of the university, Mercator achieved his release in seven months.

Eight years later Mercator left Louvain for Duisberg, a German city that was then part of a small state called the Duchy of Cleves. He spent the rest of his life at Duisberg, working as a teacher, cartographer, overseer of a mapmaking workshop, and scholar. In 1564 Duke Wilhelm of Cleves honored Mercator with the grand title of court cosmographer*. Mercator died 30 years later and his son Rumold Mercator carried on the family business, publishing cartographic work left unfinished by his father.

Mercator's most important work was a map projection he invented. Every cartographer faces the challenge of portraying the round earth on a flat sheet of paper. The method of arranging geographic data on a map is called a projection, because it projects an image of the three-dimensional world onto a two-dimensional sheet. Mapmakers use many kinds of projections, but none is perfectly accurate, although each has its advantages and disadvantages. Mercator's projection, first used in a world map he published in 1569, gave mariners a tremendous advantage. On this projection, the lines of latitude and longitude are at right angles to one another everywhere on the map. This enables navigators to plot a course using a single compass bearing over long distances instead of making frequent changes of bearing, as was necessary with other projections. Although the Mercator projection distorts landforms close to the poles—making Greenland look larger than it really is, for example—its usefulness made it one of the most universally familiar maps in the world. Generations of schoolchildren learned geography by studying maps made using Mercator's projection.

The second of Mercator's contributions to cartography began in the late 1560s, when he began to publish sets of maps, each set covering a different part of Europe. After his death his son issued a volume containing all the maps. Drawing from the ancient Greek myth of Atlas, the giant who bore the world on his shoulders, Rumold called the 1595 book *Atlas—or Cosmographic Meditations on the Structure of the World*. The term *atlas* is still used to refer to a bound collection of maps.

Fridtjof
NANSEN
1861–1930

ZOOLOGY, OCEANOGRAPHY,
POLAR EXPLORATION

Fridtjof Nansen was one of the most remarkable figures in the world of science and exploration. He pursued three separate careers and achieved outstanding distinction in each. As a young man he was one of the world's great Arctic explorers and an inspiration to other polar explorers, especially fellow Norwegian Roald AMUNDSEN. In his middle age, he was a prominent oceanographer*. Near the end of his life, he led some of the greatest humanitarian* efforts of modern times, for which he received the 1922 Nobel Peace Prize.

Explorer and Scientist. Nansen was born in Store-Fröen, near the city of Oslo, Norway, to a relatively wealthy family. As a youth he was an outstanding athlete, excelling at skating, skiing, and other outdoor activities. He attended the University of Christiania (now Oslo), earning a degree in zoology. Nansen got his first taste of Arctic adventure as a student when, in 1882, he accompanied the *Viking* on a trip to Greenland. His job was to observe and record winds, currents, the movement of ice, and animal life.

This voyage sparked in Nansen a plan to explore the interior of Greenland. However, when he returned to Norway, he was offered the position of curator* of the natural history collection at the Bergen Museum. He accepted the post and spent the next six years studying microscopic animal life. The work formed the basis of his doctoral dissertation, now considered a classic work on animal nervous systems.

In 1887 Nansen began planning for his Greenland expedition. On July 17, 1888, Nansen and his five-member party arrived near the east coast of Greenland. Delayed by adverse currents, the team did not reach the coast until August 16. After a difficult 9,000-foot climb to the plateau and an arduous journey through ice, snow, and night-time temperatures as low as -50°, they reached the village of Godthaab on the west coast on October 3. The men were forced to winter on Greenland, and Nansen recorded their experiences in *Eskimo Life,* which also contains rich ethnographic* details about the people of Greenland. The expedition confirmed that Greenland is completely covered with ice.

Nansen returned to Norway in 1889, and the following year he proposed a new expedition. He had found evidence that there was an east-west ocean current that caused the polar ice to drift in the Arctic Ocean from Siberia to the North Pole and from there to Greenland. To prove his theory, he wanted to design and build a ship that, when trapped in ice, would rise and float with the ice instead of being crushed. He planned to set sail off the coast of eastern Siberia and allow the ice to capture the ship and carry it to the Spitsbergen archipelago*, 360 miles north of Norway. The government reluctantly approved the plan and Nansen built the ship, which he named the *Fram* ("Forward").

On June 24, 1893, the *Fram* began its eastward journey from Oslofjord with a 12-member crew. Skirting ice packs along the Siberian coast, the vessel passed Cape Chelyuskin, the northernmost point on the Siberian coast, on September 10. Nine days later it set course straight north in open water, and on September 22, the *Fram* was trapped in ice and began to drift. The ship became a floating laboratory, and Nansen and the crew made important discoveries. On March 14, 1895, nearly 18 months later, when it became clear that the ship was not drifting toward the North Pole, Nansen decided to leave the ship with one companion, dog sleds, and kayaks, and made a dash for the pole. They did not reach the pole but came within 268 miles of their goal, having traveled farther north than had any previous explorer. Nansen and his companion were forced to winter on the ice in a hut they built using whalebones, bearskins, and sleds; they shot bears and walrus for food.

oceanographer one who practices oceanography, the study of oceans

humanitarian one who is concerned with human welfare and social reform

curator caretaker

ethnographic of or relating to ethnography, the branch of anthropology dealing with the scientific description of different cultures

archipelago group of islands

Nansen, Fridtjof

Refuge for the Homeless

In 1921, a year after Nansen was appointed a Norwegian delegate to the League of Nations, the league selected him to manage its High Commission for Refugees. As part of his duties, Nansen invented a passport for refugees whose plight left them citizens of no country. Known as the "Nansen Passport," the document was eventually recognized by 52 nations. After Nansen's death in 1931, the Nansen International Office for Refugees was established in Geneva. The office helped many thousands of refugees including Jews fleeing Nazi Germany.

See the routes of Nansen's voyages in the "Maps" section.

*delegate representative

Meanwhile, on May 19, 1896, the *Fram* became free of the ice north of Spitsbergen and began to drift southward. It reached Norway on June 19, after almost three years at sea, proving Nansen's theory about the east-west current. The ship had also reached the farthest northerly latitude yet reached 85'55"N, a record that remained intact until 1958, when a U.S. submarine transited under the polar ice cap. The *Fram* is preserved in the Fram Museum in Oslo.

The most important contributions of the *Fram* expedition were the discoveries of the depth of the Arctic Ocean and of the locations of land and water masses. Nansen's studies also showed that the Arctic Ocean was warmer and deeper than people had thought it was and proved that there was no landmass near the North Pole.

Scientist and Humanitarian. After the *Fram* expedition, Nansen accepted a professorship in zoology from the University of Christiania. However, by this time he had become more interested in oceanography, and his post was later changed to a professorship in that field. For the next 20 years, he helped establish the International Council for Exploration of the Sea and made several scientific ocean expeditions.

Nansen's cruises took him to the Norwegian Sea, the North Atlantic, the Azores Islands, the Barents Sea, the Kara Sea, and once again to Siberia. In addition to publishing reports on these voyages, he made several material contributions to oceanography. These include designing new scientific instruments and improving existing ones, explaining the action of wind in producing ocean currents, increasing knowledge of the waters of the Arctic, and developing theories on the formation of deep water and bottom water in the oceans.

In 1905 Nansen took a break from science to involve himself in politics. At the time, Norway was seeking independence from the kingdom of Sweden. He convinced the British to intervene on behalf of Norway and after a year of negotiation, Norway became an independent kingdom. Nansen became Norway's first minister to Great Britain, a post he held for the next two years.

During World War I (1914–1918), when the Allied powers conducted a continent-wide blockade to prevent food, fuel, and arms from reaching Germany, Nansen negotiated an agreement with the United States to allow vital supplies to reach Norway. In 1920 he became the first Norwegian delegate* to the League of Nations, a post he held until his death.

One of Nansen's first duties at the league was to organize the return of German and Austrian prisoners of war from the former Soviet Union. Because of his efforts, more than 425,000 prisoners returned home over the next two years. In 1921 the International Committee of the Red Cross chose Nansen to lead a famine relief effort in Russia. The Western powers were reluctant to deal with the Soviets, even when millions of people were at risk of starvation. Overcoming indifference and resistance, Nansen expended tremendous energy to organize the delivery of food that helped save countless lives.

When Fridtjof Nansen heard that the skiing was excellent in Greenland, he decided to ski across the island. It took Nansen and his companions, all expert skiers, little more than a month to ski across Greenland from east to west.

In 1922 the league asked Nansen to deal with the refugee problem caused by the war between Greece and Turkey. He arranged the return of some 500,000 Turks from Greece in exchange for 1,250,000 Greeks from Turkey. For his outstanding service to humanity, Nansen was awarded the 1922 Nobel Peace Prize. In keeping with his character, he used the one million dollar prize to further his humanitarian activities. Three years later he worked to alleviate the suffering of Armenians who were being persecuted in Turkey. Nansen died in Oslo at the age of 68.

The Finnish-born Swedish scientist Nils Adolf Erik Nordenskiöld ranks among the greatest Arctic explorers of his time. He is best known for successfully navigating the Northeast Passage, a sea route across the Arctic Ocean from Europe to Asia.

Early Life and Explorations. Nordenskiöld was born into a prominent family in the city of Helsinki, Finland. His father was the superintendent of mining, and as a youth Nordenskiöld accompanied him on trips to explore Russia's Ural Mountains. Nordenskiöld entered the University of Helsinki, where he studied chemistry and geology, receiv-

Nils Adolf Erik
NORDENSKIÖLD

1832–1901

ARCTIC EXPLORATION, GEOGRAPHY, HISTORY OF CARTOGRAPHY

Seafood Platter

During the long winter months when the *Vega* was trapped in the Arctic ice, Nordenskiöld made scientific observations and established friendly relations with the local Chukchi people. In his report on the expedition, he describes a breakfast he was served at a Chukchi household: "first seals' flesh and fat, with a sort of sauerkraut of fermented willow-leaves, then seals' liver, and finally seals' blood—all frozen."

---

*mineralogical referring to mineralogy, the study of the properties of minerals

*archipelago group of islands

See the route of Nordenskiöld's 1878–79 voyage in the "Maps" section.

*strait narrow waterway that runs between two landmasses and links two bodies of water

ing his M.A. and Ph.D. in 1853 and 1855. After earning his doctorate, he continued his studies in Germany.

In 1857 Nordenskiöld made a speech in favor of Finnish independence—at the time, Finland was part of the Russian Empire. The speech angered Russian authorities, who banished Nordenskiöld from the country. He went to Sweden where, the following year, he became superintendent of the Swedish Royal Museum's Mineralogical* Department. That same year he made his first Arctic trip as a member of the noted Swedish geologist Otto Martin Torrell's expedition to the Spitsbergen archipelago*, 360 miles north of Norway.

Three years later Nordenskiöld again accompanied Torrell to Spitsbergen, and in 1864, he commanded his own party to the islands. Four years later Nordenskiöld attracted international attention when, aboard the steamer *Sofia*, he led an expedition that went farther north into the Arctic Ocean than any explorer before him. London's Royal Geographic Society honored him for his feat, as did scientists in Sweden.

In 1870 Nordenskiöld turned his attention to Greenland. His goal was to experiment with the use of dog sleds to aid in polar exploration. On the trip he became the first scientist to venture into the interior of Greenland to study its ice cap. Two years later he was back in Spitsbergen, hoping to use the archipelago as the starting point for an attempt to reach the North Pole. However, he lost the reindeers he took along as pack animals, and an ice storm forced his party to winter on Spitsbergen. Stranded, Nordenskiöld and his companions traveled across the island of Nordaustlandet (now North East Land) to study its nature.

The Northeast Passage. After his 1872 experience in Spitsbergen, Nordenskiöld gave up his quest to reach the North Pole. For two years he served in the Swedish legislature before resuming his explorations. He then undertook two journeys sailing across the Kara Sea north of Russia to Siberia's Yenisey River. These explorations convinced him that the ocean north of Russia was navigable. He then conceived the idea of sailing directly from Sweden to the Pacific Ocean via this northern sea route.

The king of Sweden and two wealthy Swedish businessmen financed the expedition, which left from Tromsø, Norway, on July 21, 1878. By August 19, Nordenskiöld had reached Cape Chelyuskin, the most northern point of land in Asia, roughly the halfway point of his journey. By late September, his steamship the *Vega* had reached within 120 miles of the Bering Strait*, which separates Asia from North America. However, the ship became frozen in ice and was stuck until the following July.

While icebound, Nordenskiöld and his crew gathered a great deal of information about the polar region, the first Arctic expedition to do so. When the ice finally broke, the expedition resumed its journey on July 20, 1879, and took just four days to push across the Bering Strait to Port Clarence, Alaska. The *Vega* became the first ship to successfully navigate the Northeast Passage.

From Alaska, Nordenskiöld returned to Norway by sailing around Japan, China, and Ceylon (now Sri Lanka), and through the Suez Canal in the Red Sea. He reached Stockholm, Sweden, on April 24, 1880, and Sweden's King Oscar II rewarded him by making him a baron. That date is now celebrated in Sweden as Vega Day. Nordenskiöld's feat came 325 years after the English navigators Hugh Willoughby and Richard Chancellor first attempted to cross the Northeast Passage and more than 230 years after the Russian fur trader Semyon Dezhnyov proved that such a voyage was possible.

The *Vega* expedition was notable not only for its successful crossing of the Northeast Passage, but also for doing so without sickness or the loss of life among the crew. Nordenskiöld's report on the journey was published as a five-volume set titled *Scientific Observations of the Vega Expedition*. It contained a wealth of information about the botany, zoology, oceanography*, geology, and anthropology* of Siberia. A best-seller, the book was translated into five languages.

Later Accomplishments. Nordenskiöld undertook one last Arctic mission after the *Vega* expedition—to prove that ice-free land existed in Greenland's interior. In 1883, accompanied by Oscar Dickson (who had financed part of the *Vega* voyage), Nordenskiöld set out to explore that possibility. He pushed as far into the interior of Greenland as possible but he did not find ice-free land.

After this voyage, Nordenskiöld retired from Arctic exploration, but he continued to serve as an adviser to fellow explorers. He devoted his later years to the study of the history of cartography (mapmaking). He wrote two groundbreaking works in the field: *Facsimile-Atlas to the Early History of Cartography* and *Periplus—An Essay on the Early History of Charts and Sailing Directions*. Although others had attempted histories of cartography, Nordenskiöld was the first to bring a truly scientific and critical approach to the filed. He died in Dalbyö, Sweden, at age 68.

***oceanography** study of oceans

***anthropology** study of human beings, especially in relation to origins and physical and cultural characteristics

---

During a ten-year career that included five major voyages to the Arctic, William Edward Parry searched unsuccessfully for a Northwest Passage* across Canada, mapped dozens of islands and bays, and came closer to the North Pole than anyone before had. He also developed techniques of polar exploration that were adopted by later explorers.

Born in Bath, England, Parry joined the Royal Navy at age 13. He spent the first 15 years of his naval career serving on various ships, some in Europe and others along the Atlantic coastline of North America. Among his assignments was a stint aboard a ship that helped protect whaling vessels in the waters off Spitsbergen, an archipelago* 360 miles north of the Norwegian coast. During these years, Parry learned the basics of seamanship and studied navigation and astronomy.

In 1818, a naval official read a report on nautical* astronomy that Parry had written. Impressed, he recommended Parry for a position on

William Edward
PARRY

1790–1855

ARCTIC EXPLORATION

***Northwest Passage** water route connecting the Atlantic and Pacific Oceans through the Arctic islands of northern Canada

***archipelago** group of islands

***nautical** of or relating to ships or seamanship

the crew of a polar expedition commanded by the English captain John Ross. The purpose of Ross's voyage was to find a Northwest Passage. Parry was placed in charge of one of the expedition's ships.

The journey was unsuccessful. Parry and Ross voyaged only as far as Lancaster Sound, just north of Baffin Island, before they turned back. Ross claimed that Lancaster Sound was a bay and therefore a dead end, but Parry believed that the water would lead them straight through to the Pacific. Intrigued by Parry's perspective, the British Admiralty (government department in charge of naval affairs) asked him to command an expedition the following year.

In Charge. Parry's 1819 voyage proved that Lancaster Sound led to open water to the west. He also voyaged several hundred miles beyond the sound, considerably farther west than any previous English ship had sailed. Parry and his crew later won a cash prize from the English government for being the first Arctic expedition to venture past the 110th meridian*. In October 1819, Parry's westward journey came to a stop, however, when the ships encountered thick ice.

Rather than retreating to a warmer climate, Parry elected to spend the winter in the Arctic. It was a bold move; no white explorer had yet attempted to spend a winter in that region, and even the closest Inuit* peoples were 500 miles away. Parry did his best to keep his crew active and occupied, fearing that the isolation, cold, and darkness could lead to insanity and illness.

When the ice broke the following August, Parry sailed west until he could see Banks Island, the westernmost island in the Canadian Arctic, but ice again blocked his path. He considered spending another winter in the region and trying to venture farther the next summer, but supplies were low and the crew's health was declining. In 1820 he returned to England and the crew received a hero's welcome. Parry's voyage added many new features to the map of northern Canada, and even though he had not found the Northwest Passage, he had at least found what many believed was its entrance.

Another Voyage. In 1821, Parry sailed on another Royal Navy voyage of discovery. This time, instead of sailing north of Baffin Island, he navigated the Hudson Strait, a passage of water south of the island. He reasoned that he might have better luck in the southern temperate waters than in the icy north. He voyaged through the strait and into Foxe Basin, where he spent weeks exploring its western shores. The only western passage out of the basin lay at its the northern tip, a narrow waterway that Parry called Fury and Hecla Strait after his two ships.

Unfortunately, this passage proved too icy to navigate and the ships were forced to spend two winters in the region. As before, Parry managed to keep his crew busy, disciplined, and healthy. Finally, in 1823, he returned to England without finding the sea route to the Pacific, but certain that there was no route through Foxe Basin. As he had done on his previous journey, Parry arrived in Europe with valuable new information about the land and waters of the Canadian Arctic.

*meridian imaginary north-south line circling the earth and passing through the poles and that is used to indicate longitude

*Inuit people of the Canadian Arctic and Greenland, sometimes called Eskimo

William Parry's expedition through ice packs in the Arctic Ocean is captured in this illustration. Here, his ship is shown near Melville Island, one of the largest islands in the Arctic.

Parry made one more attempt to find the Northwest Passage. In 1824, he sailed through Lancaster Sound and headed southwest into Prince Regent Inlet. He intended to explore the western coast of the inlet in the hope of finding a passage to the Pacific, but one of his two ships was crushed in the ice and sank. The disaster cut short the expedition and Parry returned to England in 1825 having made no headway in finding the Northwest Passage.

Later Journeys. In 1827 Parry made his last voyage to the Arctic. He sailed to the island group of Spitsbergen, where he had once come to the aid of whaling ships. From there he set off across the polar ice on a sledge*, hoping to reach the North Pole. Although he did not succeed in his goal, he reached the northern latitude of 82'45"N, setting a record for venturing farther north than anyone had in recorded history. The record remained unbroken until 1896, when the Norwegian explorer Fridtjof NANSEN reached 85'55"N. When Parry returned to England, he was knighted and awarded an honorary degree from Oxford University.

For the next two decades, Parry worked as an administrator for businesses, hospitals, and the English government. In 1845, he returned briefly to his polar interests when he helped John FRANKLIN plan an expedition to find the Northwest Passage. When Franklin and his men disappeared, Parry helped plan a search. Parry died in Ems, Germany.

His Legacy. Parry's methods of keeping sailors active and focused during Arctic winters were revolutionary. Before his time, few had dared to spend the winter in the Arctic, and those that did had done so accidentally, after having ventured too far out into the ice pack too late

*sledge heavy sled that is mounted on runners for traveling over snow and ice

in the year. Parry, however, wintered in the Arctic on purpose and planned accordingly. He kept his men busy, reasoning that active men were more likely to keep their health and less likely to fall victims to depression. He also provided plenty of recreational opportunities by establishing a shipboard newspaper and engaging his men in amateur dramatics. His strategies for surviving the brutal Arctic winter were used by later polar explorers.

Robert Edwin
PEARY

1856–1920

ARCTIC EXPLORATION

The American naval officer Robert Edwin Peary devoted more than 20 years of his life to exploring the Arctic. Peary and his companions have generally been considered the first people to reach the North Pole, although Peary's claim to polar fame has never been completely secure. In 1909, when Peary announced his feat to the world, a rival explorer claimed to have reached the North Pole before him, and in the 1980s, researchers began to doubt whether Peary had reached the pole at all. Others, however, consider Peary the conqueror of the North Pole.

Background and Early Career. Peary was born in Cresson, Pennsylvania. His father died when he was quite young, and from the age of three he lived in Maine, where his mother had moved to be near her family. After graduating from high school in Portland, Maine, Peary attended Bowdoin College, where he studied civil engineering.

Peary graduated in 1877 and went to work as the town surveyor of Fryeburg, Maine. He then moved to Washington, D.C., to work for a government department responsible for surveying and mapping. In 1881 he joined the Civil Engineers Corps of the U.S. Navy. Three years later he went to Nicaragua as part of a team that was surveying possible routes for a canal that would connect the Atlantic and Pacific Oceans—an alternative to the Panama Canal that was never built.

By 1887 Peary had become the chief engineer of the Nicaragua canal survey. He had also hired a personal servant, an African-American man named Matthew HENSON, who proved to be skilled in mathematics and navigation. Henson rapidly became a valuable addition to the survey crew and shared Peary's later adventures and explorations. Those adventures would take both men into a realm very different from the Nicaraguan tropics—the Arctic.

Exploring Greenland. Like many others of his day, Peary was deeply interested in the unexplored geographic frontiers of the polar regions. Arctic explorers no longer searched for the fabled Northwest Passage*, the goal of many expeditions in earlier centuries. Geographers had finally confirmed that the easy shipping route they had once hoped to find through North America did not exist. Many geographic mysteries, however, remained to be solved in the Arctic, and a glittering prize waited to be claimed. In a time when explorers were hailed as national and international heroes, the first person to reach the North Pole would certainly become famous worldwide.

*Northwest Passage water route connecting the Atlantic and Pacific Oceans through the Arctic islands of northern Canada

Peary, an ambitious man, realized that successful exploration in the north might do more to advance his career than steady work in the tropics. In the summer of 1886, the year before he met and hired Henson, he took a leave of absence from the U.S. Navy and traveled to Greenland. This enormous, ice-covered landmass in the northern Atlantic between Canada and Europe was and still is a sparsely populated territory of Denmark, home to the Inuit* and to a few Europeans who live in settlements along the coast. It was a well-chosen destination. Not only did Greenland deserve further exploration in its own right, but some explorers also believed that it would prove to be a highway to the North Pole. Its northern extent had not yet been mapped, and geographers did not know whether it reached all the way to the pole.

On Peary's first expedition to Greenland, he and a companion, Christian Maigaard, traveled 100 miles inland from Disko Bay on the west coast, but they turned back after three weeks. Peary left Greenland and did not return until five years later as the leader of a seven-person expedition sponsored by the Philadelphia Academy of Natural Sciences. One member of the expedition was a geologist who had paid $2,000 to join. Other members included Peary's wife, Josephine, his associate Henson, and Frederick A. Cook, a physician.

Peary had again taken an 18-month leave of absence from the Navy, spending 13 months in Greenland. During that time he led a 1,300-mile trek across northern Greenland. He learned how to move supplies across the ice on the sturdy sleds called sledges, pulled by men or dogs, and he also learned much about a group of Inuit he called the "Arctic Highlanders" who lived in Greenland's remote northern reaches. Peary discovered Independence Fjord, an inlet in northeastern Greenland, and gathered evidence that suggested that Greenland is an island whose northern coast falls several hundred miles short of the Pole. He realized that any approach to the pole might have to be made across the ice pack that covers the frozen Arctic Ocean, not over land.

By this time Peary had become determined to do more than explore Greenland—he wanted to reach the North Pole. Between 1893 and 1895 he returned with Henson to northeastern Greenland and made a long journey over the ice, using sledges pulled by dogs. Although the pole remained out of reach, Peary was becoming a skilled and experienced Arctic traveler. He adopted some of the tools and techniques, such as fur clothing and snow shelters, that the Inuit had devised over the centuries to help them survive in the region's harsh climate. In time Peary also developed a method of preparing for a long journey by making several shorter trips along the planned route to store supplies at a series of depots, or stockpiles. Supply depots meant that the main expedition party would not have to carry all of its supplies at once and that food would be available along the way in case of emergencies, such as the loss of a sledge through a hole in the ice. This method came to be called the Peary System of Arctic Travel.

In 1895 Peary explored the part of northern Greenland that today bears his name. During the two summers that followed he devoted his efforts to taking meteorites—large chunks of rock and metal that had

*Inuit people of the Canadian Arctic and Greenland, sometimes called Eskimo

*ethnological referring to ethnology, the scientific study of the physical and cultural differences between human races

*meteorological referring to meteorology, the science that deals with the atmosphere, especially the weather and weather predictions

fallen to earth from space—from Greenland to the United States. In 1898 he published his first book, *Northward over the "Great Ice,"* which told of his geographic, ethnological*, and meteorological* studies in Greenland. Peary had not lost his desire to reach the North Pole.

Attempts on the Pole. In 1898 Peary launched a serious and long-lasting attack on the pole. During the course of four years he investigated several routes to the pole, one of which began in Etah, an Inuit settlement in northwestern Greenland. Two years later Peary completed his exploration of Greenland's northern coast, naming its northernmost point Cape Morris Jesup in honor of the president of the American Museum of Natural History, who had provided Peary with considerable support during his many expeditions.

By this time, Peary had confirmed that Greenland is an island, not a polar continent. (The island ends at 82°N latitude, while the North Pole lies at 90°N.) Knowing that traveling to the northern end of Greenland would not take him to the pole, Peary began to focus on other possible routes. In 1902 he tried to reach the pole by starting from Ellesmere Island, part of the Canadian Arctic. However, he only reached as far as 84°17'N. From this failed attempt, Peary gained important knowledge about conditions on the polar ice pack and about the pack's drift, or movement.

As news of Peary's attempts spread, he won the support of wealthy people who formed a group called the Peary Club to raise funds for his expeditions. In 1904 the club had a ship, the *Theodore Roosevelt,* built to Peary's requirements. The following year the *Roosevelt* sailed north to Cape Sheridan on Ellesmere Island. From there Peary and Henson hoped to sledge to the pole, but weather and ice conditions were against them. They reached a latitude of 87°6'N, just 174 miles from the pole—a new "farthest north" record and a significant achievement. Peary wrote about it in *Nearest the Pole,* published in 1907.

Peary and Henson again sailed north in 1908 to make one last push to the North Pole. They set up a base camp at Cape Columbia, on the northern coast of Ellesmere Island, and in March 1909 set out with 24 men, 133 dogs, and 19 sledges to cover the more than 400 miles to the pole. Teams of men moved ahead to set up supply depots. The last of them turned back 140 miles from the pole, leaving Peary, Henson, and four Inuit companions to proceed with 40 dogs and 5 sledges.

On April 6, 1909, Peary announced that he and his companions had reached the North Pole. The victorious explorers turned back and reached their base at Cape Columbia before the end of April, but they could not sail home until July because of ice. In September the *Roosevelt* reached a telegraph station in Labrador, Canada, where Peary sent a telegraph to the world claiming, "Stars and Stripes nailed to the North Pole."

Before setting out for Ellesmere Island, Peary had learned that fellow American Frederick Cook, a member of his second Greenland expedition, was also attempting to reach the pole. To his astonishment, he discovered that Cook claimed to have reached the pole in April 1908, a

The Fate of Frederick Cook

Fighting with Peary over the North Pole was just one episode in the stormy life of Frederick Albert Cook, a physician interested in polar exploration—and the chance for fame it offered. After traveling to Greenland with Peary, Cook went to Antarctica with a Belgian expedition. In 1906 he claimed to have made the first climb up Alaska's Mount McKinley (known today as Denali), but this claim was later proven false. Some years after the dispute with Peary, Cook went to prison for fraud in a scheme involving Texas oil fields. Released in 1930, he spent the last years of his life trying in vain to prove his Alaskan and polar claims.

Robert Peary's passion for Arctic exploration lay in the challenge of conquering the pole. He did not try to be a natural part of the environment nor did he feel a sense of kinship with the Inuit. However, he admired the Inuit for their survival skills, which he also adopted.

full year before Peary and Henson. Peary accused Cook of lying, and those who had believed Cook lost faith when he failed to produce the detailed records—navigational sightings and calculations of distances covered—that would have supported his claim. Soon almost everyone had rejected Cook's claim. Scientific and official organizations throughout the world, such as the National Geographic Society, the Royal Geographical Society of Great Britain, and the U.S. Congress, honored Peary as the first to reach the pole. Ironically, however, Peary's own navigational records came under the microscope in the 1980s, when one researcher's review of them suggested that Peary had only reached a point some 30 to 60 miles from the pole. Although the experts continue to argue in support of and against Peary's claim, most agree that even if Peary did not actually reach the pole, he came very close.

Hailed as a hero of exploration, Peary went on to publish *The North Pole* in 1910 and *Secrets of Polar Travel* in 1917. He retired from the Navy in 1911 with the rank of rear admiral and died nine years later in Washington, D.C.

See Jones and Piccard.

One of the most famous travelers of all time was a young Italian man named Marco Polo, who traveled from Europe to China during the late Middle Ages*. After living in China for many years as a guest of the emperor Kublai Khan, Polo returned to his homeland and produced a book that became a well-known and influential piece of travel writing.

PICCARD, *Bertrand*

Marco
POLO

ca. 1254–1324

TRAVEL

Polo, Marco

Called *Il Milione* (The Million) or *The Description of the World,* the work encouraged Europeans to search for trade routes to Asia—Christopher COLUMBUS was just one of many who read and was inspired by the story of Polo's travels. Although critics have questioned the accuracy and honesty of his tales, scholars agree that his contribution to geography was an important one. Polo played a key role in educating Europeans about the lands and peoples beyond their borders.

The Polo Family. Historians have not been able to find much information about Marco Polo's early life. Even the date of his birth is an estimate. Most accounts claim that he was born in Venice, a city on the coast of northern Italy that became a major trade center during the late Middle Ages. Some sources, however, say that he was born in Curzola, an island off the coast of Dalmatia (today the eastern European nation of Croatia), which was ruled by Venice at the time.

Whatever his place of birth, Polo was raised in Venice and considered the city his home. He belonged to a family of prosperous merchants with connections in the Middle East, Turkey, and ports of the Black Sea. These markets were rich sources of Asian goods—silk, pottery, and other items from China, carried across Central Asia for thousands of miles by caravans*—that were highly prized in Europe.

Marco's father, Niccolò Polo, and his uncle, Maffeo Polo, were bold and successful men of business. Around 1260 they set off with a fortune in jewels to trade among the Mongols, horsemen from Mongolia who, under the leadership of Genghis Khan, had just conquered much of Asia. The Polos spent some time with Barka Khan, who ruled the western reaches of the Mongol empire from his camp near the Volga River in present-day Russia. Because war within the Mongol domain prevented the Polos from returning to Venice, they headed east to Bukhara, a city in the present-day Central Asian republic of Uzbekistan. It was located on the Silk Road, the caravan route linking the West with China.

From Bukhara, the Polos were escorted across the Gobi Desert and into China, which had also been conquered by the Mongols. There they visited the court of Kublai, the ruler of the Mongols and the grandson of Genghis Khan, who treated them kindly and sent them on their way home with a foot-long golden plaque—a special pass that entitled the Polos to horses, food, protection, and safe passage through his empire. In 1269 Niccolò and Maffeo arrived in Venice and told of their journey. They were not the first Europeans to visit the Mongol kingdom, but they were the first to have gone to China and to have returned safely.

Journey Across Asia. Marco Polo was about 15 when his father and uncle came home after their long absence. Niccolò and Maffeo Polo had promised Kublai Khan that they would return to his court, bringing people to teach the Mongols about Christianity and the arts and sciences of Western Europe. When they set off again in 1271, young Marco accompanied them, as did two monks.

The three Polos followed a route different from the one that Niccolò and Maffeo had taken before. They traveled east through Turkey, Armenia, and western Persia (now Iran) before reaching the port of Hormuz on the Persian Gulf. They had traveled through snow-covered mountains and scorching deserts and had overcome hostile attacks by robbers. At this point in the journey, the monks refused to travel any farther and turned back. The Polos considered continuing their journey to the Mongol kingdom by sea because a sea trade existed between the Arabian and Middle Eastern shores of the Indian Ocean and ports in India, Southeast Asia, and China. They changed their minds, however, when they saw the vessels at Hormuz, which Marco later described as "wretched affairs . . . only stitched together with twine made from the husk of the Indian nut [coconut]."

The Polos headed northeast across the deserts of eastern Iran. They were better pleased with the climate of Badakhshan, a highland region in northern Afghanistan, where they may have stayed for as long as a year. Marco Polo's account of the journey suggests that in Badakhshan he recovered from an illness, possibly malaria, a mosquito-born disease found in warm regions. Because Marco also described regions that lie south of Afghanistan, including present-day Pakistan and Kashmir, some readers think that he made at least one visit to these places from Badakhshan. Other scholars, however, claim that he did not necessarily visit the places he described—he may have simply repeated information gathered from other travelers. Here as in many other places, his account of the journey is vague and does not paint a clear picture of his activities and of his itinerary.

From Badakhshan the Polos went north across the Pamir Mountains, which Marco called "the highest place in the world." The Himalayas are higher, but the Pamirs are rugged and forbidding, with many peaks reaching heights greater than 13,000 feet. This region later became known as the rooftop of the world. North of the mountains the Polos were again in Central Asia. They reached the caravan city of Kashgar, which is now part of western China. From there they followed a branch of the Silk Road from oasis to oasis along the southern fringe of the two major deserts of the region, the Taklamakan and the Gobi. Marco later described this region as a wasteland that "looks as if it had never been traversed by man or beast," and where they found little to eat. Around 1274 or 1275, as the Polos followed the Huang He (also known as the Yellow River), they were met by representatives of Kublai Khan who guided them to Shangdu, the summer capital of the Great Khan. Later they moved to his winter capital, Cambulac (present-day Beijing).

Life in China. The Polos spent 16 or 17 years in China, which they called Cathay. Because Marco Polo's later account of those years was more concerned with geography and history than with autobiography, scholars cannot be certain how he and his father and uncle spent their time. They are known to have become very wealthy, either through trade or because of gifts from Kublai Khan, who regarded them highly

After 25 years of traveling through much of Asia, Marco Polo returned to Venice. However, when Polo reunited with his family, they did not believe at first that he was their long-lost relative.

See the route taken by Marco Polo in the "Maps" section.

*imperial of or relating to an empire or emperor

*besiege to force surrender by surrounding a fortress or city with armed troops, cutting it off from supplies and aid

and employed them in various imperial* positions. The Mongols felt that the Chinese, whom they had conquered just a decade earlier, could not be trusted, and so they employed many foreigners in their courts.

Niccolò and Maffeo may have worked as technical advisers. Marco's account says that they designed machines called *mangonels*, which threw large rocks, for the Khan's forces to use against a city they were besieging*. Although such machines were known to exist in Europe, and although it is possible that the incident occurred as Marco described it, many historians doubt the veracity of the story.

Marco Polo was a favorite of the emperor, who enjoyed hearing Polo tell of his journey through Asia. Kublai Khan also sent Marco to distant parts of the empire to gather information; Polo traveled to the Sichuan and Yunnan regions of southern China and possibly even into Burma (now called Myanmar). Yet another trip took him into southeastern China. Some interpretations of Marco Polo's book suggest that he may have served as governor of the city of Yangzhou for three years. Although most historians doubt this claim, many point out that he may well have held a lesser government post. Marco's account contains a great deal of information about the salt trade, and it is possible that he was an official in charge of taxing or regulating that industry.

The Mongols fascinated Marco Polo, who gave a detailed account of their history and customs in his book. He dwelled on the wealth and splendor of Kublai Khan's palaces, especially the lavish summer palace. He praised the speed and efficiency of the Mongols' system of mail carriers, which used both runners and riders to carry messages swiftly throughout the empire. Polo also marveled at many features of Chinese society, including the use of paper money, which was unknown in Europe, and the extensive network of canals that connected the major rivers and carried goods throughout the country.

Return to Italy. Around 1290, the Polos became anxious to return to Venice. Moreover, Kublai Khan was in his late 70s, and the Polos were aware that his death might bring changes that would make it hard for them to leave China with the fortunes they had acquired. Each time they asked the emperor for permission to return to Venice, he refused because he did not want to lose them. Around 1292, however, Kublai Khan agreed to let them go, but they would have to perform a final service for him on the way—escorting a Mongol princess to Persia to be married to Arghun, the Persian khan. The Polos were very willing to do so.

On the trip home the Polos covered most of the distance by sea. A fleet of 14 Chinese ships carried the large party of nobles and attendants who accompanied the princess. The fleet set sail from Quanzhou, a port in southern China that Polo called Zaiton. The ships rounded Southeast Asia, stopping in Vietnam and at several islands in the South China and Malay Seas. At Sumatra the fleet halted for six months to allow the monsoon* season to pass. When they resumed the journey, they sailed to Ceylon (now called Sri Lanka) and stopped there and at various ports along the Indian coastline. From India, the fleet sailed west of Pakistan until it reached the Persian city of Hormuz.

*monsoon annual season of strong winds and heavy rains

There the Polos learned that Arghun Khan had died and that the princess would be married to his son instead. They also learned that Kublai Khan had died. Even after the emperor's passing, his word was powerful throughout the Mongol realm. The Polos traveled through Persia and Turkey, protected from bandits by the golden imperial safe-passage plaque they carried. From the city of Trebizond on the Black Sea they sailed to Constantinople (now Istanbul, Turkey), where the Polos had long had business interests, and then on to Italy. The voyage took many years and was plagued by problems. Many of the crew and passengers died, although Polo's account does not make clear whether they perished from disease or because of attacks by pirates or warriors.

The arrival of the Polos in Venice in 1295 caused a stir—friends and relatives had long believed that they had died long ago. Many years after his return, Polo participated in a war between Venice and Genoa, a rival Italian city-state. Captured by the Genoese, he was put into prison along with a writer named Rustichello. Polo told the story of his travels to and in China to Rustichello, who wrote it down. Modern scholars think that Rustichello, a writer of flowery tales of romance and knighthood, made contributions of his own to Polo's descriptions of court life and battles. The book was published as *The Description of the World,* but it was also known as *Il Milione* (The Million). Polo himself acquired the nickname "Il Milione," perhaps a reference to his wealth but more likely because people said that he had a million tales to tell. Nonbelievers in his tales said he had a million lies.

In 1299, when Polo was freed from prison, he returned to Venice and continued to trade. He also married and raised a family. Polo died at the age of 70. One often-repeated legend is that on his deathbed Polo said, "I did not write half of what I saw," responding to critics' claims about the truthfulness of the details in his book.

Polo's Legacy. Polo's book became a medieval best-seller and appeared in many editions in the principal languages of Europe. But anyone who copied it felt free to make changes or additions, creating enormous problems for modern scholars who labor to reconstruct the text as composed by Rustichello. About 140 different manuscripts survive. Today the book is most often published under the title *The Travels of Marco Polo.*

In addition to describing places and people that he saw, Marco Polo included the descriptions of places that he probably never visited, such as Japan, India, Siberia, and Ethiopia. He obtained some of his information from other travelers of unknown reliability and honesty, and some of it may have been little more than hearsay or rumor. Researchers who have compared Polo's account with other sources, however, believe that he accurately reported the things he saw. As for what he heard, he probably passed it along with little exaggeration, but he had no way of knowing how accurate his sources were.

Pointing to the myth, fable, and fantasy that occur throughout Polo's travelogue, a few modern investigators have questioned whether Polo ever went to China at all. They have asked why his name does not

Ghosts of the Gobi

Marco Polo's account of crossing the Gobi Desert includes legends about that lonely wasteland: "When a man is riding through this desert by night and . . . gets separated from his companions and wants to rejoin them, he hears spirit voices talking to him as if they were his companions, sometimes even calling him by name. Often these voices lure him away from the path and he never finds it again, and many travelers have got lost and died because of this. . . . Even by daylight men hear these spirit voices, and often you fancy you are listening to the strains of instruments, especially drums, and the clash of arms. For this reason bands of travelers make a point of keeping very close together."

appear in Chinese court records and why he fails to mention such things as the Great Wall and the binding of Chinese women's feet. Other researchers, however, point out that Polo's name might be recorded in an unrecognizable Chinese form, that the Great Wall was incomplete in Polo's time, and that he associated mostly with Mongols, not with Chinese, and cannot be expected to have known every Chinese custom. The verdict of most historians is that Polo did make the journey he claimed to have made. His great travel work is not only a compelling story but also a generally accurate contribution to geography as well.

PTOLEMY

ca. 100–ca. 170

GEOGRAPHY, CARTOGRAPHY

*medieval referring to the European Middle Ages, a period from about A.D. 500 to 1500

*celestial relating to the heavens or heavenly bodies

Claudius Ptolemaeus, called Ptolemy, was a scientist who lived in Alexandria, Egypt, at a time when Egypt was part of the Roman Empire. An astronomer and mathematician by profession, Ptolemy made important early contributions to geography and cartography (mapmaking).

Very little is known about Ptolemy's life. The works of some ancient and medieval* writers contain a few pieces of information about him, but these may not be accurate. Historians base their estimates of Ptolemy's birth and death dates on the celestial* observations that he describes in his own book, the *Almagest,* a work on astronomy that has survived to the modern day. The last name "Ptolemaeus" suggests that Ptolemy lived in Egypt but was born into a family with Greek ancestry, while his first name, "Claudius," shows that he was a citizen of Rome—perhaps the emperor Claudius had granted citizenship to one of his ancestors. There is no evidence, however, that Ptolemy ever lived anywhere but in Alexandria. Once a major center of learning in the Mediterranean world, Alexandria had declined by Ptolemy's time, but it still had great libraries and a tradition of scholarship.

Ptolemy's fame as a geographer rests on his *Guide to Geography,* usually called simply the *Geography.* Divided into eight parts or books, the *Geography* is an attempt to map the entire known world and to establish the scientific principles of mapmaking. Ptolemy's original text was undoubtedly accompanied by many maps, but those have been lost. Ptolemy included enough detailed information in the text, however, that the maps could be reconstructed.

In Book I of *Geography,* Ptolemy tells how to draw a map of the world as he knew it. He describes several kinds of projections, or methods of depicting the curved, three-dimensional surface of the round earth on a flat, two-dimensional map. One of Ptolemy's projections gives the map something of the appearance of a globe, with curved lines representing latitude and longitude.

Ptolemy was not the first geographer to use latitude and longitude to locate points on the earth's surface, but he was probably the first to list systematically many places by their coordinates of latitude and longitude. Books II through VII contain the coordinates of about 8,000 places in the Roman Empire and beyond. In Book VIII he explains how the world map can be divided into 26 smaller maps of particular regions. The combination of a system of projection and the lists of coordinates makes it possible for any mapmaker to reproduce Ptolemy's maps.

Many of Ptolemy's coordinates were incorrect, however. Although scientists of his time could measure latitude almost accurately by their astronomical observations, few such observations had been made. Longitude was even more difficult to measure. Consequently, like other ancient geographers, Ptolemy possessed accurate coordinates for only a few places. In calculating the coordinates for other places, he used distance estimates based on the milestones along main roads. He also gathered information from traveling soldiers and traders. As a result, Ptolemy's information contained significant errors. For example, he made the Mediterranean Sea too large, and when dealing with more distant places, such as southern Africa or India, he made even greater mistakes, such as extending Africa's southern coast eastward to enclose the Indian Ocean.

Around the 800s, Arabic scholars translated the *Geography* into their language, and the work greatly influenced Arab geographers. In the 1400s, when the *Geography* reached Western Europe in a Latin translation, it became extremely popular because it was the best available guide to the known world. Most European maps of the 1400s and 1500s are based on Ptolemy's geography. The work was used as late as the 1490s, when the explorer Christopher COLUMBUS used the Ptolemaic world map, which shows Asia as much wider than it really is, to support his argument that Asia lay within easy sailing distance of western Europe.

Élisée Reclus wrote some of the most ambitious and best-known geographical treatises of the late nineteenth century. Much of his work was on the topic of physical geography but his interests spanned natural history* and the relationships between people and their environments. Few other geographers of the time succeeded in bringing together so many different aspects of science in their work.

Born in Sainte-Foy-la-Grande, France, Reclus was educated at the University of Berlin, where he studied theology* and attended lectures on geography given by Carl RITTER. Although Reclus found these lectures interesting and inspiring, he did not immediately become a geographer. Instead he returned to France and became involved in antigovernment politics there. In 1851, after a military coup*, he left France to live in England, Louisiana, and Colombia. For the next six years he worked as a tutor and a farmer, and he traveled as much as possible.

In 1857 Reclus returned to France and this time devoted himself to the study of geography. He read extensively on the subject and wrote and published several articles on geography and travel. He also found a job with a publishing company. For the next ten years, Reclus traveled

Élisée
RECLUS
1830–1905
GEOGRAPHY

natural history systematic study of nature and natural objects in their original settings

theology study of religion

coup sudden, often violent, overthrow of a ruler or government

throughout France and neighboring countries to gather information for the company's *Guides Joanne* travel books.

Around the same time, Reclus began to approach geography from an academic perspective. He wrote scholarly articles that were well received by other geographers and won him admission to the Société de Géographie, an organization of French geographers. In 1868 he published the first volume of *La Terre* (The Earth), a treatise that dealt with physical geography and natural history and helped establish his fame as a geographer. The second volume was published the following year.

Geography, however, was not Reclus's only passion. He continued to play an active role in politics, eventually adopting an anarchist perspective, opposing all forms of government. In 1872, he was imprisoned and then banished from France for his antigovernment activities. Settling in Switzerland, Reclus began work on what would become his most famous project—*Nouvelle géographie universelle* (New Universal Geography), a multivolume geography of the world that was illustrated with carefully drawn maps and charts.

The first volume appeared in 1876. To gather information for the work, Reclus visited parts of Africa and the Americas, as well as much of Europe; he also read the ideas of other geographers. At first he intended for there to be five or six volumes, but he soon discovered he could not fit all he wanted to say in that space. When the final installment was published in 1894, the work was 19 volumes long and had taken nearly as many years to complete. The Société de Géographie awarded him a gold medal for the work and the Royal Geographical Society in England recognized the value of his contribution.

Reclus then moved to Belgium to take a teaching position at a new university in Brussels. He also began to write a new six-volume work, *L'Homme et la terre* (Humans and the Earth), in which he examined the connections between people and their environment; it was an early example of a social and cultural geography. Much of the work was published after his death.

Toward the end of his life, Reclus grew increasingly interested in cartography (mapmaking). He proposed the construction of several enormous globes with relief features, which he hoped would be symbols of world unity and brotherhood. One such proposal would have resulted in a globe with a diameter of about 420 feet. He was able to interest several colleagues in the project, but the cost was prohibitive, and none of these globes was ever built. Reclus died in Thourout, Belgium, at the age of 75.

Ferdinand von
RICHTHOFEN

1833–1905

GEOGRAPHY, GEOLOGY

Ferdinand von Richthofen was an important figure in the fields of geography and geology. His knowledge of Chinese geography was unsurpassed among scientists of his time, and he is known for his analysis of rocks in Asia, Europe, and North America.

Richthofen was born in the town of Karlsruhe in present-day Poland. He studied geology at two universities, graduating from the

University of Berlin in 1856. The next year he joined a geological expedition that toured a section of the Alps. Richthofen's assignment was to compile a report on the group's findings; he also produced a publication of his own that described some of the geological features he had seen. Both were well received by experts in the field.

In the years that followed, Richthofen conducted geological research in the Carpathian range of Eastern Europe. Between 1860 and 1862 he served as a staff geologist on a Prussian* government-sponsored trip to eastern Asia. Richthofen visited Sri Lanka, Japan, Thailand, and several other countries that he found fascinating and was especially intrigued by tropical environments, which he had never seen before. Unfortunately, his notes relating to this trip were lost.

Richthofen next traveled to California to study the Sierra Nevada range, where he made important geological discoveries, such as the location of new gold fields in the mountains. In 1868 Richthofen again traveled to Asia and spent the next four years studying the geology and geography of China. He made seven journeys through the Chinese provinces, recording what he saw in sketchbooks and hand-drawn maps.

Returning to Germany in 1872, Richthofen prepared his notes for publication in book form. His finished work, *China: Ergebnisse eigener Reisen und darauf gegründeter Studien* (China: The Results of My Travels and the Studies Based Thereon), which appeared in three volumes between 1877 and 1912, discusses and analyzes the geological heritage of China. Illustrated with detailed maps, the books contain descriptions of the kinds of rocks typical of various parts of the country and explanations of how the land had affected the movement of people.

Richthofen was also active in the scientific community. He served as president of a German geographical society, and he was instrumental in establishing an oceanographic* institute. He taught at universities in Bonn, Leipzig, and Berlin, and at the same time he continued to work on research and writing projects. Foremost among these was *Führer für Forschungsreisende* (A Guide for Research Expeditions)—a manual for geographers doing fieldwork. Richthofen asserted that scientists should begin with a clear, unbiased description of a region's physical features and from there, move toward more complex questions, such as the relationships between various landforms. Richthofen's guide was a practical tool for young scientists, and it provided a way of defining and structuring the study of geography.

At the age of 72, Richthofen died of a stroke in Berlin. His influence, however, continued for years; many of his students went on to become professors of geography themselves.

In 1983, when Sally Kristen Ride undertook a six-day flight aboard the space shuttle *Challenger*, she became the first American woman in outer space. Trained in astrophysics*, Ride served in support capacities on various shuttle missions before she made the first of her two flights. Although she spent less than ten years working for the space program, her name and face became recognized quickly in households through-

Sally Kristen
RIDE

born 1951

SPACE EXPLORATION

*astrophysics branch of astronomy that seeks to explain the movement and the physical and chemical properties of heavenly bodies

out the United States. Moreover, her status as the first American woman to travel in space made her a symbol of women's progress.

Ride was born in Encino, California. Her father was a professor of political science, and her mother worked as a volunteer at a local prison. Early on, Ride showed a penchant for physical activity. After graduating from high school, she attempted to become a professional tennis player, but she gave up when she realized that her skills were not sufficient to enable her to play at the highest levels of the sport.

Instead, Ride enrolled at Stanford University in Palo Alto, California, where she studied both physics and English literature, graduating in 1973 with two bachelor's degrees. Although she knew that she wanted to pursue graduate studies, she was at first uncertain which discipline to follow. In the end she chose physics, earning her master's and doctoral degrees from Stanford in 1975 and 1978.

NASA. Shortly before receiving her doctorate, Ride saw a newspaper advertisement from the National Aeronautics and Space Administration (NASA), the U.S. government agency in charge of space exploration. NASA was looking for young scientists interested in becoming mission specialists for future space flights. These specialists would serve in various capacities, some in flight and some on the ground; typically, they would be responsible for one aspect of a shuttle launch.

Although Ride had never seriously considered being an astronaut, she decided to apply. She was one of about 8,000 people who expressed interest. After a long and grueling application process that included physical and psychological examinations as well as interviews with NASA officials, 35 applicants were admitted into the program. Six of the 35 were women; they became the first group of American women to be accepted into an astronaut-training program—Ride was among the six.

In 1978, immediately after her graduation, Ride began a yearlong course of training to prepare for the demands of space travel. There was no guarantee that she would ever actually make a journey into outer space; few NASA trainees did. However, the training helped prepare her mentally and physically for the possibility of spaceflight. Her studies included navigation, water survival, and pilot training, among the many disciplines that potential astronauts need to learn.

Crew Member. Ride's specific responsibility was to work with a team of scientists to design and construct a mechanical arm controlled by a remote radio. Using the arm, shuttle crews would launch satellites deeper into space. The crews would also use the arm to capture the satellites from space once they had obtained sufficient data.

After completing her training, Ride served as a member of the support staff for shuttle launches. Twice, she served as a communications officer during flights of the shuttle *Columbia.* Working from the ground, she sent radio messages to the crew and was in charge of receiving the messages that the astronauts sent in reply. Ride won

Sally Ride was a heroine to feminists everywhere, but while she was the first American woman to travel into space, other women had been there before her. Nearly 20 years earlier, Russia sent the first woman cosmonaut into space, and only one year before Ride's mission, sent another woman cosmonaut into space.

respect from her colleagues for her work; she was considered intelligent, a flexible thinker, and an excellent team player.

In March 1982 Ride was selected as a member of the crew for an upcoming flight of the space shuttle *Challenger*. Many Americans, who saw Ride's selection as an important symbol of progress for women everywhere, greeted the announcement with enthusiasm. Ride would not be the first woman in space; the former Soviet Union had sent Valentina TERESHKOVA on a mission in 1963 and Svetlana Savitskaya in 1982. Still, NASA's decision to include Ride on the flight struck a chord across the country, and Ride quickly became a hero and role model.

Wanted: Pilots and Scientists

The advertisement to which Sally Ride responded represented a significant policy change for NASA. In the past, department officials had looked exclusively to military test pilots when they needed to recruit new astronauts. Shortly before Ride joined NASA, however, the department had decided to expand its horizons and consider hiring scientists as well. The reason was practical—NASA was increasingly taking on scientific research and space exploration projects. With scientific skills and knowledge becoming more significant than the ability to fly an airplane, Ride and other scientists became eligible to hold important positions in the space program.

In preparation for the flight, Ride again underwent rigorous training. On June 18, 1983, she and four other astronauts, all male, lifted off from the *Challenger*'s base in Cape Canaveral, Florida. Several hundred thousand spectators watched the launch, many of whom were present just to support Ride. Many onlookers wore T-shirts bearing the inscription "Ride, Sally Ride."

Satellites and Experiments. Ride's responsibilities aboard *Challenger* were varied. She helped release and deploy two communication satellites. One of these was a Canadian satellite called Anik-C; the other, known as Palapa B, belonged to Indonesia. Both of the satellites were released as scheduled, and both launches were successful.

Another assignment involved the mechanical arm that Ride had helped design. The shuttle crew ran several tests on the arm to see how well it performed in actual space conditions. Ride was pleased with its success. Among the tests she conducted was a successful release and capture of a 3,300-pound space laboratory. It soon became evident that the arm could be used to retrieve broken satellites, to bring them to the shuttle for repairs, and to release them back into space.

Ride also served as flight engineer aboard the shuttle mission and participated in scientific experiments involving the effects of zero gravity. On June 24 *Challenger* returned successfully to earth, this time landing at Edwards Air Force Base in California. Back on land, Ride was the subject of many profiles and interview requests. It was clear that she had greatly enjoyed her time in space. She said, "The thing I'll remember most about the flight is that it was fun," and, "In fact, I'm sure it was the most fun that I'll ever have in my life."

Afterward. In October 1984 Ride served on a second shuttle mission, again on board the *Challenger*. On this voyage her crew included another woman, Kathryn Sullivan, who became the first American woman to walk in space. Ride and the rest of the crew deployed a new satellite and experimented with ways of refueling satellites in space. They also made extensive observations of earth using a large camera. This journey lasted eight days and was Ride's last venture into space.

Although Ride made no further space flights, she remained with NASA for several years. She became a liaison between NASA and private corporations that collaborated on the space program. Her responsibility was to coordinate planning and make sure that partnerships benefited all parties. As the role of the private sector within the space program increased, her position gradually took on more importance.

In 1986 a shuttle mission ended in tragedy when the *Challenger* exploded immediately after launch, killing all seven of its crew. Ride was named to a 13-member commission to study what had gone wrong. The commission determined that several technical mistakes had occurred. Its report also pointed out several flaws in NASA's policies and procedures. The following year, Ride retired from NASA and accepted a fellowship at Stanford University. Two years later she moved on to a position as director of the Space Science Institute at the

University of California at San Diego. She also taught in the university's physics department and wrote books for children and adults about her experiences in space and as a scientist.

As the first American woman to travel into space, Ride had an enormous impact on the U.S. space program, especially where public awareness of the program was concerned. Today Ride is an enthusiastic advocate for the cause of women in science and in the space program.

Carl
RITTER

1779–1859

GEOGRAPHY, HISTORY

Carl Ritter is generally considered one of the most important figures in the development of geography as an academic discipline. Many historians of geography believe that his ideas were so influential as to make him the founder of the field. In his roles as teacher, scholar, and writer, Ritter helped shape many generations of geographers, and his work continues to influence scholars.

Ritter, one of six children, was born in the town of Quedlinburg in the Harz Mountains of central Germany. In 1796, he enrolled at the University of Halle where he studied a range of subjects, but concentrated on the management of government land. Ritter's interest in geography was sparked two years later when he took a position in Frankfurt as a private tutor for the children of a wealthy banker. He took his students on field trips and taught them about the history, people, and physical formations of the region they were visiting. In his spare time Ritter worked on several geographical projects of his own; he drew maps of the countryside and worked on a book about European geography.

Interdisciplinary Studies. Published in two volumes in 1804 and 1807, *Europa: ein geographisch-historisch-statistisches Gemälde* (Europe: A Geographic, Historical, and Statistical Portrait) broke ground in the study of geography. Earlier books on the topic had often consisted of facts about landforms, political boundaries, and geology, but Ritter's work moved well beyond lists. He posed interesting questions about why different lands and people were the way they were. He also looked at geographical research from a broad, interdisciplinary perspective. The emphasis on history, in particular, became a hallmark of Ritter's work.

In 1807 Ritter met the Swiss educator Johann Heinrich Pestalozzi and the German scientist Alexander von HUMBOLDT, who was recognized at the time as the world's foremost geographer. Both men encouraged Ritter to build on his success as a geographer and writer, influencing him to return to school to become a geography professor. Before long, Ritter was enrolled at the University of Göttingen in central Germany.

During his years at Göttingen, Ritter began a new writing project—a geographical examination of the entire world. The first volume of *Die Erdkunde im Verhältniss zur Natur und zur Geschichte des Menschen* (Geography in Relation to Nature and the History of Man) was published in 1817 and met with critical approval. It was followed the next year by a second volume. In all, the series contained 19 volumes

Converting to Geography

Many students at the Universities of Frankfurt and Berlin took courses from Carl Ritter. In several cases, he helped change the direction of these students' lives and careers. Élisée Reclus came to Berlin with the intention of studying religion, and Ferdinand von Richthofen planned to study the sciences. After attending Ritter's lectures, both men opted for careers in geography. Few geographers have had such an influence on their students as Ritter.

Instead of writing textbooks that served merely as a catalog of facts to be memorized, Carl Ritter concentrated on creating geographical works that intellectually stimulated his students.

*Prussian of or relating to Prussia, a country that existed from the 1400s until 1947 in the area of present-day eastern and central Europe

*cartographic of or relating to cartography, or mapmaking

that were published during a span of more than 40 years; even then, Ritter believed he was far from finished with the work. Modern scholars believe that *Die Erdkunde* is one of the most comprehensive works ever undertaken by an individual.

Academia. *Die Erdkunde* represented something new in the study of geography. Ritter's main focus was not on the descriptions of land and boundaries but on larger questions. In particular, his new work examined how physical environments had shaped and influenced human activities over the years. Although the work was considered difficult to read and often somewhat obscure, it established Ritter's reputation as a scholar of importance. In 1819 he accepted a post teaching history at the University of Frankfurt, and the following year he went to the University of Berlin to take a newly created position in the geography department—becoming the first geography professor in Germany.

That Ritter's first university job was in the history department at Frankfurt was no accident. His academic interests were rooted in history and geography, and he often stressed the connection between the two disciplines. Some geographers, during his time as well as afterward, considered Ritter primarily a historian because of his emphasis on the impact of landforms and terrain over time. Today, many believe that Ritter was both a geographer and a historian—he was probably the first advocate of a geographical interpretation of history.

Ritter brought more than history into the study of geography, however. He was interested in all kinds of scientific study and was eager to develop the relationships between each of these disciplines and geography. In his view, geography was a science: that is, land and people behave according to certain rules and natural laws. He was an observer and was more inclined to report what he had seen than to formulate and prove hypotheses; indeed, in his writings he did not devote much time to describing the natural laws that he believed underlay geographical science.

Teaching, Awards, and Travels. Ritter spent the rest of his career at the University of Berlin. In 1821 he formally received his doctoral degree. He was noted as an outstanding teacher whose lectures, in contrast to some of his writings, were structured carefully and easy to understand. In a time when professors typically taught by simply reading aloud their lecture notes, Ritter preferred to use more interesting methods. For example, he used the blackboard extensively while he lectured—perhaps a small point today but a decided break with the traditions of the time.

Ritter received many honors and awards for his work. In 1822 he was chosen to join the Prussian* Academy of Sciences, and six years later he founded the Berlin Geographical Society. Toward the end of his career, he was named curator (caretaker) of the Prussian Royal Cartographic* Institute. Well respected by their colleagues, Ritter and Humboldt were most likely the two best-known geographers of the time.

Ritter also undertook travels in and around Europe, especially during the 1830s. During these trips he learned about the people and places he visited, often with an eye toward writing about them in an academic paper or book. Although he was willing to learn from the descriptions of other travelers and writers—he explored very little of Asia and none of Africa, despite writing extensively about each—he preferred firsthand experience whenever possible. Ritter also hoped to meet with fellow geographers and other scientists on his travels, eager to learn more about current trends in his own and related fields. His journeys included trips to Ireland, Turkey, Norway, and France, and he returned with a wealth of new knowledge and experiences each time.

His Legacy. Ritter died in Berlin at age 80; he was still serving as a professor. Much of his work remained unfinished at the time of his death; his teaching and travel schedules had limited the amount of time available for research and writing. In particular, the massive *Erdkunde,* although 19 volumes and about 20,000 pages long, was not as far along as he had hoped. In fact, the volumes dealt mainly with Asia; he had barely begun to cover Europe or the Americas. Nevertheless, *Die Erdkunde* stands as one of the great works on geography, and its creator ranks among the world's finest and most influential geographers. With the possible exception of his friend and colleague Humboldt, no one is more deserving of the title of the first modern geographer.

James Clark Ross was one of the few early explorers who traveled in both the Arctic and the Antarctic. Interested in magnetism and its effects on the earth, Ross discovered the north magnetic pole and attempted to locate the one at the South Pole as well. (The north and south magnetic poles are the areas near the earth's geographic poles that attract magnetic compass needles.)

Born in London, England, Ross joined the Royal Navy at age 11. For several years he served under his uncle, the explorer John Ross, when the latter surveyed the North Sea, the Baltic Sea, and other northern European waters. In 1818 Ross accompanied his uncle and William PARRY on a mission to find a Northwest Passage*. The voyage was unsuccessful, but for the next nine years, the young Ross accompanied Parry on four more Arctic expeditions. Three of these expeditions were a search for a Northwest Passage; the fourth was an attempt to reach the North Pole. These voyages also gave Ross the experience of spending winters in the Arctic, unusual among explorers at the time.

The North Magnetic Pole. In 1827 Ross was promoted to the rank of commander in the navy. Two years later he received a compelling offer. A wealthy English businessman named Felix Booth was willing to underwrite the costs of another expedition to locate the Northwest Passage. Booth chose John Ross as the commander, who then asked James to serve as his second-in-command.

James Clark
ROSS

1800–1862

POLAR EXPLORATION,
NAVIGATION, GEOMAGNETISM

*Northwest Passage water route connecting the Atlantic and Pacific Oceans through the Arctic islands of northern Canada

*sledge heavy sled that is mounted on runners for traveling over snow and ice

The voyage was more difficult than expected. The officers spent four years in the central Canadian Arctic, two more than any European polar explorer had previously spent. James Ross used the time well, however. He explored the region surrounding King William Island and the Boothia Peninsula—named after the expedition's backer—where the ships were trapped. Traveling by sledge* and by boat, he recorded his observations and impressions.

In the spring of 1831, Ross found the north magnetic pole at a location not far from the camp on the Boothia Peninsula. "It almost seemed as if we had accomplished every thing that we had come so far to see and do," he wrote, thrilled with the discovery. The expedition returned to England in 1833.

In 1836 Ross made one more trip to the Arctic. He sailed aboard the HMS *Cove* to Baffin Bay to aid a group of whaling ships caught in the ice. After that voyage, he spent some time doing magnetic surveys in England. When he resumed his exploring interests, he turned his attention southward. In 1839 a British scientific organization sponsored an expedition to the Antarctic and placed Ross in command.

Antarctic Research. The primary goal of the journey was to gather scientific information. Ross was instructed to carry out magnetic surveys and to chart and map Antarctic territory. He also hoped to locate the southern magnetic pole.

Ross planned carefully for the voyage. From the winters he had spent in the Arctic, he knew that eating a variety of foods would help preserve the crew's health, so he carried vegetables, berries, and meats aboard his ships, the *Terror* and the *Erebus*. Knowing, too, the importance of comfort during dark, cold winters, he redesigned the ships' interiors. He also made certain that the two ships were strong enough to survive the ice they might encounter. In September 1839, when Ross was satisfied with the preparations, the ships left England.

Ross's route did not lead directly to Antarctica. Instead, he made several stops to set up stations where scientists could observe and study the earth's magnetism. The *Erebus* and the *Terror* docked near the Cape of Good Hope at the southernmost tip of Africa to establish an observatory; another was set up in Tasmania, Australia. Throughout the voyage Ross recorded his observations of the oceans and the stars.

*floe floating mass of ice

The Continent. On January 1, 1841, 15 months after setting out from England, Ross's expedition finally crossed the Antarctic Circle. They soon encountered heavy ice that threatened to destroy the ships, but Ross pushed his way through the floes*. A week later, the vessels broke through the ice and sailed into an open sea that now bears his name.

Ross sailed along the edge of the continent, exploring and surveying from aboard his ship. He located and named many mountains, islands, and other features. His discoveries included the active volcano that he named Mount Erebus and a section of the continent that he called Victoria Land in honor of the queen of England. By the end of January, Ross had voyaged farther south than any previous expedition

James Ross is shown here with a few members of his crew, braving the cold Antarctic waters to discover Victoria Land, which he so named in honor of England's queen. Soon after that discovery, Ross uncovered a sea and an ice shelf, both of which today bear his name.

had done. The *Terror* and the *Erebus* continued sailing along the coast. In mid-February, Ross decided to abandon his search for a sea passage that would lead through the land to the south magnetic pole.

Hoping to avoid the furies of an Antarctic winter, the expedition sailed to Australia, arriving at Derwent River in Tasmania on April 6, 1841. On November 23 the expedition set out again for Antarctica. Conditions were miserable, however; the ships narrowly avoided being crushed between ice floes, and ice formed daily on the sides and masts of the vessels. Ross could not find a break in the land. Although he knew from his observations and experiments that he was close to the south magnetic pole, he was nevertheless forced to give up the attempt. The ships left Antarctica in March 1842 and spent the winter in the Falkland Islands off the eastern coast of South America.

On December 17, 1842, Ross and his crew left the Falklands for one last attempt to penetrate the Antarctic continent. The ships reached the Weddell Sea south of South America, but met "dense, impenetrable, pack ice." Ross again abandoned his plan and returned to England on March 5, 1843, armed with extensive scientific information. In 1847 Ross published a two-volume account of his voyage, in which he made contributions to geology, biology, and the study of geomagnetism*.

In 1848 Ross was appointed to lead an unsuccessful search party for Sir John FRANKLIN, whose expedition had been lost in the Canadian Arctic. The unsuccessful search for Franklin was Ross's last expedition. Ross spent his last years as an acknowledged authority on polar exploration and the magnetism of the earth. Knighted and awarded several prizes for his contributions to science and exploration, Ross died in Aylesbury, England, shortly before his 62nd birthday.

*geomagnetism study of the earth's magnetic field

Rollin Daniel
SALISBURY

1858–1922

GEOLOGY, PHYSICAL GEOGRAPHY

Rollin Daniel Salisbury was a major influence on the study of earth sciences during the early twentieth century. A professor of geology and a college administrator, he was perhaps best known for his textbooks and journal articles. Through fieldwork in Wisconsin, New Jersey, and Greenland, he contributed to the then-new science of glaciology, or the study of glaciers and their effect on the earth.

Salisbury was born in Spring Prairie, Wisconsin, where he grew up as the son of farmers. At first he studied to be a teacher, but after teaching for one year he decided to pursue further education. He enrolled at Beloit College in southern Wisconsin, where he became intrigued by the work of a geology professor named T.C. Chamberlin. In 1881 Salisbury graduated with a bachelor's degree and worked for one year as Chamberlin's assistant at the United States Geological Survey.

In 1884, when Chamberlin left Beloit, the college appointed Salisbury to take his place. The following year Salisbury published his first geological paper, a collaboration with Chamberlin. His work at Beloit was interrupted for a year (1887–1888) by a trip to Heidelberg, Germany. There Salisbury continued his education and conducted research on European glaciation. This experience led to another paper, which like the first brought him some prominence among geologists.

Salisbury stayed at Beloit until 1891, when Chamberlin, then the president of the University of Wisconsin, offered him a job. The following year, however, Salisbury and Chamberlin moved to the newly founded University of Chicago, where Chamberlin became the chair of the geology department and Salisbury a professor of geographic geology.

Salisbury continued to focus his research on glaciers. He joined an expedition to Greenland in 1895; he also studied glacial development in Wisconsin, the Rocky Mountains, and New Jersey. Collaborating with Chamberlin or with his students, Salisbury published influential articles on glaciology that were based on his research and field trips.

In 1893 Salisbury was appointed a managing editor for the *Journal of Geography;* he later became the journal's editor in chief. Salisbury also served as president of the Geographic Society of Chicago and was active in other professional organizations. Salisbury also took on important administrative posts. In 1899 he became dean of the university's graduate school, a position he held for more than 20 years. He also served as head of the geological department and later as chair of the department of geography.

In spite of his administrative responsibilities, he continued to teach and to write textbooks that shaped the study of earth science and geography. His first text, *Geology,* coauthored with Chamberlin, was a three-volume work that appeared between 1904 and 1906. Later, he wrote or coauthored three books: *Physiography*, Elements of Geography,* and *Modern Geography,* all of which were widely used in college classrooms. Salisbury died in Chicago shortly before his 64th birthday, having devoted his life and his energies to work.

*physiography physical geography

A naval officer with an interest in the Antarctic, Robert Falcon Scott led the second official British expedition to reach the South Pole. Although Scott and his four companions died while returning to base camp, their heroic and courageous expedition remains among the most compelling narratives in the history of exploration.

Scott was born in Devonport, England, and he joined the Royal Navy at age 14. Stationed in western Canada, the Mediterranean Sea, and the Caribbean Sea, he rose quickly through the ranks. In June 1900, having risen to the position of first lieutenant, Scott was invited to command a British expedition to Antarctica. The continent was still a mystery at that time, although many previous expeditions had reached the coastline and many explorers had spent time on the continent itself. Scott's sponsors were motivated to mount an expedition, hoping to fill in the missing areas on the map. Moreover, patriotic feeling ran high, and British officials were anxious to send a British explorer to bolster a British claim to the continent and to the South Pole.

Scott Explores Antarctica. Scott spent a year planning and outfitting the expedition, working out the smallest details. Finally, on August 6, 1901, he set sail from England aboard the *Discovery,* which was built especially for this voyage, with a 47-member crew consisting of experienced seamen, naval officers, geologists, naturalists*, and physicians. After stopping at the Madeira Islands, the *Discovery* continued along to Cape Town, arriving there on October 3. Because the voyage was progressing slower than Scott had planned, he decided to sail directly to Lyttleton, New Zealand, without stopping in Australia as he had planned. He arrived at Lyttleton at the end of November, and about a month later he set out for Antarctica.

On January 8, 1902, Scott and his men arrived at McMurdo Sound in Antarctica, which they would use as base camp for the next two years. Although conditions were often miserable and many men suffered from disease and frostbite, the expedition was a success. Scott explored large stretches of Antarctica, coming at one point within 500 miles of the South Pole—easily the farthest south that any explorer had yet traveled. He explored the Ross Ice Shelf and traveled as far as the Edward VII Peninsula, which he named in honor of the English king. Scott and his crew recorded information about ice, penguins, and other features of Antarctica. The expedition returned to England in 1904.

Fundraising for Another Expedition. During the years that followed, Scott resumed his naval career, but Antarctica was constantly on his mind. He hoped to undertake a second expedition to the South Pole, but raising the funds proved difficult. Meanwhile, the goal of reaching the pole was beginning to attract other explorers as well. Ernest SHACK-LETON, who had accompanied Scott on his first voyage, was planning an expedition to the continent; so were several explorers from other European nations. Eager to be the first to set foot at the bottom of the world, Scott devoted himself to gaining financial support for another expedition.

Robert Falcon
SCOTT

1868–1912

POLAR EXPLORATION

See Scott's route to the South Pole in the "Maps" section.

*naturalist one who studies objects in their natural settings

By early 1910 Scott had secured the necessary funds. The South Pole was still unconquered; Shackleton had come close and had even surpassed Scott's "farthest south" mark. As before, Scott's journey had a scientific purpose; he hired three geologists, a naturalist, and a physicist. However, he was clear that scientific and geographic exploration would be subordinated to his main goal—reaching the pole.

Expedition to the South Pole.

In June 1910 Scott embarked on his voyage. He arrived at Cape Evans on McMurdo Sound on January 4, 1911, and immediately went to work. He planned to use a combination of ponies, skis, sledges*, and sled dogs to make the overland journey to the pole. He also set up supply stations along his intended route and stocked them with food, fuel, and other supplies. For the rest of the year, Scott's party explored and studied the region surrounding their camp; mostly, they readied themselves for a push to the pole. Scott also learned that he was not the only explorer in the region. The Norwegian Roald AMUNDSEN, an experienced Arctic adventurer, was encamped nearby and had the same goal as Scott did. Although his rival's polar experience worried Scott, he did not to change his plans.

On November 1, 1911, Scott left Cape Evans with 11 men. Travel proved more difficult than Scott had expected. He had brought along several motorized sledges, which he hoped would make transport easier, but they proved virtually useless. Scott had also brought along ponies, but they lasted just over a month. Because he had not brought along sled dogs, the strenuous work of hauling the sledges and supplies up the 10,000-foot-high Beardmore Glacier fell to the men. After they had climbed the glacier, seven men returned to the McMurdo camp.

The five-member party endured many blizzards that slowed their progress; one in early December delayed them by four days. When conditions improved, they moved quickly and by late December, their goal was in sight. Unfortunately, the delays had cost them time and energy. The men were growing exhausted and increasingly weak, but Scott persisted. They began the final trek to their destination. Scott and his companions reached the pole on January 18, 1912, but were disappointed when they realized that Amundsen had already been there. "Great God!" Scott wrote. "This is an awful place and terrible enough for us to have laboured to it without the reward of priority."

Back to Camp.

Having conquered the pole, Scott and his party began the journey back to camp. The weather was bitterly cold, and the crew's run-down condition became increasingly worrisome. One man's feet ached continually; another fell and strained a leg muscle. Food supplies ran low, and only became worse. It was taking too long to make their way between supply depots, but they simply could not move faster. Scott lowered their daily rations in the hope of making food last longer, but his decision only further weakened the men.

*sledge heavy sled that is mounted on runners for traveling over snow and ice

Robert Scott is shown here in his expedition hut writing in his journal. His journal, which contains a detailed account of his findings and activities, was found in the tent where he died.

The situation became desperate. They discovered that their fuel supplies at many of the depots had leaked. Temperatures dropped far below zero, yet in some spots the snow was so soft that travel through it was virtually impossible. In the middle of February one man died and a month later another frostbitten crewmember walked out of his tent and was never seen again. "I am just going outside," Scott quoted him as saying, "and may be some time." There is little doubt that he committed suicide to avoid slowing down his companions.

The three remaining men continued the journey, but before they reached the next supply depot, another blizzard hit. The end was near. For several days the men lay weakly in their tent. "Have decided it shall be natural," wrote Scott, referring to death. "We shall march for the depot and die in our tracks." However, the storm proved too long and too severe for them to make an attempt. On March 29, Scott wrote the final entry in his diary. "We shall stick it out to the end," he wrote, "but we are getting weaker, of course, and the end cannot be far. It seems a pity, but I do not think I can write more. For God's sake look after our people." He died that day or the next at age 43.

On November 12, 1912, a search party from Cape Evans found the tent in which Scott and his two companions had died. His journal, which gave a complete account of the expedition, was found as well. The story of Scott's attempt and death did not become known until the winter of 1913, when the rest of the expedition returned to England. Scott became a hero and his wife was knighted in his place. Nearly a century later, Scott is still considered a gallant and courageous explorer.

Ellen Churchill
SEMPLE

1863–1932

GEOGRAPHY

Ellen Churchill Semple was the first well-known American female geographer. A writer and a teacher, she was the first to propose that human behavior was influenced by the physical environment. Although this perspective has since fallen out of fashion, Semple's influence during her time was great.

Semple was born in Louisville, Kentucky, and was educated at public schools and at home. Admitted to Vassar College at age 16, she graduated three years later near the top of her class. While at Vassar, she took two trips to Europe and another after her graduation. She returned to Louisville where she taught history and languages at various schools. Although she was a good teacher, she was not fully satisfied. Claiming "there was insufficient intellectual stimulation," she began to study other subjects on her own.

In 1889 Semple returned to Vassar to work on a master's degree. Although the college did not offer a formal program in geography, Semple, inspired by the works of the well-known German geographer Friedrich Ratzel, grew increasingly interested in the subject. She received her M.A. in 1891 and went to the University of Leipzig in Germany, hoping to take courses taught by Ratzel himself.

In keeping with the standards of German universities at the time, Leipzig did not allow women to enroll as students, but Ratzel allowed Semple to attend some of his lectures. Although Semple soon returned to Louisville to resume her teaching duties, the study of geography had become her main interest. In 1894 she published her first article on the subject, and the following year she traveled once more to Leipzig for further instruction by Ratzel. When she returned to Kentucky this time, she became a full-time geographer.

A Career in Geography. In the years that followed, Semple wrote many articles about Louisville and the nearby Appalachian Mountains. Her interest was not simply in describing the physical features of these regions, but also in making connections between the area's landforms and the people who lived and traveled there. One article, for example, dealt with the effect of the Appalachians on colonial American history; another investigated the relationship between the mountaineers of eastern Kentucky and the hills in which they lived. She also wrote on the geography of Alaska and Germany, and she studied oceans as well.

In 1903 Semple published her first book, *American History and Its Geographic Conditions*, which was soon adopted as a textbook in many colleges and won her acclaim as a first-class geographer. Semple then took a job as an associate editor of a geography journal, and she became a charter member of the Association of American Geographers (AAG). In 1906 the University of Chicago hired her as a part-time lecturer.

In addition to her teaching duties, Semple busied herself with planning a new book. She planned this volume to be an English version of her mentor Ratzel's ideas on geography; although Ratzel was respected in Europe, many of his ideas were unknown in the United States. However, after Ratzel's death in 1904, Semple's version began to diverge somewhat from her original ideas. When *Influences of Geographic Environment* appeared in 1911, the work was a combination of Ratzel's views and Semple's own ideas.

Determinism. The work summed up Semple's perspective on the connection between human behavior and land: "Man is a product of the earth's surface." In her view, geographical features presented people with specific problems. Agriculture, for example, is especially difficult in areas where there is a shortage of water or in locations near steep mountain slopes. She also argued that geography often provided solutions to these problems. Although she was careful to say that the environment does not control people, it was clear that she subscribed to the "determinist" theory of geography, which states that landforms play a vital role in the development of human history.

Critics applauded Semple's achievement and her colleagues agreed that the book was an important contribution to geography. Institutions across the country invited her to lecture, and after several years of serving as a visiting lecturer, she accepted a professorship at Clark University in Worcester, Massachusetts. Her work also brought honors; she received a medal from the American Geographical Association and she became the first female president of the AAG.

Immediately after completing *Influences of Geographic Environment,* Semple took a trip around the world. Particularly intrigued by the region surrounding the Mediterranean Sea, she began to work on a book on its geography. The work, titled *The Geography of the Mediterranean Region: Its Relation to Ancient History,* was published in 1931. It combines her interests in landforms, ancient languages, and human history. By this time, however, Semple's health had begun to decline because of heart problems. She died in West Palm Beach, Florida, at age 69.

Junípero SERRA

1713–1784

EXPLORATION OF NORTH AMERICA

*missionary person who works to convert nonbelievers to his or her faith

*theology study of religion

*indigenous referring to the original inhabitants of a region

Known as the "Apostle of California," Father Junípero Serra was a missionary* who played an important role in the Spanish colonization of North America. He founded several missions in parts of present-day California, and he used these missions to extend both the religious power of Christianity and the political power of Spain.

Miguel José Serra was born on the island of Mallorca, off the coast of Spain. He adopted the name Junípero in 1730, when he joined the Franciscan order of monks, and he was ordained a priest in 1738. Serra received a doctoral degree in theology* and worked as a professor in Mallorca's capital. In 1749 he decided to become a missionary in North America. Besides preaching and other priestly duties, his main task was to convert the indigenous* people to Christianity. For the next 18 years he lived and worked in northern and central Mexico.

In 1767 Serra was placed in charge of the Spanish missions in Baja, or Lower, California (part of present-day Mexico). He was also asked to help Spanish leaders move into Alta, or Upper, California (an area

Junípero Serra is under consideration for sainthood by the Catholic Church. Native Americans criticize this decision, however, claiming that Serra enslaved, whipped, and shackled their ancestors, and that his strict, religious way of life destroyed Indian culture.

*beatify to sanctify a person

within present-day California). Although Spain had laid its claim to the region, its political leaders worried that another nation might try to take it away. They asked Serra to establish missions in areas they hoped to colonize. Two years later Serra headed north in spite of his poor health—he suffered from asthma and had difficulty walking.

Serra's first stop was San Diego, where he founded California's earliest mission. In the years that followed, Serra set up another eight missions, including some near present-day San Francisco and Los Angeles, and established his headquarters at San Carlos Borromeo (near present-day Carmel). His missions were designed to encourage Spanish settlement of California and to make the Indians allies of Spain.

On the one hand, Serra offered a more "civilized" way of life to those who came voluntarily to the missions. He introduced the indigenous people to livestock, grains, and fruits that later became staple crops and offered them protection from their enemies. He also taught them crafts, and, as a result, the missions produced goods that were used in other places in California under Spanish control. On the other hand, Serra used force to get the Indians to do what he wanted—most were required to work in the mission's agricultural fields. People who came freely soon found that they were not permitted to leave; Serra authorized brutal punishments for those who tried. The hard work and harsh punishments contributed to many deaths. Some modern observers liken his control over the indigenous people to a form of slavery.

In political and economic terms, the missions fared very well. By attracting settlers and converting about 6,000 Indians to Christianity, the missions indicated that Spain's control over the land was real. The missions also made money, producing enough farm products to send a surplus to Mexico. Serra served in the area as head of the Franciscans until he died at the age of 70 at the Mission San Carlos Borromeo.

Serra's defenders at the end of the twentieth century point to these successes as evidence of Serra's greatness. They also cite his religious enthusiasm. His critics, however, find Serra's willingness to use force for conversion impossible to justify. For better or worse, Serra remains an important figure in California's history and settlement. He was beatified* by the Roman Catholic Church in 1988.

Ernest Henry
SHACKLETON
1874–1922

POLAR EXPLORATION, GEOGRAPHY

A great leader and navigator, Ernest Henry Shackleton was among the great polar explorers of his day. He made several attempts to reach the South Pole and at one point held the record for traveling the farthest south. However, Shackleton is best remembered today for the voyage of the ship *Endurance* and the ill-fated journey into the Antarctic that tested the limits of his crew's physical and mental stamina.

Shackleton was born in County Kildare, Ireland, and he spent his childhood in London. At the age of 16 he left school to join England's merchant marine. Fascinated with boats and ships, he became a member of the Royal Naval Reserve in 1901. That same year he volunteered for duty in the British National Antarctic Expedition commanded by Robert Falcon SCOTT.

The expedition encountered many navigational problems and ended unhappily because Scott had failed to make the proper preparations. Scott was also unprepared for the long, difficult land journeys and made an unrealistic plan to travel a distance of 1,500 miles in 91 days to reach the South Pole. Scott took Shackleton and another companion on this land trip, but the explorers were forced to turn back because of an outbreak of scurvy*. They had traveled just 270 miles in 60 days. Shackleton resolved to return to Antarctica for further exploration.

He returned to London and began to work as a writer. Some years later he became secretary of the Scottish Royal Geographic Society, and because he was still interested in Antarctica, organized his own expedition. Although other members of his expedition would climb Mount Erebus on Ross Island, explore Victoria Land Plateau, and discover the South Magnetic Pole, Shackleton's primary goal was to reach the South Pole itself. Using sledges* and ponies, Shackleton set a new record by coming within 97 miles of the pole, beating Scott's record by 360 miles. Concerned about his ability to return safely, however, he ventured no farther. Returning to England, he was hailed as a hero and knighted by Edward VII.

Shackleton's "farthest south" mark was soon bettered by the Norwegian explorer Roald AMUNDSEN, who in 1912 became the first person to reach the South Pole. In the process, Amundsen beat Scott in the famous race to the South Pole. Shackleton subsequently turned his attention to another goal—becoming the first to travel across the continent of Antarctica. In 1914 he again set out for Antarctica aboard the ship *Endurance*. His first destination was the coastline of the Weddell Sea, a part of the South Atlantic Ocean, where he planned to disembark. From there he planned to journey by land past the South Pole to McMurdo Sound on the opposite side of the continent; a supporting party was assigned to lay supply depots on the McMurdo side.

The voyage, however, was a disaster. The *Endurance* was caught in ice and was unable to reach the shore. Several months later the ship was crushed between ice floes*, forcing Shackleton and his men to encamp on the ice itself. When the ice began to break up, the men launched three small boats they salvaged from the ship. However, winds and currents did not permit them to reach the safety of the Antarctic Peninsula, so they sailed instead to Elephant Island, a rocky and deserted piece of land in the South Atlantic.

Elephant Island, unfortunately, was not an answer to Shackleton's problems. After months of dealing with cold, hunger, and illness, the men were weak and tired. The nearest habitation was on the island of South Georgia, 800 miles away. Despite the risks of sailing on the open sea in the small boat, the *James Caird*, Shackleton decided to attempt the voyage. He chose five members to accompany him to South Georgia and promised to return for the rest once he had found help.

*scurvy disease caused by a lack of vitamin C and characterized by bleeding gums, bleeding under the skin, and extreme weakness

*sledge heavy sled that is mounted on runners for traveling over snow and ice

*floe floating mass of ice

The voyage to South Georgia took 15 days and is one of the most remarkable in history. The men were forced to survive both bitter cold and a dwindling supply of water. It took another two days to find a safe landing on the island. Once ashore, they had to cross a mountain range to the opposite side of the island. After a 36-hour march, Shackleton and two companions arrived at a Norwegian whaling station on the island of South Georgia. With the help of the Norwegians, Shackleton later retuned to rescue the men he had left on Elephant Island. Owing in part to Shackleton's bravery and steady leadership, all of the members of that expedition returned home alive.

Shackleton planned one more journey to Antarctica. In 1921, he sailed from England to conduct geological studies and to chart the Antarctic coastline. The ship had only reached South Georgia, however, when Shackleton's health gave out. He died at age 47 of a heart attack, and was buried in Grytviken, South Georgia. Shackleton published the accounts of his two expeditions: *The Heart of the Antarctic,* published in 1909, contains the story of his journey 97 miles shy of the South Pole, and *South,* published in 1919, contains a report of his Trans-Antarctic Expedition.

THE SINGHS

Nain Singh
ca. 1830–ca. 1882
EXPLORATION OF TIBET

Kishen Singh
ca. 1850–ca. 1921
EXPLORATION OF TIBET

During the second half of the 1800s, people of Asian descent helped the British explore regions in Asia that were off-limits to Europeans. Two of the most successful "geography spies" were cousins, Nain Singh and Kishen Singh. Each made important contributions to the exploration of the Himalaya Mountains, Tibet, and the other regions of Central Asia.

The Geography Spies. The Indian subcontinent was Great Britain's most important foreign colony during the 1800s. As part of their administration of India, the British made a geographic survey. The British surveyors, however, ran into difficulties near the northern edge of India. The Himalaya Mountains, which have the highest peaks in the world, rise like a vast, snow-capped wall along India's northern border. In addition to the challenges of the harsh mountainous terrain, the British encountered hostility from people who were determined to keep Europeans from entering and seizing their territories. Europeans who ventured into these regions were, at best, forcibly turned back across the border and at worst, killed.

Foreigners were especially unwelcome in Tibet, which today occupies a vast plateau north of the Himalaya Mountains. Few outsiders had ever visited Tibet and the British were particularly anxious to gather information because they knew that two great powers, Russia and China, were both exploring Central Asia and maneuvering to increase their power and influence in that part of the world. Geographic information about Tibet, the British believed, would not just be a valuable addition to science, but it would also give them an advantage against the other powers. How could the

British survey Tibet, even when their agents, disguised as Asians, had been discovered?

T.C. Montgomerie of the British survey corps in India came up with the idea of training Indians in surveying techniques. He believed that such individuals could enter Tibet and other forbidden lands without arousing suspicion. If they were careful and secretive, they might be able to carry out scientific measurements. In 1863 Nain Singh was one of the first Indians chosen for training as a secret agent.

Nain Singh's Achievements. Nain Singh ran a village school in northern India. People called him a *pandit*, the Hindi term for a person of learning. The British referred to him by this term, although they pronounced it "pundit," and in time all Indian secret agents were known as pundits.

The British spent two years preparing Nain Singh before sending him into Tibet. They created a false identity for him because it would have been unwise to allow him to travel as a schoolmaster who had connections with the British. Finally, they trained Nain to take survey measurements, such as altitude, latitude, longitude, and the distance and direction of each day's travel. He was instructed to keep these measurements secret, and they would later be converted into maps.

Nain Singh entered Tibet successfully and spent three months in the country's capital, Lhasa, located in the south. He not only carried out the scientific observations necessary to position Lhasa correctly on the map but also learned much about the city and its inhabitants. He even saw the Dalai Lama, leader of the Tibetan Buddhists and head of the country.

By 1866, when Nain returned to Dehra Dun, a city in northeastern India that served as the base of operations for the pundits, he had traveled a distance of more than 1,200 miles. On his way to and from Lhasa he took readings that enabled the British surveyors to map trade routes through the mountains and the Zangbo River (the name of India's upper Brahmaputra River in southern Tibet); its course through the Himalayas had been a geographic mystery until that time.

A year later Nain made his second trip into Tibet. This time he went to Thok Jalung, a place in western Tibet known for its gold mines. He succeeded in observing the mines, and his report helped the British understand that gold was an important Tibetan resource.

Nain's most ambitious journey began in 1873 when he accompanied a British diplomatic* mission from India to the city of Yarkant (now Shache) in the Xinjiang Uygur region in western China. On its way back from Yarkant, he stopped at Leh, the capital of Ladakh—a country in the western Himalayas now divided between India and Pakistan. Although Nain Singh was tired of exploration, his employers urged him to go on one more mission. They wanted him to travel from Leh through northern Tibet—a region almost entirely unknown—to Lhasa. There, he was to join a caravan* that traveled every three years from Lhasa to Beijing, the capital of China. A British official in Beijing would send him back to India by ship. If Nain could

Tricks of the Spy Trade

The Singhs and other pundits, or secret agents, who explored Tibet and Central Asia for the British had to pass themselves off as innocent pilgrims, merchants, or shepherds. They could not be seen measuring distances or making technical observations, which were necessary to produce accurate maps. To this end, they learned clever tricks to conceal the purpose of their journeys. For instance, they learned to communicate in code and to hide tools in secret pockets in their clothing. They practiced taking steps of a specific length so that they could measure distance by counting their paces.

*diplomatic of or relating to diplomacy, the practice of conducting official relations between nations

*caravan large group of people traveling together across a desert or other dangerous region

not join the caravan, he was instructed to journey south through the Himalayas back to India.

By now, Nain Singh was known in Leh and on the Tibetan frontier as a British employee. To sneak into Tibet for a third time, he used an especially complicated scheme in which he pretended to be taking a herd of sheep back to Yarkant. The trick worked, and Nain and four of his companions entered Tibet with the sheep. They made their way across central Tibet—a huge plain dotted with lakes—taking care to avoid the bandits who infested the region. Most of the lakes in this part of Tibet had never been seen by a foreign explorer. Nain Singh mapped all that he passed.

After a brief visit to the gold mines of Thok Daurakpa in central Tibet, which produced less gold than the mines Nain had seen on his earlier trip, the party proceeded southeast. They saw mountains south of their route—today called the Nain Singh Range. In late 1874 Nain and his companions reached Lhasa, four months after they had left Leh and covered a distance of 1,095 miles. Unfortunately, one of the first people they saw in Lhasa was a man from Leh who knew Nain Singh. Fearful that the man might reveal Nain's identity and purpose to the local authorities, Nain decided not to wait for the caravan but to leave Lhasa at once. He sent two of his companions back to Leh with his survey records, and he headed south across the Himalayas. He again mapped the course of the Zangbo River on his journey through the mountains, reaching British India in the spring of 1875, two months after his survey records arrived in Leh.

Nain Singh went on no further expeditions, but he helped train other pundits. He later retired to the Rohilkhand region in northern India, where the British government had given him land as a reward for his services. He also received an income from the British and awards from the Paris Geographical Society and the Royal Geographical Society in London.

Kishen Singh's Achievements. Before retiring from exploration, Nain Singh had helped train a cousin named Kishen Singh. Kishen's first secret mission into Tibet occurred in 1871 and was not a success. He and his companions were robbed by bandits and had to turn back short of their goal, the large lake called Koko Nor (also known as Qinghai) in northern Tibet.

In 1873 Kishen accompanied his cousin Nain on a diplomatic mission to Yarkant. Afterward he traveled southwest of Yarkant into the Pamir Mountains, located in Tajikistan and Kashmir northwest of India. Five years later he and two assistants left India on a mission that would last more than four years and cover 2,800 miles.

Kishen Singh had been instructed to travel north across Tibet and into Mongolia to explore part of the Gobi Desert. The best way to reach Mongolia was to accompany a caravan from Lhasa, so the three travelers made their way to the Tibetan capital. Just as his cousin Nain had done, Kishen and his men pretended to be merchants. They lived in

Lhasa for more than a year observing the people and their customs until they were able to join a caravan for Mongolia.

The caravan, composed of Tibetan and Mongolian merchants, was attacked by bandits in a remote region of the Tibetan plateau. Although Kishen lost everything but his surveying tools, he decided to continue. He led his companions past Koko Nor, where they herded camels for many months to support themselves. One assistant deserted with most of their supplies, but Kishen and the other assistant persisted. In early 1881 they reached the Chinese town of Dunhuang, the entry to the Silk Road, the ancient trade route that ran east and west across Central Asia.

Detained by a suspicious local governor, Kishen and his companion won their freedom with the help of a Buddhist monk, who accompanied them south through China. After parting ways with the monk, they turned west, entered Tibet, and completed the final stretch of their journey through the Himalayas to British India. Exhausted and at the end of their strength, they arrived at their base in late 1882 with their secret information intact.

Kishen received medals and awards and spent the rest of his life in retirement. Together the two men had provided many details regarding one of the remaining blank areas on the world map. One British official said of Nain: "His observations have added a larger amount of important knowledge to the map of Asia than those of any other living man," and claimed that Kishen's trek was a "marvelous journey."

One of the most important women of science during the 1800s, Mary Somerville not only presented the world with new and interesting scientific ideas but she also had to overcome many difficult barriers in order to do so. Her career spanned more than 50 years and resulted in discoveries in astronomy, mathematics, and geography.

Somerville was born in Jedburgh, Scotland. Her early education was limited to one year at a boarding school and a series of lessons in ballroom dancing, needlework, and other spheres of activity that, at the time, were considered feminine. Despite this limited exposure, Somerville became intrigued by mathematics as a teenager. Her parents forbade her to study it, however; they feared the strain would destroy her mind. Somerville, however, found information on her own. During the next decade or so, she studied the subject sporadically. She also married and had two children.

After her husband Samuel Greig died in 1807, Somerville resolved to continue her studies openly. She avidly read works in astronomy and mathematics, including the English physicist Isaac Newton's *Principia*. In 1812, she married again and this time her husband, a physician named William Somerville, encouraged her to learn. Before long Somerville was studying botany and geology in addition to advanced mathematics.

Somerville did not learn solely from books; she also learned from great scientists. As she and her husband traveled throughout Europe,

Mary Fairfax Greig SOMERVILLE

1780–1872

ASTRONOMY, GEOGRAPHY

Mary Somerville was a great supporter of women's education and women's emancipation, and she opposed vivisection (the practice of dissecting the body of a living animal for scientific research).

suffrage right to vote

they were welcomed into the homes of many important thinkers. Most of these men shared their ideas and enthusiasms with the couple, and they typically treated Mary as a fellow scientist.

In 1826 Somerville published her first original paper on the magnetizing effects of sunlight. Later, she would write other experimental papers on light and the spectrum. Her first major scientific success, however, was a book called *The Mechanism of the Heavens*. Partly an explanation of the French scientist Pierre Laplace's theories and partly her ideas, the book was a critical success when it appeared in 1831. Its popularity was a surprise to its publisher, who had only printed 750 copies. It was an even bigger surprise to the author. Worried because she lacked a college degree, Somerville had insisted that the work be kept secret until publication and specified that the manuscript be destroyed if it was not to the editor's liking.

Somerville followed this success three years later with a volume titled *On the Connexion of the Physical Sciences*. This book brought her further acclaim, including honorary memberships in astronomical and scientific societies, most of which barred women from full membership; and an annual pension. The influence of the book would last many years. The astronomer who later discovered the planet Neptune credited his finding to Somerville's observations about the orbit of nearby Uranus.

In 1848, at the age of 68, Somerville published her third and most successful book, *Physical Geography*. Although she was a relative latecomer to the study of geography, she had been working on this volume for at least ten years before its publication. This book focused primarily on landforms, vegetation, and other aspects of the earth's surface; Somerville also investigated the effect of people in changing their environment. As had been true of her other works, *Physical Geography* brought her many awards and honors.

Physical Geography was not Somerville's last work, however. Her final book, on microscopic plants, appeared when she was 89. By then her science was widely considered out-of-date but her publisher, out of loyalty, printed the book anyway. In her later years, Somerville mixed her scientific research with the cause of women's education and suffrage*. She served as a model for many young women interested in science. Appropriately, one of the first women's colleges established at Oxford University was named after her.

Somerville died in Naples, Italy, where she had lived for many years. Perhaps unsurprisingly, she had been hard at work on a mathematical paper until the day before her death.

Henry Morton
STANLEY

1841–1904

EXPLORATION OF AFRICA

Henry Morton Stanley was a journalist whose fame as an explorer rests on three long African expeditions. His first and third trips were to "rescue" Europeans who were believed to be in trouble in the heart of Africa. Although neither of these individuals really needed rescuing, the publicity given to Stanley's efforts made him a popular hero. His most significant achievements were his journeys through the Congo River region and his help in establishing the Belgian Congo colony.

Background and Early Career. Although born in Great Britain, Stanley considered himself an American. He was born in Denbigh, Wales, as John Rowlands. His parents were not married, and he received little love or attention from his mother. His childhood was divided between a workhouse* and relatives who did not care much about him.

Later in life, Rowlands claimed to have suffered cruel treatment at the workhouse and to have escaped from the place. Investigation by modern biographers, however, has shown that these stories were greatly exaggerated. There is no doubt that Rowlands felt the lack of love from his mother and the embarrassment of being an illegitimate child, but he appears to have received an education and to have left the workhouse under ordinary circumstances when he was 15.

A few years later Rowlands went to sea as a cabin boy and traveled from Liverpool, England, to New Orleans, Louisiana. There he found a friend and patron in an American businessman named Henry Stanley. The meeting prompted Rowlands to change his name to that of his new friend, and he later added "Morton" as a middle name.

During the years that followed, Stanley held many positions. He was a soldier in the American Civil War, and he returned to the sea, serving on ships in both the merchant fleet and the U.S. Navy. He also gained experience as a journalist by reporting on events on the frontier of the American West. In 1867 he went to work for James Gordon Bennett, publisher of a major newspaper, the *New York Herald*.

In Search of Livingstone. The *Herald* sent Stanley to East Africa to report on a conflict between British and local forces in the mountainous country of Ethiopia. Stanley then covered the Middle East until an assignment from Bennett took him into Africa on the expedition that made his name—the search for Livingstone.

David LIVINGSTONE was a well-known British missionary* and explorer who had set off in 1866 to search for the source of the Nile River. Since that time, almost no news of Livingstone had reached the outside world, and fears rose about his condition and fate. The *Herald* sent Stanley into Africa to look for the missing explorer and to help him in any way necessary. Stanley did not, however, reveal his purpose to colonial officials in Africa. He wanted his story to be a surprise and did not want other journalists to find Livingstone before he did.

Stanley's journey began in January 1871 in Zanzibar, an island off the coast of Kenya in East Africa. He crossed over to the mainland and made his way inland under difficult conditions—the region was troubled by both war and disease. In November he reached Livingstone's last known location, a town called Ujiji on the shore of Lake Tanganyika. There Stanley encountered the man he had come to find. In his 1872 book *How I Found Livingstone*, Stanley wrote that he greeted the explorer by saying, "Dr. Livingstone, I presume?" The phrase became famous.

The two men together explored the area around Lake Tanganyika. Stanley came to greatly admire Livingstone, who was dedicated to wiping out the slave trade and to exploring Central Africa. Because Living-

workhouse home for orphans, the poor, and others with no means of supporting themselves; residents sometimes had to work for their keep

missionary person who works to convert nonbelievers to his or her faith

The Governor of Equatoria

Emin Pasha, whom Stanley crossed Africa to rescue, was a colorful and somewhat mysterious figure. Born Eduard Schnitzer in Germany, Emin became a doctor before traveling in Turkey and Albania. Sometime around 1870 he changed his name to Emin Pasha and probably also became a Muslim. Abandoning his family, he went to Egypt, where he became the physician of the British governor, who put him in charge of Equatoria, a southern territory ruled by Egypt. A lover of solitude and nature studies, Emin Pasha enjoyed the position. After Stanley "rescued" him, he returned to the interior with a German expedition. Slave traders killed him in 1892.

stone did not want to return to the coast and to "civilization," Stanley, when he reached the coast, sent supplies inland for Livingstone. Stanley headed for London, where he published his book and received a gold medal from Britain's Royal Geographical Society. In 1873 the *Herald* sent Stanley to Ghana, in western Africa, as a war reporter.

Second Expedition. The same year, word of Livingstone's death in Central Africa reached the world. Hearing the news, Stanley decided to carry on Livingstone's work and to complete the exploration and mapping of Central Africa's complex tangle of rivers and lakes. The *Herald* and London's *Daily Telegraph,* in exchange for exclusive rights to print Stanley's stories, financed the expedition.

Stanley set an ambitious goal for his second African journey. He planned to settle the matter of the source of the Nile and to answer questions raised by Livingstone and Richard Francis BURTON, who had also explored Africa. Stanley's journey would have important results for both geography and politics.

As before, he launched his expedition from Zanzibar. In August 1874 Stanley entered Central Africa from the east and made his way to Lake Victoria. He traveled completely around it, confirming the British explorer John Hanning Speke's opinion that the lake was indeed the source of the Nile. While in the region of present-day Uganda, Stanley visited the king of the Buganda people, and as a result of his visit, the king allowed the British to send missionaries into the area a few years later. Uganda later came under British control. Stanley continued to Lake Tanganyika and from there he pushed westward to the Lualaba River. Earlier, Livingstone had thought that this river might feed into the Nile, but Stanley followed it and found that it eventually became the Congo River, which flows in a great semicircle through central Africa before emptying into the Atlantic Ocean on the continent's western shore.

Journeying along the Congo, Stanley and his men faced hostile attacks from local people and they battled malnutrition and starvation as well. Notwithstanding the problems, Stanley made a thorough exploration of the Ituri River, a tributary of the Congo. Traveling sometimes by boat and sometimes overland, the expedition made its way downstream, past a series of huge waterfalls that Stanley named the Livingstone Falls, to the European trading settlements at the mouth of the Congo. Stanley reached the Atlantic Coast in November 1877 after nearly three years of difficult travel. The following year he published *Through the Dark Continent,* in which he described the journey. The book won him a reputation for bravery but also brought criticism of his aggressive, militaristic style of exploration.

The expedition made Stanley an authority on the people and resources of the almost entirely unknown Congo region. He hoped to interest Great Britain in establishing a colony there, but when British authorities failed to act he took his information to King Leopold II of Belgium, who was eager to claim a colony in Africa. Stanley spent five years working in the Congo, overseeing the building of a railroad

This drawing of Henry Stanley meeting David Livingstone at Ujiji, Lake Tanganyika, was drawn from Livingstone's material. When Stanley saw the drawing he said, "It is as correct as if the scene had been photographed."

around the Livingstone Falls and the launching of steamboats on the upper part of the Congo River. The strength and determination he showed in the arduous task of railroad building earned him the African nickname Bula Matari, or "Breaker of Rocks." King Leopold annexed a huge region around the river as the Congo Free State, later renamed the Belgian Congo. Stanley continued to write about his adventures, publishing *The Congo and the Founding of Its Free State* in 1885.

Third Expedition. In 1887 the British government asked Stanley to lead an expedition to help Emin Pasha, a European official who had been stranded near Lake Albert in Central Africa following an uprising of Muslim rebels. Stanley agreed to lead the mission. Having already crossed Africa from east to west, he decided to approach Lake Albert from the west and enter the continent by traveling up the Congo River.

The expedition set out from the mouth of the Congo River on the Atlantic coast in March 1877. Three months later the search party crossed the Livingstone Falls and reached the point where the Congo becomes navigable. The following year Stanley reached Emin Pasha's outpost. Although Emin insisted that it was not necessary for him to leave his territory, Stanley convinced him to leave the area. Stanley then guided about 1,500 people, his own men and Emin's followers, eastward to the Pacific coast, which they reached in December 1889.

During this final journey through eastern Africa, Stanley made some important geographic discoveries. He located the Ruwenzori Mountains, which PTOLEMY and other geographers of the ancient world had called the Mountains of the Moon, and he found a river connecting Lakes Albert and Edward. The Royal Geographical Society awarded Stanley another gold medal after the trip, which he described in his 1890 book, *In Darkest Africa*. Among other notable features, the book contains an account of the little-known Pygmies of the central African rain forest.

His Last Years and Legacy. Stanley spent his final years in England. He was elected to the British Parliament in 1895 and was knighted four years later. He last visited Africa in 1897, an account of which he published in *Through South Africa*. Stanley died in London at age 63, having gained a reputation as a ruthless and aggressive explorer with often-rude manners. However, he has since been praised as one of Africa's more successful explorers.

Vilhjalmur
STEFANSSON

1879–1962

GEOGRAPHY, POLAR
EXPLORATION, ANTHROPOLOGY

*anthropologist scientist who specializes in the study of human beings, especially in relation to origins and physical and cultural characteristics

*Inuit people of the Canadian Arctic and Greenland, sometimes called Eskimo

*archaeological of or relating to archaeology, the scientific study of past human life and activities, usually by excavating ruins

Vilhjalmur Stefansson made valuable contributions to the scientific understanding of the Arctic. As an explorer, he traveled across large stretches of the Canadian Arctic; as an anthropologist*, he spent many years living among the Inuit* and learning their ways. He believed strongly that Europeans could find the Arctic as friendly a place as the Inuit did, and he devoted much of his career to making this case.

Of Icelandic ancestry, Stefansson was born in Arnes in Northwest Territories, Canada, and educated at universities in the United States. In 1905, he joined an archaeological* expedition to Iceland, and the following year he began his career as an explorer when he agreed to serve as staff anthropologist on the Anglo-American Polar Expedition. He traveled by boat to Herschel Island in northwestern Canada, where he was to meet the rest of the expedition.

The expedition, however, never arrived there but the egotistical Stefansson did not go home; he decided to proceed by rail and river to Mackenzie Bay, the intended destination. He felt that being alone rather than a member of large expedition would enable him to develop closer relations with the Inuit. He spent that winter, from October 1906 to March 1907, with the Inuit, living in their homes and gradually learning their complex language and customs.

The following spring Stefansson heard rumors of Inuit who lived on isolated Arctic islands east of Herschel Island, people who had had no contact with Europeans whatsoever. Even the map issued in 1906 by the Canadian government had marked these areas as "uninhabited." Eager to find and study these people, Stefansson returned to Canada and won a research and travel grant from the American Museum of Natural History.

In May 1908 he and a zoologist friend, Rudolph Martin Anderson, traveled north to the Canadian territory of Yukon. They carried with them the simplest equipment—cameras, film, rifles, ammunition, silk tents, writing materials, cooking utensils, and field glasses. The two men and their Inuit guides arrived in Herschel Island by mid-August 1908 but Stefansson did not reach his destination—Victoria Island off the coast of north central Canada—until May 1910. In the meantime, Anderson had contracted pneumonia and returned to Mackenzie delta.

Stefansson remained in the Arctic until May 1912. He explored much of the western part of the Canadian Arctic, visited many Inuit villages along the way, and lived for a time with a group of Inuit he called the "Copper Eskimos" because of the copper tools they used. Stefansson was greatly taken with these peoples, whom he considered among the friendliest and most generous he had ever encountered. He was also impressed by the quality of their lives. Although most Europeans considered the Arctic a frozen wasteland, Stefansson recognized that the Inuit thrived on the extreme conditions they faced. In his view, other people could do the same if they learned and adopted Inuit ways.

After a brief return to the United States, Stefansson again led an exploring party, consisting of two companions, six dogs, and one sledge*, to the Arctic in 1913. This was an official Government of Canada expedition. During the next five years he traveled more than 500 miles through various parts of Alaska and the Yukon and the Northwest Territories of Canada. The expedition carried out scientific experiments; explored uncharted territory; learned more about the Inuit; and mapped previously unexplored territories, including the Borden, Meighen, and Lougheed Islands, extending Canadian sovereignty in the high Arctic. Stefansson also established a floating research laboratory in the Beaufort Sea, a method that became an accepted way of making long-term observations of the region. During all these travels Stefansson successfully made use of Inuit techniques for staying warm, traveling, and finding food. This expedition marked the longest prolonged exploration of the Canadian Arctic.

For the rest of his life Stefansson remained involved in projects related to the Arctic. During World War II (1939–1945), he studied the United States defenses in Alaska; he also served as an adviser to the U.S. government on polar matters. Later, he held the position of Arctic consultant at Dartmouth College in New Hampshire, and he ultimately donated his library of more than 35,000 volumes on polar life and exploration to the college.

Stefansson was a tireless advocate for the Arctic and its people. He wrote several books on the region's geography and ethnology*, including *My Life with the Eskimo, The Friendly Arctic,* and *Unsolved Mysteries of the Arctic.* These accounts of his travels, which were often self-promoting and sensational, became best-sellers. Stefansson was able to convince observers that the Arctic was not a place to be feared, but a region that could be settled and developed with the help of Inuit techniques. He died in Hanover, New Hampshire, at age 82.

*sledge heavy sled that is mounted on runners for traveling over snow and ice

*ethnology scientific study of the physical and cultural differences between human races

The Greek geographer and historian Strabo described the world as known to the Romans and the Greeks of his time in *Geographica,* a work that became important because it marked the first known attempt to assemble all geographical knowledge into a single source. Although Strabo was interested in physical geography, his greatest focus was on the culture, politics, and history of the lands he discussed.

Early Life and Career. Of Greek ancestry, Strabo was born to wealthy parents in Amasia, Asia Minor (present-day Turkey). Instructed by Greek tutors, he studied religion, geography, philoso-

STRABO

ca. 64 B.C.–ca. A.D. 33

HISTORY, GEOGRAPHY

phy, and mathematics. Around 44 B.C. he went to Rome to continue his education, and he stayed there until about 31 B.C. Thereafter he traveled in Greece and northern Africa, returning to his birthplace for his final years.

While in Rome, Strabo began to write a multivolume history of the ancient world that was intended to serve as a sequel to an earlier history by the Greek scholar Polybius, whose writings had covered the history of the world through about 145 B.C. Strabo's history began where Polybius's ended and may have extended until about 25 B.C. Other than a few isolated excerpts quoted by contemporaries and later writers, very little of Strabo's historical work has survived.

After completing the history, Strabo turned his attention to geographical research, which was to occupy his interests for the rest of his life. The result of his labor, *Geographica,* appeared in 17 volumes during a period of more than 20 years. To gather information for these books, Strabo relied partly on personal experience. He traveled extensively around the Mediterranean Sea, visiting Crete, Corinth, Sardinia, and Alexandria. Later, he traveled up the Nile River as far as the Ethiopian frontier. Strabo also visited Armenia and the region around the Black Sea, and it is possible that he journeyed to areas other than those included in the written records.

Sources for the Masterwork. The bulk of Strabo's information came not from firsthand experience, but from the works of other scientists, travelers, and explorers. He read widely and drew from the experiences and knowledge of earlier writers, most of them Greek; he either ignored, or was unaware of, the works of Roman writers. His sources included cartographers (mapmakers), astronomers, and experts in various other fields. For example, when discussing Europe, Strabo cited Polybius and a scholar named Posidonius, both of whom had traveled through parts of the continent and had recorded their impressions. Similarly, Strabo's astronomical information was freely borrowed from the works of the Greek scientists Eudoxus of Cnidus and Hipparchus.

Strabo, however, did not always accept these writers' observations at face value. In the first two books of the *Geographica,* he surveyed the works and ideas of earlier geographers, often in harsh terms. While acknowledging the value of Hipparchus's astronomical observations, for instance, he criticized the scientist for failing to provide his readers with much information about the earth itself. Similarly, he argued that ERATOSTHENES, an earlier Greek geographer, was imprecise in his measurements of the earth and that Posidonius was wrong on several important geographical theories. At the same time, Strabo was willing to give credit where he felt his sources deserved it, singling out Polybius, among others, for general excellence in his studies.

In the remaining volumes Strabo described the physical, cultural, and historical geography of the known parts of the world. He began with Spain and worked his way roughly clockwise around the Mediterranean Sea, ending in northern Africa. His subjects included regions as far northwest as Great Britain and as far east as India, although the accuracy of his descriptions tended to diminish as he moved away from the Mediterranean region.

The Earth's Size and Shape. Strabo adopted the ideas of earlier scientists with regard to the size of the globe and the shape of its landmasses. He ignored the great unknown stretches of eastern and northern Asia, and he treated Africa as an area smaller than Europe, lying wholly north of the equator; outside Egypt, he noted, that continent was largely desert. Strabo followed Eratosthenes in showing the land area of the world as consisting of one large continent encompassing most of Europe, Africa, and Asia.

Strabo represented the landmass as parallelogram-shaped and extending about 7,000 miles from Spain to the Ganges River in India. In breadth, the mass extended about 3,000 miles and was interrupted by bays, inlets, and other waterways, most notably the Mediterranean Sea itself. In Strabo's view, this landmass took up about a quarter of the globe and was restricted entirely to the northern hemisphere. Strabo did acknowledge that there might be other unknown landmasses elsewhere.

Much of Strabo's work was concerned with physical aspects of the world, such as the geology of coastlines and the landscapes in each country. Marshes, tides, and riverbeds also intrigued him; he used information from geological studies to suggest that much of the known world had, at some point, been submerged under water. He also discussed and evaluated theories of how the land might have been formed.

Strabo investigated other scientific matters in the *Geographica* as well. He relied on established astronomical observations and conclusions to establish the location of the equator, the ecliptic*, and the tropics, and accepted the system of dividing the equator into 360 degrees. He also adopted the notion of five climatic zones or belts based on latitude, with only the temperate zones being habitable.

Science and Culture. Although Strabo was generally willing to include scientific information in the work, he did not consider science central to the study of geography. Perhaps because he was not primarily a scientist himself, he tended to place more emphasis on his own observations and on those who had traveled and had observed the peoples of unfamiliar lands. When he provided scientific data, it was more background information than an end in itself.

The focus of the *Geographica* was the cultural and historical elements of the lands that Strabo described. He took care to write about the major agricultural and industrial products of each country. Religious practices intrigued him, too, as did legal systems, which varied from place to place. When he knew the history of a country, he included that in his description. Because of the emphasis on the people and cultures of the known world, Strabo's work developed into an excellent political and cultural atlas.

Strabo also speculated on the origins of civilization. In his view, geography played an important role in determining whether a particu-

Strabo's only extant work, *Geographica*, provides a detailed physical and historical geography of the ancient world.

*ecliptic path of the sun among the stars; also the orbit of the earth around the sun

lar society would develop a superior culture. The most important factors, he argued, were a varied coastline together with a mild climate. Perhaps not coincidentally, those were the very conditions found around much of the Mediterranean Sea.

His Legacy. Strabo's date and place of death are unknown; it is likely that he died in his birthplace about A.D. 33. His work was little known during the centuries that followed, but around the A.D. 400s the *Geographica* came to the attention of scholars, and its influence increased steadily after that. While there were other geographies produced during ancient and classical times, none approached the subject from the same perspective. Not strictly a physical geography or a natural history*, not concerned entirely with culture, Strabo's *Geographica* was a truly comprehensive work.

*natural history systematic study of nature and natural objects in their original settings

Charles
STURT

1795–1869

EXPLORATION OF AUSTRALIA

One of the most famous explorers of Australia, Charles Sturt undertook several expeditions into the interior of the continent. He journeyed down the Murray and Murrumbidgee Rivers in the southeast and mapped large sections of the southern Australian outback. His work helped British officials determine where to locate new colonial settlements.

Sturt was born in Bengal, India, and educated in England. He joined the British Army at age 18, and in 1827 his regiment was sent to Australia, where he was appointed military secretary to Sir Ralph Darling, the governor of New South Wales. At the time little was known about the interior of Australia, and Darling was eager to learn more. His first goal was to explore the areas west and north of Sydney. The Macquarie River had its source in that area and flowed to the northwest, but no one had ventured far along the riverbed. Some speculated that the river eventually drained into a great inland sea.

In 1828 Darling appointed Sturt and another explorer, Hamilton Hume, to follow the Macquarie and explore the interior of Australia. Tracking the Macquarie to its end, Sturt and Hume learned that it flowed into a river that they named Darling. They also charted other rivers and streams, but they were hampered in their investigations by a drought that had dried up many of the waterways. However, they had proved that there was no inland sea in that part of Australia.

The following year, Sturt convinced Darling to send him on another expedition, this time down the Murrumbidgee River, whose source was south of the Macquarie's. The river was wide and fast moving, and Sturt needed both sails and oars to move his boat downstream. Along the way he received help from aborigines (original inhabitants of the continent) who knew the area well. He discovered that the Murrumbidgee flowed into a broad river that he named Murray.

Sturt decided to continue his explorations along the Murray River. Before long it was evident that the river was flowing into the ocean near the location of the present-day city of Adelaide. Arriving at the coast, Sturt looked for signs of ships that might carry him and his crew to Sydney, but finding none, they resumed the journey upstream. This leg of the journey proved difficult. The river was in flood stage, and the currents made rowing upstream exhausting work. The travelers ran short of supplies and barely managed to safely reach Sydney. Sturt suffered because of the ordeal: he lost his eyesight for several months afterward and had vision problems for the rest of his life.

Sturt returned briefly to England after this expedition. He wrote *Two Expeditions into the Interior of Southern Australia,* carefully describing the terrain that he had crossed and explored. The city of Adelaide was founded partly on Sturt's recommendation. His health restored, he journeyed again to Australia to serve as surveyor general.

Sturt's final expedition began in Adelaide in 1844. Leading a party of 16 men, he headed north into the wilderness, hoping to travel all the way to the center of the continent. The journey was a near disaster. High temperatures, lack of water, and disease threatened to kill all the men; one died and several others were forced to return to Adelaide, but Sturt pressed on. Although he did not reach the center of Australia, he came close. His journey added much information to the map of the continent. He published an account of this expedition in *Narrative of an Expedition into Central Australia.*

In 1851 Sturt returned to England, never returning to Australia. He died in Gloucestershire at the age of 74.

The Dutch navigator and sea captain Abel Janszoon Tasman was among the greatest explorers of his time. He undertook two important voyages to the Indian Ocean and to the southern Pacific, becoming one of the earliest Europeans to investigate the region and the first European to sight New Zealand and Tasmania.

Tasman was born about 1603 in Lutjegast in the Netherlands. Very little is known of his early years. Around age 30 he was hired by the Dutch East India Company, a corporation that carried out extensive trade in Indonesia, Malaysia, and other areas of the eastern Indian Ocean. Tasman signed on as a first mate aboard the *Weesp* and explored the region. Around 1644 he was promoted to the rank of captain and he commanded the *Mocha* on a voyage of exploration to Indonesia.

During the years that followed, Tasman led trading and exploration voyages in Asia, traveling to Japan, Cambodia, and Sumatra among other places. Most of his journeys were within waters relatively well known to traders of the time. In 1639 he was part of an expedition that ventured into the northern Pacific Ocean. The goal of the voyage was to find islands that had been rumored to contain gold and silver. Unfortunately for Tasman and his employers, the ships returned empty.

Farther South. In 1642 the East India Company decided to mount an expedition into the uncharted waters of the southern Indian Ocean.

Abel Janszoon
TASMAN

ca. 1603–ca. 1659

EXPLORATION OF AUSTRALIA
AND THE SOUTH PACIFIC

Pleasures of the Tongan Islands

When Tasman and his men reached the Tongan Islands, they were greeted by a warm and friendly people at Atu, the most southerly island. The people, whom Tasman called Southlanders, danced and entertained his crew. Tasman was also impressed by their by their neat and well-decorated homes and gardens. He and his crew spent several weeks relaxing on the island and later, when they had replenished their food and water supplies, proceeded to their next destination. These islands became known as the Friendly Islands.

*Maori original inhabitants of New Zealand

Knowledge of the area was sketchy at best. Some geographers believed that a large southern continent divided the Pacific and Indian Oceans, just as South America separated the Pacific from the Atlantic. Others suggested that there might be open sea. Several Dutch captains had sighted sections of the coast of the Great South Land (later renamed Australia), but not enough to determine whether these were unconnected stretches of island coastline or the sign of a southern continent.

Tasman was to sail from west to east across the southern Indian Ocean, farther south than any vessels had ever ventured. Although the voyage would certainly add to European knowledge of the outside world, the East India Company was the journey's main sponsor and so its main goal was commercial. Company officials hoped there would be a clear sea passage from the western reaches of the Indian Ocean through the Pacific Ocean to Chile in South America. The other goals of the voyage were to rediscover the Solomon Islands and to explore New Guinea.

On August 14, 1642, Tasman sailed from Batavia (present-day Jakarta), Indonesia, with two ships, the *Heemskerk* and the *Zeehaen*. First he sailed west until he reached the island of Mauritius, then he turned south and east, reaching 49° south, the farthest southerly latitude he would travel. From there he headed generally east and north until he sighted land on November 24. He called it Van Diemen's Land after the Dutch governor general of Indonesia (the island was later renamed Tasmania in the explorer's honor). Tasman believed erroneously that the island was actually a part of a continent, but he and his officers chose not to explore the area. He simply noted that the island seemed too barren to be of much commercial use; he also believed it was inhabited, although he had seen no people. He claimed the land by planting a Dutch flag, and on December 5 the ships left Tasmania and continued sailing east.

New Zealand and Beyond. Eight days later, Tasman reached the South Island of New Zealand. He named it Staten Landt after the Dutch Legislature. He believed that the South Island represented the western shore of the supposed southern continent; he also suggested that the land might be somehow joined to the Staten Landt near Cape Horn, South America. Tasman again decided to move on rather than spend further time exploring partly because of poor weather and partly because of the hostilities he faced from the Maori* people of the island.

Shortly after the expedition had reached the South Island's coast, several Maori canoes paddled out from the land. A fight ensued in which four of Tasman's men were killed. Tasman decided to stay away from the land. After journeying along the western coast, he rounded the northern tip of the North Island and headed northeast. Because of the strength of the swells from the southeast, Tasman decided that there was most likely an ocean between him and Chile; he believed he had found a passage to South America. On January 21, 1643, Tasman arrived at the Tongan Islands in the southern Pacific, where he found the inhabitants to be warm and friendly. After visiting a few nearby islands, he headed west to Indonesia, skirting the northern coast of New Guinea along the way. He reached Batavia on June 14.

From a geographical perspective, Tasman's journey had been a success. He had sailed around Great South Land, proving that it was not connected to any southern continent. He had also found several new lands and possibly a new route to South America. However, company officials were not entirely pleased because Tasman had failed to discover new sources of wealth and he had not explored the region as carefully as they had hoped. In particular, the company wanted more information on Tasmania and on the sea route to Chile. Nevertheless, the company's leaders were delighted by the news that Tasman had found a possible passage to South America.

Second Voyage. In 1644 Tasman set out on another voyage. This time the East India Company ordered him to explore the western and southern coasts of New Guinea and to determine if the island was connected to the Great South Land or if the island was separated by a passage of water.

On February 29, 1644, Tasman set out again from Batavia and reached New Guinea's south coast. He sailed as far east as the mouth of Torres Strait*, which runs between New Guinea and the northern coast of Australia. Although it was possible to sail through this passage and into the Pacific Ocean, Tasman did not navigate the strait, believing it was only a bay. Instead, he explored much of the northern and western coasts of Australia before returning home.

*strait narrow waterway that runs between two landmasses and links two bodies of water

Tasman was awarded the rank of commander and appointed to the Council of Justice of Batavia. However, his superiors were disappointed with the results of his voyage. Governor-general Van Diemen regretted that Tasman had not discovered anything of commercial interest. He expressed his disappointment that the explorer had not ventured in search of valuable minerals or other trade goods. In Tasman's later years he led trading and battle fleets, but he never again commanded a voyage of exploration. He died around 1659 in Jakarta, Indonesia.

Valentina Tereshkova was a cosmonaut, or "sailor of the universe," in the space program of the former Soviet Union. In 1963 she became the first woman in space, orbiting the earth 48 times in 71 hours before returning safely.

Tereshkova was born in Maslennikovo, a village on Russia's Volga River. Her father, a soldier in World War II (1939–1945), died when she was just two years old. Because she had to help her mother, a worker in a cotton mill, Tereshkova did not start school until she was ten. At the age of 18 she went to work in the mill where her mother worked. She also took technical courses by mail and became a member of the Communist* Party, which controlled the Soviet government. In 1959 Tereshkova joined the Air Sports Club and began parachuting—a hobby that gave her entry into the space program.

Valentina Vladimirovna
TERESHKOVA

born 1937

SPACE EXPLORATION

*Communist of or referring to communism, the system in which land, goods, and the means of production are owned by the state or community rather than by individuals

Valentina Tereshkova made history in 1963 when she became the first woman ever to fly in space.

During the late 1950s and early 1960s, the Soviet Union and the United States were locked in a state of mutual hostility and suspicion called the Cold War. The two nations competed in many technical fields, including space exploration. The Soviet Union scored a major victory when Yuri GAGARIN, a Soviet cosmonaut, became the first person in space. The Soviet space program then began recruiting women cosmonauts, partly in the hope of achieving another first. Inspired by Gagarin's spaceflight, Tereshkova volunteered. The ideal cosmonaut was a pilot, but because of the shortage of trained women pilots, several parachutists were admitted to the top-secret program. Tereshkova was a member of this group and the only one to make it into space.

Tereshkova and the other women in the space program spent a year and a half in training, which included parachute jumping and studying rocketry and piloting. As the launch date approached, Tereshkova learned that she had been chosen to pilot the spacecraft *Vostok 6*.

On June 16, 1963, Tereshkova's spacecraft was successfully launched. She reported over the radio, "I see the horizon. A light blue, a beautiful band. This is the Earth. How beautiful it is! All goes well." She remained in space for nearly three days, traveling a distance of 1.2

million miles. The time she spent in space was longer than the combined total for all of the astronauts of the Mercury missions, the first manned space program of the United States. When it was time to return to earth, Tereshkova left the *Vostok 6* at an altitude of about 20,000 feet and parachuted to the ground in present-day Kazakhstan, then a part of the Soviet Union.

Although Tereshkova's voyage had shown that women can withstand the stresses of launch, space travel, and re-entry as well as men, the Soviet Union did not send another woman into space until 1982, one year before the American astronaut Sally RIDE entered space. Tereshkova herself never returned to space. A few months after her historic flight she married a fellow cosmonaut. In the years that followed, she traveled the world as a symbol of Soviet women's achievements, served as an engineer in the Soviet space program, and held various positions in the Soviet government.

Marie Tharp became influential in the fields of oceanography and cartography; she studied the oceans and drew maps of the ocean floor. From around 1950 through the late 1970s, she was part of a group of researchers who revolutionized the scientific understanding of the ocean floor and its role in world geography.

Marie
THARP
born 1920
OCEANOGRAPHY, CARTOGRAPHY, GEOLOGY

Confirming Continental Drift. Tharp was familiar with mapmaking from an early age. Her father, in his job as a soil surveyor for the U.S. Department of Agriculture, was responsible for producing maps that showed the various types of soil in certain areas. At Ohio University, however, Tharp studied English and music. It was shortly thereafter that the door opened to a career in science.

The United States entered World War II (1939–1945), and with men enlisted in the armed forces, scientific and technical jobs became available to women. "I would never have gotten the chance to study geology if it hadn't been for Pearl Harbor," she said. In 1942 "the geology department at the University of Michigan opened its doors to women . . . about ten of us girls responded to one of their flyers, which promised a job in the petroleum industry if we got a degree in geology." Tharp earned her master's degree in geology the following year.

Tharp spent the next four years working for an oil and gas company in Tulsa, Oklahoma. In 1948 Tharp went to New York City, where she met the oceanographer* Maurice Ewing of Columbia University. Ewing hired Tharp to draft, or prepare, scientific drawings. Within a few years she was working closely with one of Ewing's students, Bruce Heezen, in the Lamont Geology Observatory, a research institute founded by Ewing. Heezen's research project was the study of the ocean floor.

*oceanographer one who practices oceanography, the study of oceans

Mapping the Atlantic. As early as the mid-1800s, the American naval officer Matthew Fontaine MAURY had discovered that the seabed is not a flat plain but has many ridges, mountains, and trenches. Based on this information, Heezen began to map the floor of the central Atlantic Ocean using echo-sounding devices. He calculated ocean depths by the amount of time it took for sound to bounce off the ocean floor at a particular location. He then mapped the landscape of sections of the ocean floor based on a series of soundings in those sections.

Tharp turned the data from the soundings into the profiles and pieced them together. When she noticed that a cleft (rift) ran down along the middle of the Atlantic Ocean, she at once knew that it supported the German scientist Alfred Wegener's controversial theory of continental drift—that continents moved apart as the oceans widened between them. The rift she found marked the location where the Atlantic Ocean was spreading apart. Although both Ewing and Heezen rejected the idea at first, Tharp persisted and continued her efforts to find evidence in support of the theory. She and Heezen worked together on seafloor charts that revealed ridges and rifts in the Indian Ocean, Red Sea, and other bodies of water. In the years that followed, the maps produced by Tharp and Heezen, with their unmistakable images of midocean ridges as "seams" between continental plates, helped convince the scientific community of the theory of continental drift.

The World Ocean Floor. Tharp's careful drafting of the seafloor led to an important discovery in the earth sciences—the realization that the Mid-Atlantic Ridge is not an isolated feature. It is part of a much larger phenomenon, a network of ridges and rifts that runs through all of the world's oceans and is the source of many earthquakes. In 1956 Ewing and Heezen announced their discovery, and during the next two decades, Tharp and Heezen produced a series of maps that illustrated it. "I thought I was lucky to have a job that was so interesting," Tharp later said. "I just had the fun of putting the puzzle together. I had the whole world to figure out."

*physiographic of or relating to physiography or physical geography

The seafloor maps produced by Tharp and Heezen are called physiographic* maps, and they illustrate the floor of the ocean as it appears from above, without water and with its high and low points shaded and contoured. In 1956 they published their first physiographic map, which showed the floor of the North Atlantic Ocean, and five years later they followed with a map of the South Atlantic. In 1964 *National Geographic* magazine published a map of the floor of the Indian Ocean. This map was so well received that Heezen and Tharp produced others for the magazine, ending with a view of the Antarctic Ocean in 1975.

Two years later Heezen and Tharp published their greatest work, a physiographic world map showing all features of the world's ocean floors. Beautifully painted and extraordinarily detailed, the map offers a view of a world that is both familiar, with its well-outlined continents, and strangely alien, with the undersea world stripped of its covering waters.

Heezen died in 1977, a few weeks after the map was completed. Since that time, Tharp has received increasing recognition for her work in mapmaking and oceanography. In 1997 the Library of Congress, home of the world's largest map collection, honored her contributions to cartography. Two years later the Woods Hole Oceanographic Institution in Woods Hole, Massachusetts, awarded Tharp the Women Pioneers in Oceanography Award.

David
THOMPSON
1770–1857
GEOGRAPHY, EXPLORATION OF NORTH AMERICA

A fur trader and a surveyor, David Thompson was an early European explorer of western North America. His charts and descriptions of the Columbia River, the northern Rocky Mountains, and many other sections of the continent were invaluable sources of information for governments and traders. Although he had many geographical achievements, he is best remembered for his maps, his exploration of several important river systems, and his travel journals.

Thompson was born in London, England, to a Welsh family. Because his parents were poor, his only formal education was several years of study at a charity school, where he excelled at mathematics. At age 14 he became an apprentice at the Hudson's Bay Company, an English fur-trading organization that obtained its furs from Canada and the northern United States. He was sent to the Hudson Bay town of Churchill, Manitoba, where he trained to become a clerk.

Between 1784 and 1786, Thompson was stationed at several trading posts between Hudson Bay and the northern Canadian Rockies. In 1787, he spent the winter with indigenous* Canadians not far from present-day Calgary; the experience gave him a solid grounding in their language and their ways. The following spring he returned to active duty at one of the company's trading posts.

*indigenous referring to the original inhabitants of a region

In December 1788, Thompson suffered a severe leg fracture because of an accident and was immobilized for nearly a year. During this period, he learned surveying skills from the company astronomer. Intrigued and something of a captive audience, Thompson soon learned enough to do surveying on his own.

The Uncharted West. At the time, Europeans knew very little about the lands north and west of Lake Superior. Other than fur trappers and their employers, few had traveled extensively in the territory. Those who had ventured there were not trained surveyors, and their accounts only gave a general picture of the land. Thompson's interest in surveying the region stemmed from the need for more information.

The Hudson's Bay Company supported Thompson's plan because his survey would give them detailed maps of Canada and the northern United States, aiding their commerce. When Thompson's leg had healed sufficiently, the company sent him into the field, equipped with sextants, almanacs, and chronometers*—the tools of the surveyor's trade. Thompson made measurements and recorded his data, all the while carrying on his clerical duties as he moved from post to post.

*chronometer instrument designed to keep precise time in spite of rough movement or variations in environmental conditions

In 1796 Thompson undertook his first major expedition for the Hudson's Bay Company, journeying to Lake Athabasca in western Canada. Although his destination was already known to the trappers

The Surveyor's Timepiece

First developed in 1659 and perfected in 1762 by the British clockmaker John Harrison, the chronometer was designed to keep precise time in the roughest weather, in extreme temperatures, and during the rolling motions when a ship is at sea. The chronometer was a necessary tool for explorers and surveyors because the precise measurement of time enabled them to calculate longitude. When used in conjunction with a quadrant (a device for measuring altitude) and a sextant (an instrument for measuring the angle between the horizon and a celestial body), the chronometer enabled navigators to determine their exact position on earth.

and traders who had traveled in the region, the route he took was not. From all accounts, Thompson enjoyed the adventure. The following year, he left the Hudson's Bay Company and joined a new fur-trading business, a Canadian concern called the North West Company. Because the new position involved extensive travel, it gave Thompson more opportunities to survey the region.

Thompson wasted little time. He spent his first winter with the company making an extensive journey through western Canada. During the next few years, he explored the Saskatchewan, Assiniboine, and Missouri Rivers as well as Lesser Slave Lake and Lake Winnipeg. Traveling by foot, canoe, and occasionally horseback, Thompson ventured south along the rivers of North America. He voyaged as far as the city of St. Louis and located the sources of several rivers, including the Mississippi.

The Rockies. Thompson's travels for the North West Company also included explorations of the Rocky Mountains. Beginning in 1800, he undertook several journeys to the region, including a two-year stay in the mountains of Alberta at a trading post known as Rocky Mountain House. He hoped to fill in missing information on the maps and to find a navigable mountain pass through the Rockies that would make it possible to ship goods easily to the Pacific. The company that found such a route first would have an advantage over its competitors.

Thompson spent much of the early 1800s searching unsuccessfully for such a passage. In 1806, by which time he had become a partner in the North West Company, he returned to Rocky Mountain House and readied himself for another attempt. Thompson hoped to find a route that would avoid territories claimed by the indigenous peoples who opposed the establishment of trade. After an extensive search, Thompson found the Howse Pass, which took him to the Columbia River. There he established Kootenay House, the first fur-trading post in the region.

For the next four years Thompson remained in the eastern Columbia Valley, setting up many new trading posts, trying to gain control of the region for his fur corporation, and carrying out extensive surveys. Although he intended to continue his voyage down the Columbia to the Pacific Ocean, he did not see any reason to hurry because there were no significant competitors in the area that pressured him.

Down the Columbia. Before long, trouble arose. British Canada and the United States both claimed ownership of parts of the Pacific Northwest. For years, the issue had been unimportant because neither nation had been able to establish a presence in the area. In 1810, however, the United States sent its merchant ships to the mouth of the Columbia River.

Thompson was traveling east on a leave of absence when the news reached him. He quickly changed his plans. It had become vital for Canada to establish a presence at the mouth of the Columbia as quickly as possible, and Thompson received immediate orders to turn around and head for the coastline. Unfortunately for Thompson, he could not travel fast enough. Indigenous Canadians who did not support cross-mountain trade stopped him near the Howse Pass. When Thompson eventually traveled through another pass, it was too late. The Americans had arrived and had established their trading post at the river's mouth.

Although Thompson arrived late, he achieved an important distinction—the first person to travel the length of the Columbia River. He later undertook extensive surveys of the lower reaches of the river, producing the earliest accurate maps of the area. Following the completion of these surveys, Thompson headed east. He settled in Quebec, where he used his notes and observations from 50,000 miles of travel to construct a large and detailed map of much of northwestern North America. He also served for a time on a commission charged with locating the boundary line between the United States and Canada.

Thompson's later years were marked by poverty; never wealthy to begin with, he lost much of his money when his private business failed. He died near Montreal in 1857. An edition of his journals was published in 1916 under the title *David Thompson's Narrative*.

Charming, gregarious, and remarkably energetic, Nikolay Ivanovich Vavilov made an impact on science as both a botanist and a geographer. His main focus was to improve Russian agriculture, but he was also known for his research to find the origins of different plants.

Vavilov was born in Moscow and received his education from the city's Agricultural Institute. As a student, he organized a science club that undertook geographical and botanical trips in Russia. After graduating in 1911, Vavilov studied plant science in England and France. He returned to teach at two Russian schools, and in 1920 he was appointed director of the government's department of applied botany.

The position was a perfect fit for Vavilov. Under his leadership the department thrived. He was passionately interested in plant geography—the distribution of plants across the globe. He led botanical expeditions to the United States, Taiwan, Ethiopia, and Argentina. These travels earned him the presidency of the U.S.S.R. Geographical Society, and an account of his journeys was published after his death.

In 1935 Vavilov announced that he and his fellow scientists had located the origins of about 600 species of cultivated plants. By 1940 he had amassed a collection of over a quarter million plant specimens. Vavilov arranged to have these samples tested and crossbred to find the hardiest and most fruitful plants for Russia. He observed that some regions of the world were astonishingly diverse in the types of plants they contained, while others were not. From this information, Vavilov formulated a theory that agriculture had begun in zones where this diversity was the greatest. Although Vavilov's theory has been altered over the years, it remains important in the study of agriculture and geography.

Vavilov also did extensive research on plant genetics*, especially attempting to improve Soviet methods of breeding plants. In his view it

Nikolay Ivanovich
VAVILOV

1887–1943

BOTANY, GEOGRAPHY

genetics branch of biology that deals with heredity

was possible to develop grains and vegetables that could be planted everywhere; given sufficient research and ingenuity, even the tundra could be turned into a breadbasket.

In 1935 Vavilov faced a challenge from fellow Russian geneticist T.D. Lysenko. Russian agriculture had not shown much improvement since Vavilov had become director of the department of applied botany, and Lysenko publicly blamed Vavilov for the lack of progress. He charged that Vavilov's scientific thinking was flawed, that his collecting trips were pointless, and that he was influenced by foreign scientists.

During the next four years, Vavilov's support in Russia dwindled as government officials began to agree with Lysenko. In 1940 Vavilov was arrested during a collecting trip and imprisoned. He suffered malnutrition and died in prison. Several years later his family appealed to the government to reopen his case. In 1955 they succeeded, and the Soviet Supreme Court officially cleared his name.

Vavilov devoted his life to science. He wrote on a variety of topics, publishing hundreds of books and articles. Many of these works were written during his travels or at odd moments. He slept just four or five hours a night, often on a couch in his office, and he never took vacations beyond his collecting trips. Outgoing and personable, he was asked to lead a number of scientific organizations. He was elected a member of the Soviet Academy of Sciences, and he received numerous awards, including honorary doctorates and medals.

Paul
VIDAL DE LA BLACHE
1845–1915
GEOGRAPHY

*archaeology scientific study of past human life and activities, usually by excavating ruins

Paul Vidal de La Blache is perhaps the most influential figure in the history of French geography. He was among the first scholars to recognize and act on the need for improving the geography curriculum in France, and to suggest that geography should combine the study of physical environments with that of the people who live in them.

Vidal was born in Pézenas, a village in southern France. At age 13 he went to Paris, where he attended preparatory school; his training was primarily in the classics. He continued his education at the école Normale Supérieure, also in Paris, where he studied history and historical geography. In 1867 after a short stint teaching school in France, Vidal accepted a position at a school in Athens, Greece. He stayed there for three years, teaching archaeology* and studying ancient cultures. Vidal traveled in and around Greece and visited Italy and Turkey as well.

Around this time, he became interested in the study of geography, especially after reading the works of two well-known German geographers—Carl RITTER and Alexander von HUMBOLDT. For a few years, however, geography remained only an interest rather than a passion. In early 1870, he returned to France and completed a doctoral degree in the humanities from the Sorbonne, a prominent university in Paris.

Professorship. After his graduation, Vidal was hired by the University of Nancy in northeastern France. The school offered him a dual appointment as a lecturer in history and geography. Although comfortable with the history portion of the job, Vidal was less certain of his ability to teach geography, especially when he found that he was expected to develop the program at Nancy; before his arrival, there was very little geography in the curriculum.

To develop his knowledge, Vidal read extensively. He also held discussions and maintained correspondences with notable geographers of the time, including Ferdinand von RICHTHOFEN of Germany. By 1875 his interests had swung decisively to geography. That same year he was named professor of geography at Nancy. Two years later he moved back to Paris, where he accepted a faculty position at the école Normale Supérieure—his alma mater.

Vidal remained at the école Normale Supérieure until 1898. During those years his reputation as a geographer steadily increased. Because of his influence, other educational institutions in France began to pay greater attention to the study of geography. In 1891 Vidal founded and became the first editor of *Annales de Géographie,* a French language journal of geography. He also published several papers and books that were widely read by geographers in France and outside the country.

Ideas. Vidal's main contribution to the field was his belief that the human element could not be ignored in the study of geography. Where some geographers concentrated more or less exclusively on describing landforms and other aspects of physical terrain, Vidal saw the study of human influence on the land as at least as important. Because people can modify the land to suit their own purposes, he reasoned, it made little sense to ignore their impact.

Vidal also gained fame for his interest in making detailed studies of the geographies of small regions. Although most of his work in this area concerned the many regions of France, he issued several studies focusing on other parts of the world. He also combined geography with his interests in history, producing one of his best-known works, *Histoire et Géographie* (History and Geography).

In 1898 Vidal accepted a professorship at the Sorbonne, where he remained for about ten years. Five years after he had joined the faculty at the Sorbonne, Vidal published what is perhaps his most famous work, *Tableau de la géographie de la France* (Outline of the Geography of France).

Even after his retirement in 1909, Vidal continued to write and conduct research until his death, which was caused by a heart attack. He died in Tamaris-sur-Mer in southern France. Many of Vidal's writings were collected by his son-in-law and published in 1922 as *Principes de Géographie Humaine* (Principles of Human Geography).

The American naval officer Charles Wilkes led a four-year expedition around the world during which he helped build America's reputation for science and learning. The expedition focused on surveying and charting parts of the Antarctic coastline and the Pacific Ocean, but it also improved scholars' knowledge about the natural history* of those regions. Wilkes's own reputation, however, was

Charles
WILKES

1798–1877

NAVAL EXPLORATION

Birth of a National Museum

In 1829, when the British scientist James Smithson died, he left his fortune to the United States to found an institution that would advance knowledge. The United States accepted the $500,000 gift, and political, educational, and scientific leaders began to debate about how to use the money. When Wilkes and the USEE returned in 1842, many were in favor of building a national museum to display the specimens and artifacts from the first U.S. scientific expedition. Congress agreed and established the Smithsonian Institution in 1846; construction was completed in 1855; and materials gathered by the USEE were showcased there in 1858.

---

*natural history systematic study of nature and natural objects in their original settings

*archipelago group of islands

*strait narrow waterway that runs between two landmasses and links two bodies of water

somewhat tarnished by his behavior during the expedition and the end of his career.

The Expedition Begins. Hunting for whales and seals was big business in the early 1800s, and by the 1830s, American whalers and sealers had begun to urge the U.S. government to sponsor explorations in the southern Pacific Ocean and the waters around Antarctica, which were largely untapped. Commercial hunters hoped that such voyages would help them locate new hunting grounds as well as produce charts to help them avoid treacherous rocks, shoals, and islands. In 1836 the U.S. Congress authorized a budget of $300,000 for a "surveying and exploring expedition to the Pacific Ocean and the South Seas." The resulting United States Exploring Expedition (USEE) was established "to extend the bounds of science and to promote knowledge," as well as to fulfill commercial and navigational goals.

By April 1838 the navy had chosen four ships for the expedition and had bought two smaller vessels for surveying work in shallow waters. After four senior officers turned down the command of the expedition for various reasons, the navy asked Wilkes, who accepted.

The Commander. Wilkes was born in New York City and joined the U.S. Navy in 1818. By 1830 he had risen to the rank of lieutenant and was also the head of the Depot of Charts and Instruments, an office of the navy responsible for surveying, making scientific observations, and producing maps and charts. Although Wilkes had spent little time at sea, he possessed knowledge of surveying and had a strong desire to make the expedition a success.

Wilkes and the USEE set sail into the Atlantic Ocean in August 1838. In addition to officers and crew, the ships carried nine scientists and artists to collect natural history samples and to draw the botanical and zoological sights encountered by the expedition. The Americans were not the only ones in the southern ocean at that time—the British explorer James Clark Ross and the French explorer Dumont d'Urville were also leading expeditions to the Antarctic coast.

Around the World. The USEE made its way south through the Atlantic Ocean to Tierra del Fuego, an archipelago* at the southern tip of South America. At that point Wilkes separated the six vessels into three units of two ships each. He led one unit south, with the goal of exploring as much of the Antarctic region as possible in February and March of 1839 before the winter began in the Southern Hemisphere. He sent one team toward Antarctica in a southwestern direction, while the third remained to survey Tierra del Fuego and the Strait* of Magellan, the waterway between the island and the South American mainland.

Wilkes's team turned back after ten days because of fog, but the other southbound team managed to approach Antarctica despite storms and bitter weather. By the end of April, however, bad weather forced all the ships to sail around South America to Valparaiso, a port on the central coast of Chile. One vessel was lost at sea during this passage.

Charles Wilkes was nicknamed "The Stormy Petrel"—a small, dark seabird that flies far from land—because of his willingness to travel the roughest of seas. There is also speculation that Wilkes was the inspiration for Captain Ahab in Herman Melville's novel *Moby Dick*.

Although the winter had made it impossible to explore Antarctica, Wilkes led the USEE into the central Pacific to conduct surveys of the islands of Tahiti, Samoa, and Hawaii. In January 1840 he led three ships on another attempt to reach the Antarctic coast, this time starting from New Zealand.

Passing through masses of floating ice in his flagship, he sighted mountains in the distance and sketched the Antarctic shoreline. Wilkes charted a long stretch of the coast, including the Shackleton Ice Shelf, named after the British explorer Ernest SHACKLETON, and the region now called Wilkes Land. These observations enabled Wilkes to prove that Antarctica was a large continent, not merely a scattering of islands and ice sheets. Sometime during this expedition, one of the three ships was nearly wrecked in the ice and headed north to Australia for safety, but the other two continued their survey. These ships passed d'Urville's ship, but the French and American captains ignored each other.

Wilkes spent the next two years in the North Pacific, surveying the west coast of North America. This work led to new and improved sailing charts. The USEE then sailed southwest, around the Philippine Islands and into the China Sea. Passing through Indonesia and Malaysia, the expedition crossed the Indian Ocean, sailed around the Cape of Good Hope, and proceeded northwest into the Atlantic Ocean. The fleet returned to New York in June 1842, having circumnavigated, or traveled completely around, the earth.

Although Wilkes's dedication to the expedition's goals was unquestioned, he had proven to be a less than ideal leader. His strictness caused 42 of his 342 sailors to desert; Wilkes himself dismissed another 62.

Later Career. The return was not as triumphant as Wilkes might have hoped. He became involved in a dispute with d'Urville over which of them had first sighted the Antarctic mainland. He also engaged in an argument with James Ross over the location of Antarctica. It turned out that some of the land that Wilkes had believed he had seen was really a mirage, and that Antarctica was farther away than he had thought.

Even more troubling than these problems were the charges made by Wilkes's officers that he had treated his men improperly. Wilkes underwent a court-martial, or military trial. In the end, most of the charges were dropped, but he was found guilty of ordering sailors to be punished with more than 12 lashes of the whip, which was the limit allowed by law at the time.

Despite his anger and humiliation, Wilkes completed a five-volume account of the expedition, *Narrative of the United States Exploring Expedition,* which was published in 1844. His account, however, was not the last word—information collected by the USEE appeared in scientific publications in the following years.

Wilkes resumed his naval career in 1861 (during the Civil War) and was placed in command of a small Union warship. Later that year, he ordered a British ship, the *Trent,* to stop so that he could forcibly remove two representatives of the Confederacy (government of 11 Southern states that broke away from the Union in 1860–61) who were on their way to Great Britain. The *Trent* affair enraged the British, who nearly entered the war on the side of the Confederates. Wilkes was again court-martialed because of the incident. The court found him guilty and retired him from the navy in 1864. He died in Washington, D.C., 13 years later.

Fanny Bullock
WORKMAN

1859–1925

GEOGRAPHY, EXPLORATION OF
MOUNTAIN RANGES

Fanny Bullock Workman was a well-known American traveler, spokesperson for women's rights, mountaineer, and writer during the late 1800s and early 1900s. Together with her husband, William, she undertook adventurous trips through various parts of Europe, Africa, and Asia. She also mapped the Himalaya and Karakoram Mountain ranges in Asia, achieving recognition as a serious geographer.

Early Life and Travels. Fanny Bullock was born in Worcester, Massachusetts, into a wealthy and prominent family. When she was seven, her father became the governor of Massachusetts. She was first educated at home by private tutors and later attended European schools. At age 22 Fanny married William Workman, a successful physician. Eight years later William retired from medicine, and the couple moved to Germany, where they spent their time hiking and climbing in the Alps.

The Workmans also developed a passion for bicycling, which had become popular in Europe and North America. They took long bicycle tours in Europe, and they traveled through Spain across the Mediterranean Sea to the North African country of Algeria. They kept careful and detailed records of their routes, distances covered, and road conditions. Their first books were guidebooks for cyclists.

At that time, women's rights were a popular issue in both the United States and Europe. Whenever she could, Fanny spoke in favor of equality between women and men. She did, however, insist on wearing skirts for her bicycling trips; she was shocked that some women wore pants for outdoor activities.

In 1897 the Workmans took their bicycles by steamship to India. They planned an ambitious tour of India, which was then a British colony. They pedaled a total of 14,000 miles "in spite of constant exposure to heat, sun, cold, wet, and malarial" conditions, Fanny wrote later, visiting and photographing many ancient palaces and temples. The Workmans spent more than three years in this effort, which they described in *Through Town and Jungle: Fourteen Thousand Miles A-wheel Among the Temples and People of the Indian Plain,* published in 1904.

Mountaineering Expeditions. Already enthusiastic mountaineers, the Workmans also explored the high peaks and glaciers of mountain ranges in Asia and conducted geographic surveys. Between 1898 and 1912 they organized and completed eight trips in the Himalaya and Karakoram Mountains along India's northern border. Although government departments or scientific organizations generally financed expeditions of this type, the Workmans paid for their trips themselves.

Fanny and William's first expedition was in the eastern Himalayas. They saw Mt. Everest, the world's highest peak, in the distance, but heavy snow forced them to turn back. In 1899 they shifted their operations to the western Himalayas and to the Karakoram range.

On several of their expeditions, Fanny set new records as a woman climber. In 1906 her most spectacular achievement came when, at the age of 47, she climbed Pinnacle Peak, a mountain in the group of Himalayan peaks called the Nun Kun Massif. At 22,815 feet, it was the highest point yet reached by a woman. William also reached the summit but made a point of praising his wife's "courage, endurance, and enthusiasm."

Two years later another American woman climber, Annie Smith Peck, claimed she had reached a higher altitude by climbing a moun-

Many of the successes that Fanny Workman achieved could not have been accomplished without the aid of porters. The porters, who sometimes carried Workman on their backs, dictated just how far her mountain treks went. Some of Workman's expeditions failed because of bad relations with her porters.

tain in South America. Sure that the peak that Peck had climbed was *not* higher than Pinnacle Peak, Fanny spent $13,000 to send a team of geographers to South America to measure it. Fanny proved to be right; her altitude record remained unbroken for the next 28 years.

Although the Workmans' competitive streak and desire to set records led many to dismiss them as pushy sportspeople, they wanted to be considered scientifically respectable. They took photographs and scientific measurements on all their climbs and wrote five books about their Himalayan and Karakoram expeditions. These publications won recognition from many scientific groups. In 1905 Fanny received an invitation to speak before London's Royal Geographical Society. She was the second woman to speak before the society and the first to lecture at the Sorbonne, a prominent university in Paris.

The high point of Fanny's geographic achievements was the 1911 expedition that she organized, in which she and William explored glaciers and discovered new routes through the Karakoram. They described this expedition in *Two Summers in the Ice Wilds of the Eastern Karakoram: The Exploration of Nineteen Hundred Square Miles of Mountains and Glaciers,* published in 1917. Even scientists and geographers who had considered the Workmans amateurs admitted that their accomplishments on this expedition were significant.

Fanny and William Workman retired from exploration after that expedition and they moved to southern France a few years later. Fanny died there at age 66; William returned to Massachusetts, where he lived until his death 12 years later.

XUAN ZANG

602–ca. 664

EXPLORATION OF
CENTRAL ASIA AND INDIA

*pilgrimage journey of religious devotion, usually to a sacred site

Xuan Zang (sometimes spelled Hsüan Tsang) was a Chinese scholar who took a pilgrimage* through Asia to learn about Buddhism. His 16-year journey brought a wealth of geographic and religious knowledge to China. His account of the trip remains a key source of information for modern researchers studying Central Asia and South Asia in the 600s.

Xuan Zang was born into a family with a tradition of scholarship and government service. As a youth he adopted Buddhism, a religion that had originated in India centuries earlier. By Xuan Zang's time, many versions of Buddhism had emerged in China. The ideas and texts differed among these schools, and Xuan Zang decided that the best way to find the original version of Buddhism would be to study in India, the birthplace of the faith and the source of its important documents.

At the time, citizens of China were not allowed to leave the empire without the proper permits. Xuan Zang could not obtain a permit, so in 629, he slipped out of China and traveled west across Central Asia, north of the Taklamakan Desert on China's western edge. He then followed the trade route known as the Silk Road, which passes through ancient oasis towns such as Tashkent and Samarkand, both in present-day Uzbekistan. Along the way, the pilgrim received invitations to stay, but each time, he continued his journey, enduring heat, cold, hunger, robbers, and other hardships.

Xuan Zang traveled south through Afghanistan. Crossing the Hindu Kush, a range of snow-capped and rugged mountains, he entered Pakistan and continued on into Kashmir in northern India. He remained there for a time, studying with a noted philosopher before continuing south and east along the Ganges River to the major centers of Buddhist learning.

Around 633, Xuan Zang arrived at Nalanda, a monastery in eastern India, where he spent considerable time studying Sanskrit, the language of ancient Buddhist texts, and philosophy. He then crisscrossed India to visit other important Buddhist sites and saw much of the land and its people. Ten years later Xuan Zang was ready to return to China with his new knowledge and about 600 Buddhist texts he had acquired.

On the trip home Xuan Zang passed through a series of cities in western China, including Kashgar, Yarkand, Khotan, and Tunhuang. He returned to China in 645, and although he had left the country illegally, the emperor welcomed him. The emperor also assigned leading scholars to help Xuan Zang translate the Buddhist texts from Sanskrit into Chinese. In addition to shaping the direction of Buddhism in eastern Asia, Xuan Zang wrote a book about his travels. Titled *Record of Western Lands,* the work describes the geography, peoples, cultures, customs, and Buddhist beliefs of the lands through which he had traveled. The book was a source of information for scholars and an inspiration for one of the most popular books of Chinese travel literature, *Journey to the West.* In this 1592 work, an inquisitive monkey accompanies a pilgrim on his travels through lands beyond China's frontier.

Xuan Zang, the traveler whose desire for religious knowledge carried him across 40,000 miles in 16 years, died in the Jade Flower Palace Monastery, where he had lived since his return to China.

SUGGESTED READINGS

Histories and Biographies

EXPLORATION

General Works and Atlases

Allen, John Logan. *Student Atlas of World Geography.* 2d ed. Guilford, Conn.: McGraw-Hill/Dushkin, 2001.

Bohlander, Richard E., ed. *World Explorers and Discoverers.* 1992. Reprint, New York: Da Capo Press, 1998.

Boorstin, Daniel J. *The Discoverers: A History of Man's Search to Know His World and Himself.* New York: Random House, 1985.

Cameron, Ian. *To the Farthest Ends of the Earth: 150 Years of World Exploration by the Royal Geographical Society.* New York: E. P. Dutton, 1980.

Delpar, Helen, ed. *The Discoverers: An Encyclopedia of Explorers and Exploration.* New York: McGraw-Hill, 1980.

Divine, David. *The Opening of the World: The Great Age of Maritime Exploration.* New York: G. P. Putnam's Sons, 1973.

Dos Passos, John. *The Portugal Story: Three Centuries of Exploration and Discovery.* Garden City, N.Y.: Doubleday, 1969.

Grolier Student Library of Explorers and Exploration. Danbury, Conn.: Grolier Educational, 1998.

Hanbury-Tenison, Robin, comp. *The Oxford Book of Exploration.* New York: Oxford University Press, 1993.

Konstam, Angus. *Historical Atlas of Exploration, 1492–1600.* New York: Checkmark Books, 2000.

Newby, Eric. *The World Atlas of Exploration.* New York: Crescent Books, 1985.

Novaresio, Paolo. *The Explorers: From the Ancient World to the Present.* New York: Stewart, Tabori, and Chang, 1996.

Royal Geographical Society. *The Oxford Atlas of Exploration.* New York: Oxford University Press, 1997.

*Stefoff, Rebecca. *The Young Oxford Companion to Maps and Mapmaking.* New York: Oxford University Press, 1995.

*Stefoff, Rebecca. *Women of the World: Women Travelers and Explorers.* New York: Oxford University Press, 1993.

Tinling, Marion. *Women into the Unknown: A Sourcebook on Women Explorers and Travelers.* New York: Greenwood, 1989.

Africa

Guadalupi, Gianni. *The Discovery of the Nile.* New York: Stewart, Tabori, and Chang, 1997.

Hugon, Anne. *The Exploration of Africa: From Cairo to the Cape.* New York: Abrams, 1993.

McLynn, F. J. *Hearts of Darkness: The European Exploration of Africa.* New York: Carroll and Graf Publishers, 1993.

Porch, Douglas. *The Conquest of the Sahara.* New York: Alfred A. Knopf, 1984.

Rotberg, Robert I., ed. *Africa and Its Explorers: Motives, Methods, and Impact.* Cambridge, Mass.: Harvard University Press, 1970.

*Sherman, Steven. *Henry Stanley and the European Explorers of Africa.* New York: Chelsea House, 1993.

Suggested Readings

*Stefoff, Rebecca. *Vasco da Gama and the Portuguese Explorers*. New York: Chelsea House, 1993.

Antarctica

Gurney, Alan. *Below the Convergence: Voyages Toward Antarctica, 1699–1839*. New York: Norton, 1997.

Land, Barbara. *The New Explorers: Women in Antarctica*. New York: Dodd, Mead, 1981.

Mickleburgh, Edwin. *Beyond the Frozen Sea: Visions of Antarctica*. New York: St. Martin's, 1987.

Mountfield, David. *A History of Polar Exploration*. New York: Dial, 1974.

Pyne, Stephen J. *The Ice: A Journey to Antarctica*. Seattle: University of Washington Press, 1998.

The Arctic

Barrow, John. *A Chronological History of Voyages into the Arctic Regions*. 1818. Reprint, Newton Abbot, U.K.: David and Charles Reprints, 1971.

Berton, Pierre. *The Arctic Grail: The Quest for the North West Passage and the North Pole, 1818–1909*. New York: Viking, 1988.

*Curlee, Lynn. *Into the Ice: The Story of Arctic Exploration*. Boston: Houghton Mifflin, 1997.

Delgado, James P. *Across the Top of the World: The Quest for the Northwest Passage*. New York: Checkmark Books, 1999.

Mountfield, David. *A History of Polar Exploration*. New York: Dial, 1974.

Neatby, Leslie Hilda. *Discovery in Russian and Siberian Waters*. Athens: Ohio University Press, 1973.

Orlob, Helen. *The Northeast Passage: Black Water, White Ice*. New York: Thomas Nelson, 1977.

Smith, William D. *Northwest Passage*. New York: American Heritage, 1970.

Asia

Dmytryshyn, Basil, et al., eds. and trans. *Russia's Conquest of Siberia, 1558–1700: A Documentary Record*. Portland, Ore.: Western Imprints, The Press of the Oregon Historical Society, 1985.

Gullick, J. M. *Adventures and Encounters: Europeans in South-East Asia*. New York: Oxford University Press, 1995.

Hopkirk, Peter. *Trespassers on the Roof of the World: The Secret Exploration of Tibet*. Los Angeles: Jeremy P. Tarcher, 1982.

Lattimore, Owen, and Eleanor Lattimore. *Silks, Spices, and Empire: Asia Seen Through the Eyes of Its Discoverers*. New York: Delacorte, 1968.

*McLoone, Margo. *Women Explorers in Asia*. Mankato, Minn.: Capstone Press, 1997.

Severin, Timothy. *The Oriental Adventure: Explorers of the East*. Boston: Little, Brown, 1976.

*Stefoff, Rebecca. *Vasco da Gama and the Portuguese Explorers*. New York: Chelsea House, 1993.

Australia

Carter, Paul. *The Road to Botany Bay: An Exploration of Landscape and History*. New York: Alfred A. Knopf, 1987.

McLaren, Glen. *Beyond Leichhardt: Bushcraft and the Exploration of Australia*. South Fremantle, Wash.: Fremantle Arts Centre Press, 1996.

Sigmond, J. P. *Dutch Discoveries of Australia: Shipwrecks, Treasures, and Early Voyages Off the West Coast*. Amsterdam, Netherlands: Batavian Lion, 1995.

Central America, Caribbean, and South America

Descola, Jean. *The Conquistadors*. Translated by Malcolm Barnes. 1954. Reprint, Fairfield, N.J.: Augustus M. Kelley, 1970.

Goodman, Edward J. *The Explorers of South America*. Norman: University of Oklahoma Press, 1992.

Kelly, Brian, and Mark London. *Amazon*. San Diego, Calif.: Harcourt Brace Jovanovich, 1983.

*Machado, Ana Maria. *Exploration into Latin America*. Parsippany, N.J.: New Discovery Books, 1995.

Morison, Samuel Eliot. *The European Discovery of America: The Southern Voyages, 1492–1616*. New York: Oxford University Press, 1974.

*Morris, John Miller. *From Coronado to Escalante: The Explorers of the Spanish Southwest*. New York: Chelsea House, 1992.

Middle East

Beckingham, C. F. *Between Islam and Christendom: Travellers, Facts, and Legends in the Mid-*

dle Ages and the Renaissance. London: Variorum Reprints, 1983.

Donini, Pier Giovanni. Arab Travelers and Geographers. London: Immel Publishing, 1991.

Simmons, James C. Passionate Pilgrims: English Travelers to the World of the Desert Arabs. New York: William Morrow, 1987.

North America

Allen, John Logan, ed. North American Exploration, 3 volumes. Lincoln: University of Nebraska Press, 1997.

Gough, Barry M. First Across the Continent: Sir Alexander Mackenzie. Norman: University of Oklahoma Press, 1997.

Lavender, David. The Rockies. New York: Harper and Row, 1968.

Leach, Douglas E. The Northern Colonial Frontier, 1607–1763. New York: Holt, Rinehart, and Winston, 1966.

Logan, Donald F. The Vikings in History. New York: Barnes and Noble, 1983.

Meredith, Roberts, and E. Brooks Smith, eds. Exploring the Great River: Early Voyagers on the Mississippi from DeSoto to LaSalle. Boston: Little, Brown, 1969.

Milanih, Jerald T., and Susan Milbrath, eds. First Encounters: Spanish Explorations in the Caribbean and the United States, 1492–1570. Gainesville: University of Florida Press, 1989.

Mirsky, Jeannette. The Westward Crossings: Balboa, Mackenzie, Lewis and Clark. 1946. Reprint, Philadelphia: Richard West, 1978.

Morison, Samuel Eliot. The European Discovery of America: The Northern Voyages, A.D. 500–1600. New York: Oxford University Press, 1971.

Nuffield, E. W. The Discovery of Canada. Vancouver, Canada: Haro, 1996.

*Xydes, Georgia. Alexander MacKenzie and the Explorers of Canada. New York: Chelsea House, 1992.

The Pacific Ocean

Cameron, Ian. Magellan and the First Circumnavigators of the World. New York: Saturday Review Press, 1973.

Dousset, Roselene, and Etienne Taillemite. The Great Book of the Pacific. Translated by Andrew Mouravieff-Apostal and Edita Lausanne. Secaucus, N.J.: Chartwell Books, 1979.

*Haney, David. Captain James Cook and the Explorers of the Pacific. New York: Chelsea House, 1992.

Silverberg, Robert. The Longest Voyage: Circumnavigators in the Age of Discovery. Athens: Ohio University Press, 1997.

Space

Launius, Roger D. Frontiers of Space Exploration. Westport, Conn.: Greenwood Press, 1998.

MacKinnon, Douglas, and Joseph Baldanza. Footprints. Washington, D.C.: Acropolis Books, 1989.

Reeves, Robert. The Superpower Space Race: An Explosive Rivalry Through the Solar System. New York: Plenum Press, 1994.

GEOGRAPHY

Baker, J.N.L. A History of Geographical Discovery and Exploration. Revised edition. New York: Cooper Square, 1967.

Dunbar, Gary S. A Biographical Dictionary of American Geography in the Twentieth Century. Baton Rouge: Louisiana State University, 1996.

Larkin, Robert, and Gary Peters, eds. Biographical Dictionary of Geography. Westport, Conn.: Greenwood Press, 1993.

On-Line Resources

British Antarctic Survey. Contains information about the research stations in and the physical and natural environment of Antarctica. Also includes information on life and work in Antarctica.

http://www.antarctica.ac.uk

Discovery and Exploration. From the Library of Congress. Contains links to manuscripts and published maps from the European Age of Discoveries (late 15th century to the 17th century), and access to the virtual Geography and Map Reading Room.

http://memory.loc.gov/ammem/gmdhtml/dsxphome.html

Geography Guide to Geographical Resources. A web site by the University of Wisconsin-Madison

Suggested Readings

containing links to information on geography and geographers.

http://www.library.wisc.edu/libraries/Geography/guide/geoglist.htm

Internet Medieval Sourcebook. *Contains links for exploration and expansion. Links focus on general exploration, maritime exploration and conquest, and voyages of discovery undertaken by specific explorers.*

http://www.fordham.edu/halsall/sbook1z.html

Kennedy Space Center. *The official web site for the Kennedy Space Center with current information about the Center and NASA as well as space flight archives about earlier flights, shuttles, and astronauts.*

http://www.ksc.nasa.gov/

Lewis and Clark Trail, Heritage Foundation, Incorporated. *Official web site for the Lewis and Clark Heritage Foundation. Contains a rich history of the Lewis and Clark expedition as described in the Foundation's quarterly journal.*

http://www.lewisandclark.org/index.htm

The European Voyages of Exploration. The Fifteenth and Sixteenth Centuries. *Web site from the Applied History Research Group at the University of Calgary. An illustrated tutorial about European discovery of sea routes.*

http://www.ucalgary.ca/HIST/tutor/eurvoya/

The Hakluyt Society. *A web site dedicated to the promotion of geographical discovery. Contains links that lead to extensive information on specific voyages, including biographies, time lines, and maps.*

http://www.hakluyt.com/

The Mariner's Museum. *A web site ideal for young students, but helpful for all. The on-line curriculum guide addresses maritime discovery from ancient times to* Captain Cook's 1768 voyage to the South Pacific. *Also includes short biographies of explorers, a time line, and information about ships.*

http://www.mariner.org/age/

The Roald Amundsen Centre for Arctic Research. *A web site dedicated to Arctic research; contains links to research organizations, polar literature, and libraries dedicated to polar study.*

http://www.arctic.uit.no/English/

University of Arizona Library Geography Resources on the Internet. *A resource of useful geography Internet links. Contains links to and information on geography journals, maps, atlases, and geographic associations.*

http://dizzy.library.arizona.edu/users/kollen/geog.htm

*Asterisk denotes book for young readers

PHOTO CREDITS

INDEX

Index

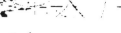

Index

Index